Europe's Eastern Crisis

In recent years a series of crises have erupted on the European Union's eastern borders. Russia's annexation of Crimea and the subsequent conflict in eastern Ukraine presented the EU with a major foreign policy challenge, in both Ukraine and across the other countries of the so-called Eastern Partnership. In response, the EU has begun to map its own form of 'liberal-redux geopolitics' that combines various strategic logics. This book traces the effect of these crises on the foreign policy of the EU, examining the changes in policies towards the countries on its eastern borders, the EU's review of the Eastern Partnership, as well as the EU's relations with Russia overall. It goes on to uncover whether the EU has contained the crisis or set up new conditions for more instability in the future.

RICHARD YOUNGS is Senior Fellow at Carnegie Europe and Professor in the Department of Politics and International Studies at the University of Warwick.

Europe's Eastern Crisis

The Geopolitics of Asymmetry

RICHARD YOUNGS
Carnegie Europe and University of Warwick

CAMBRIDGE
UNIVERSITY PRESS

University Printing House, Cambridge CB2 8BS, United Kingdom
One Liberty Plaza, 20th Floor, New York, NY 10006, USA
477 Williamstown Road, Port Melbourne, VIC 3207, Australia
4843/24, 2nd Floor, Ansari Road, Daryaganj, Delhi – 110002, India
79 Anson Road, #06-04/06, Singapore 079906

Cambridge University Press is part of the University of Cambridge.

It furthers the University's mission by disseminating knowledge in the pursuit of education, learning, and research at the highest international levels of excellence.

www.cambridge.org
Information on this title: www.cambridge.org/9781107121379

DOI: 10.1017/9781316344033

First published 2017

Printed in the United Kingdom by Clays, St Ives plc

A catalogue record for this publication is available from the British Library.

ISBN 978-1-107-12137-9 Hardback
ISBN 978-1-107-54731-5 Paperback

Contents

Maps

Preface

This book had its genesis in the dramatic summit of the so-called Eastern Partnership (EaP) held in Vilnius in November 2013. Like others attending the plethora of side events accompanying the formal summit, I was taken aback by the palpable sense of confusion and jolting bewilderment that pervaded the discussions. The countries of Eastern Europe and the Southern Caucasus – most crucially, of course, Ukraine – suddenly seemed to be slipping out of the orbit of the European Union (EU). The fluctuation of political developments within Eastern Partnership (EaP) states and the abruptness of Russia's apparent wrecking of European goals revealed a whole series of EU miscalculations. Since then, the crisis that burst onto the agenda in late 2013 has deepened and dragged on with tragic and sobering consequences, never far from the daily media headlines. Everyone in Vilnius was clear that EU policies had to change – and fundamentally. In charting developments in the three years since the first rumblings of the eastern crisis, I have been motivated to explore exactly what this conviction that the EU requires profound geo-strategic adjustment amounts to in practice. My concern has not been to stress any particular ideological or normative point of view on the highly charged and emotive issues that now surround Russian and Ukrainian matters; rather it has been to unpack, understand and conceptualise the different components of the European response to the post-2013 crisis.

I am grateful to officials and civil society representatives for the more than 100 interviews I have been able to carry out across the EaP states and EU capitals since 2013. These interviews were generally granted on the condition of anonymity and are therefore not cited individually in the text but they are drawn on extensively in the book's empirical chapters. Half a dozen trips to Ukraine, in particular, have impressed upon me how local views have shifted back and forth in complex and varied ways, as the crisis dominates the lives of a whole generation of political and civic leaders – in ways that are sad, enervating and inspiring all at the same time. Thanks go to several experts for their comments on drafts of the manuscript, including Sven Biscop, Michael Emerson, Giovanni Grevi, Balazs Jarabik, Svetlana Kozbar, Tsveta Petrova, Yauheni Preiherman, Gwendolyn Sasse, Natalia Shapovalova, Mike Smith and Tom de Waal. The text also benefited from the suggestions provided by four anonymous reviewers.

I would also like to thank the Department of Politics and International Studies at Warwick University, especially Nick Vaughan-Williams, along with the Carnegie Endowment for International Peace, and in particular Thomas Carothers and Maria Koomen, for their support in relation to my preparing the book.

1 *Introduction*

The early months of 2014 unleashed a series of dramatic crises on the European Union's eastern borders, and especially in Ukraine. Between November 2013 and February 2014, Ukrainian protestors rose up to eject President Viktor Yanukovich from power. Russia sought to stop this from happening and to prevent a more pro-European and democratic government taking office in Ukraine. When Yanukovich fled Kiev and a new interim government took power, Russia annexed the Crimean peninsula. Russia then stirred tensions in eastern Ukraine, supporting local separatists throughout the remainder of 2014, 2015 and 2016. By the end of 2016, conflict in Ukraine's Donbas region had claimed nearly 10,000 lives, left 20,000 seriously injured and driven 2.5 million people from their homes.

Many analysts and politicians argued that this cluster of events constituted the most profound menace to European security for many decades. Some called time on the whole post-Cold War international order. Visceral Russian power intensified as a major factor across Eastern Europe and the Southern Caucasus, as the Ukraine crisis took on regional proportions. Amidst frenzied talk of a new Cold War, the foundations of the whole European order seemed to be on the verge of crumbling.

Geopolitical tension had been brewing for some time prior to 2014. As the European Union (EU) endeavoured to use its Eastern Partnership (EaP) initiative to extend a range of cooperative measures to Eastern Europe and the Southern Caucasus, Russia played an increasingly nefarious hand of realpolitik to neuter this intent. The EaP partners – Armenia, Azerbaijan, Belarus, Georgia, Moldova and Ukraine – seemed increasingly divided between pro-European and pro-Russian factions, while some politicians sought to play off these two external powers against each other. The EU appeared to have a geopolitical battle on its hands in an eastern region it had rather too easily assumed would be inexorably drawn towards European partnership.

Many analysts admonished the EU and its member states for their languorous and insipid response to Russian aggression and failure to provide EaP states with effective backing. In contrast, other critics accused European governments of causing instability through ill-designed EU association agreements (AAs), stoking acrimony in the pursuit of regional hegemony and not adapting to Russia's legitimate interests. Arriving at a more nuanced conclusion, this book shows that European responses contained a more eclectic mix of strategies and policy dynamics than these rather one-dimensional critiques are able to capture. From 2014, the European Union and its member states undertook a distinctive, multi-layered geopolitical turn. This entailed significant changes to the EU's familiar modes of foreign policy action. The book argues that the EU's geopolitical adjustments to the crisis were more meaningful, far-reaching and balanced than has been commonly argued, and yet insufficiently decisive for the EU unequivocally to achieve its strategic objectives.

A European Crisis

There were many important elements of the new geopolitical context – Russian aims and policies, the domestic complexities of the region's different conflicts and ethnic compositions, and the likely evolution of simmering conflicts. This book examines one element of the strategic mix: namely, the way that the European Union and its member states responded to the fraught rise of geopolitical tensions from the end of 2013. It does not claim to present a complete picture of all regionally relevant factors, but examines how one important actor moulded its foreign policies to the new environment. The book assesses how the EU responded to the strategic challenges unleashed by Ukraine's political drama and by Russian policies towards EaP states – a constellation of factors that the book refers to in shorthand as 'the eastern crisis'.

The new situation certainly appeared to represent a serious threat to European interests and influence. It both curtailed the EU's pretensions to wield influence over eastern partners and raised the prospect of direct threats to its own security and strategic interests. It raised the question of whether EU cooperation and agreements were a source of instability rather than a fillip to successful modernisation in EaP states. Enticing Eastern European and Caucasian states into a deep partnership with the EU, based on the values of democracy, cooperative security and open markets, was now a more challenging enterprise. Russia's threat to the region's territorial borders, along with the tactics it adopted to prevent eastern states democratising and prioritising trade relations with the EU, raised broader risks to the 'European order'.

A geopolitical triangle increasingly defined Europe's strategic framework. This rested on a three-way interaction between EU policies, Russian policy and domestic political trends in Eastern European and the south Caucasian states. This invited the EU to rethink the whole basis of its foreign policy: no longer could it assume that the bloc's technocratic, rules-based gravitational pull would suffice to mitigate the need for high geopolitics. The question of how the EU would respond to crisis in its eastern borderlands was intriguing in part because the EU had traditionally shunned the kind of power politics that Russia brought to the eastern region. As tensions intensified in the years after 2013, would the EU now judge it necessary to adopt a more overtly geopolitical strategy in the east?

This had resonance for theoretical explanations of EU foreign policy dynamics in the region. For many years, there was a tendency to see what the EU termed its 'eastern Neighbourhood' as part of a natural 'Euro-sphere'. Theorists focused on explaining the gradual extension of EU rules into the region and the way in which European governments increasingly pursued their interests through the prism of the EU's external policy instruments. Many believed that, whatever the fluctuations in day-to-day politics, the region's core, underlying dynamic was that of a gradual, almost inexorable approximation with an EU governance space. The post-2013 geopolitical context raised serious questions about how far this remained a useful conceptual lens and invited deeper reflection on the future analytical drivers of European foreign policies.

The Key Questions

In light of these concerns, this book does three things. First, *it categorises the nature of EU responses to the eastern crisis*. The book examines how far the EU and member state leaders and diplomats really saw themselves facing a high-order strategic crisis in the east from 2013. It addresses a number of questions in this regard. Did EU and member state policy-makers really see this as the most existential threat to European order for a generation, or as something of a false alarm? To what extent did the EU qualitatively change its strategic approach to the EaP region? Did the crisis change how EU member states defined security in relation to the EaP? How exactly did the EU conceive the notion of a 'geopolitical' response? Did the basic European approach switch to one of wanting a weak not prosperous Russia?

Second, the book explores how far the crisis changed the *policy-making dynamics of EU foreign policy coordination.* It does this by tackling a number of crucial questions. Was the external shock of Russia's actions the long-overdue catalyst for a more united and committed EU foreign policy? Was it now this external factor that drove foreign policy cooperation between European governments, to a greater extent than its internally rooted identities and institutional structures? Did carefully rationalised interest calculations come more clearly to propel overall EU foreign policy, with deeper member state involvement? What was the balance between common EU endeavour and member states' national diplomacy? How did the mutually conditioning triangle of EU policy, Russian actions and domestic politics in the Eastern Partnership states play itself out as the crisis deepened?

Third, the book assesses *the impact of European policies.* How effective was the overall European response, as pursued through national, EU and other organisational choices? Should European strategy be classified as a success or a failure? Did the crisis suggest that the EU could still make a profound, transformative difference on its borders or did it reveal the Union's restricted reach and power? What factors accounted for the successes and failures of European responses to the eastern crisis? Which had the more effective impact: regular, existing EU policies or member states' national diplomacy? Did the crisis reinforce the standard conclusion that the EU has influence at the level of technical cooperation and soft power but much less in the realm of hard geopolitics or did it render this standard assumption less convincing?

The book also explores what the longer-term legacy of the crisis is likely to be, for both the eastern region and European interests. Did the EU as a whole gain or lose influence after the crisis? How did the crisis reshape the long-term relationships between the EU and EaP partners, as well as Russia? Was the crisis really a game-changer – as commentators ritually insisted – or likely to have a more ephemeral impact?

From late 2013, a recurrent theme in policy and analytical debates was that the eastern crisis was profoundly 'geopolitical' and required the EU to react in a way that was fully seized of this uncomfortable reality. This ubiquitous claim begged for a sharper definition of what was meant by a geopolitical response. The book's analytical approach is predicated on an open exploration of whether or not the key actors in EU foreign policy saw themselves as being engaged in a new strategic struggle, and how they defined a geopolitical approach. To orientate the empirical account of post-2013 developments, Chapter 2 sets up a conceptual framework to measure the European response to the crisis. This draws from both existing theoretical accounts of EU foreign policy and from debates over different definitions of geopolitics. The framework offers a fourfold classification of different types of geopolitical strategy: a standard EU approach; defensive geopolitics; offensive geopolitics; and the notion of *liberal-redux geopolitics*, that is described below.

Guided by this classification, the book offers a detailed empirical account of different aspects of Europe's eastern policies. To provide a baseline for comparison, the book first summarises the EU's eastern policies before 2013. It then unpacks the different ways in which the EU and member states introduced new elements to these policies as a result of events in the period 2013 to 2016, uncovering the multifaceted nature of the EU's response. In counterpoint, the book then explains the ways in which the changes to EU and national policies were limited – reflecting the Union's reluctance to adopt radically different approaches to the region's new geopolitical challenges. Three chapters then offer greater detail on the specific case of Ukraine, looking in turn at the Maidan protests that ousted the Yanukovich regime, the conflict in the country's eastern region and the post-2014 political reform process. A final empirical chapter charts the evolution of European policies elsewhere in the region, examining how far the Union modified its policies towards each EaP state, ordered by degree of strategic convergence: Georgia, Moldova, Armenia, Belarus and Azerbaijan.

In its conclusion, the book takes a step back from the dramatic and tragic day-to-day details of the eastern crisis and explores the broader analytical implications for European foreign policy. The concluding chapter assesses how far the crisis engendered changes to the EU's core strategic philosophy; what impact it had on the causal drivers of European foreign policy; and what it meant for the effectiveness of different types of EU action.

The book is concerned with the overall 'European' response to the crisis in the sense of strategies pursued at different institutional levels by countries that are members of the European Union. This includes the actions of member states pursued collectively through EU channels; individually through their own national diplomacy; and within other organisations like NATO and the Organisation for Cooperation and Security in Europe (OSCE). In this multi-level definition, the focus is on policy responses of the EU area rather than EU institutional initiatives alone. Where the book refers to the EU stance it does so to mean either a common stance broadly shared by EU member states or EU institutional initiatives. Where finer nuance is required, the book unpacks variations between different member states, between national governments and EU institutions, and between the EU and other international organisations. In each empirical component, the book charts in detail the positions of different member states, including their role in collective EU initiatives, their positions in other regional bodies and their pursuit of separate national policy initiatives. The relationship between national and European levels is one of the core issues upon which the book seeks to shed analytical light.

A Half-New Eastern Policy

The book's main findings can be summarised in the following terms. In order to *conceptualise the European response*, Chapter 2 unpacks different types of geopolitical strategy and suggests a category of *liberal-redux geopolitics*. The book's empirical chapters lead toward the conclusion that this is the category that best captures the nature of European responses to the eastern crisis. The category is 'redux' liberal in the sense of describing a situation where core liberal-cooperative practices are used in ways that are more selective, calibrated and sharply instrumental than in previous European policies, and superimposed with a layer of geo-strategic diplomacy. The liberal-redux geopolitics category features several core balances between assertive and conciliatory foreign policies.

As the eastern crisis deepened, the EU increased its level of foreign policy commitment, but not so far as to justify dramatically securitised or offensive strategic options. It reduced engagement with Russia, developing a 'lite' form of containment that did not entirely foreclose the pursuit of better cooperation with Russia in the EaP space. While several EU member states upgraded their hard-power defensive capabilities and pressed to galvanise security cooperation through NATO, an aim to maximise relative military power was not the primary metric of the overall European response. The EU offered stronger support for the six EaP partners, but there was no effort to gain strategic control or primacy in the EaP space. EU support for certain political values and reforms in EaP partners was pursued as a geopolitical comparative advantage over Russia, but combined with less normative levels of engagement. The reform-oriented dimensions of EU policies were framed and calibrated more instrumentally as a tool of purposive power – sometimes enhanced for this use, other times set aside where this was judged to be geopolitically optimal.

The EU developed a response to the crisis that combined more targeted support for and engagement with Ukraine and the other EaP partners; greater pressure on Russia; and high-level diplomatic mediation efforts. While European governments and EU collective institutions saw the shift in policies as representing a geopolitical turn, the approach adopted amounted to a relatively *soft geopolitics*. The change was not absolute; the EU did not completely eschew geopolitics before the crisis and member states did not entirely remove their support for institutionally embedded, low-politics EU approaches after 2013. The shift was one of balance, but nevertheless represented a tilt of meaningful magnitude.

In the triangular relationship between the EU, Russia and EaP partners, a *geopolitics of asymmetry* took root. European governments adopted some new elements of strategic policy in response to Russian actions and developments in the EaP states. But they did not seek to mirror the Russian understanding of geopolitics and nor did the EU as a whole understand security challenges in the same way as the EaP partners. There were differences between member states over the response to Russian actions. While many of these existed before 2013, Russia's actions accentuated some areas of internal divergence and brought them more starkly into the open. However, beneath these differences, there was European commonality on the 'asymmetrical geopolitics' spine of EU strategy.

The EU certainly applied new forms of pressure on Russia. One strand of its policies aimed to constrict Russian power. This represented a change in strategic logic from the decade-long European efforts to work in partnership to help Russia. But this shift was far from absolute. In parallel to restrictive measures, some European governments focused on more classical forms of diplomacy that sought trade-offs with Russia outside the scope of EU institutional instruments. The crisis marked the end of an era in a subtle yet profound sense: EU policies to the east now built in 'the Russia factor' in a way that the EaP had conspicuously not previously done.

A recurrent theme in post-2013 debates was whether the EU should accept Ukrainian neutrality as the solution that best protected member states' geopolitical interests. While the EU did not do so and indeed formally rejected the notion, several member states were drawn to the logic of what might be termed de facto *neutrality-lite*. This discouraged most EU governments from maximising support for Ukraine. Ultimately, the EU as a whole appeared willing to accept a degree of implicit 'defeat' in eastern Ukraine and allow Russia to take practical control not only of Crimea but also limited parts of the Donbas region. This was judged to be an outcome less damaging to European interests that open conflict with Russia.

The EU upgraded many of its commitments to the EaP states. It frequently claimed that this was the most effective means of dealing with the new geopolitics of the region and pushing back against Russian tactics. This did not fit the script of realists who argued the smartest strategic response would be for the EU to pull back from the region completely, on the grounds that the EaP was letting relations with relatively unimportant states ruin the vitally important strategic partnership with Russia. The EU did not fully embrace this form of geopolitical 'tactical retreat'.

Conversely, neither did the EU move far in the other direction of seeking to assert greater tutelage over the region as the best way of protecting its interests. European responses seemed to be seeking relatively *low-cost system maintenance*. The EU declined to offer EaP states full protection or assume responsibility for their security and territorial integrity. It offered neither the prospect of EU accession, nor major new benefits short of membership. Overall European financial support to EaP partners increased, but not dramatically. If the EU did not fully retreat from the region, neither did it strike out resolutely to do whatever it might take to gain more strategic influence over the EaP states. While there was a significant degree of change in EU policy, there was also a bedrock of continuity. While the tonality of much diplomacy changed, another strand of the response adhered to a 'more of the same' logic.

On balance, it could be said that the EU moved some way towards a strategic logic of balancing of the kind it had eschewed in its relations with Russia since the early 1990s. But this was a very moderate form of *soft-balancing*. The EU surprised many with its resolute sanctions against Russia and did not fully accept that the EaP region should be treated as a neutral buffer zone. Yet it sought to strike a middle ground between two opposing geopolitical logics: the 'buffer zone' and the 'full integration into Europe' options. Policy was an uneasy balance of engagement and containment, and was redolent of an '*engage and hedge*' geopolitical script.

Liberal-redux geopolitics entailed important shifts in the book's second area of concern: *the policy-making dynamics of EU foreign policy cooperation*. In some contrast to the most commonly applied theoretical understandings of EU foreign policy (outlined in Chapter 2 of this book), the EU moved towards a more *consequentialist-utilitarian* foreign policy, less clearly driven by institutionally embedded norms and identity. The most powerful European foreign policy dynamic prior to the crisis was that of a somewhat automatic, isomorphic rollover of internal EU rules and norms into the EaP; after the crisis this dynamic ceded ground to a more consequentialist balancing of different policy options' geopolitical impact.

The EU's multi-layered response was finely calibrated to its different types of interests: punitive measures to stop Russia extending its intrusions too far; continued cooperation with Russia where this was directly beneficial to the EU on other geopolitical challenges or on energy matters; signals of a longer-term steeliness that would militate against further Russian menace to systemic order; and extended cooperation with EaP states designed to attract these states towards alliance with the EU but without this involving too much in terms of costs and adjustments for the Union itself.

Many critics lambasted the EU and European governments for failing to respond to the crisis in a sufficiently geopolitical manner. Yet, in practice, the picture was highly nuanced; much of the delicate balance in EU policy was shot through with acutely geopolitical intent. The EU certainly eschewed a geopolitics of open confrontation with Russia in its defence of Ukrainian self-determination. However, in some ways its response was highly attuned to a judgement of where its own strategic interests lay, shifting unpredictably in the nebulous *grey zone mixing concession and assertive power.*

If the European policy mix was far from being blind to geopolitics, this entailed a shift in policy and institutional dynamics. While both external-structural and internal-identity drivers played a role in EU foreign policy, the balance tipped towards the former. The multilevel response also meant that a number of member states became more influential actors in driving forward Eastern policy and in conditioning the EaP's evolution. Relative to the EU's *sui generis* types of institutional foreign policy instruments, the more normal foreign policy dynamics of high-level diplomacy became more significant after 2013. This is not to say that institutional dynamics lost their force entirely. Indeed, they played a role in limiting the shift in European geopolitical thinking and in explaining the 'soft geopolitics' outcome. However, national governments' carefully weighted strategic calculations were undoubtedly more of an explanatory factor than was the case in the pre-2013 Eastern Partnership. This was in line with a broader interlacing of national and European levels that analysts detected across a range of EU foreign policy decisions. While many features of European responses were common to the EU area, they were increasingly advanced by national governments rather than EU institutional instruments.

In terms of the book's third aim of assessing *the impact of EU policies*, the positive view was that the EU stood just firm enough to scupper Vladimir Putin's plans. The Russian president did not win firm control over any large part of eastern Ukraine; turned the rest of Ukraine against Russia; bore a heavy cost economically; struggled to enthuse post-Soviet states with his flagship Eurasian Economic Union initiative; and failed fully to assuage Russian nationalists. However, if Putin's broader aim was to expose Western weakness and widen emergent cracks in the prevailing liberal world order, he partially succeeded. In some ways it was simply easier for Russia to have the bigger impact, as it played the role of spoiler and could run risks in a region that mattered more to Russian identity than it did to EU member states. Russia disrupted nascent patterns of domestic governance and cross-border cooperation, but was not able to offer an attractive, all-embracing ideological alternative to a European or wider Western influence.

From many perspectives – and in particular those of EaP states – the EU's success was at best highly qualified. Before the crisis erupted in late 2013, the EU's impact was problematic because the EaP was a half-way house. It extended European presence into the Eastern region but without full strategic protection. It was intrusive enough to provoke Russia, but not robust enough to deal with the consequences. Yet, many aspects of the EU's response to the post-2013 crisis if anything reinforced this half-way approach. This was the curious paradox of the crisis' legacy: the approach that contributed to triggering the crisis was the same one the EU relied on in its response to the Ukraine conflict. This continued to detract from the EU's effectiveness in contributing to a stable resolution to the eastern crisis.

In some areas the EU stuck too fast to its traditional approach of resisting geopolitical competition and offering simply to export the its own rules and norms. The EU's standard approach was increasingly an engrained foreign policy style in search of a still-receptive customer. While there was some technical sector-level convergence and the EU's power of attraction remained high for some EaP countries, the EU's diplomatic pre-eminence diminished in many parts of the region. Its ability to influence high politics was uneven. The EU contributed to – or at least could not prevent – a split between two groups of EaP states, geopolitically at odds with each other. While these states wanted firmer security backing, the European imprint remained limited – including through the institutionally separate avenue of NATO, whose role most EU governments sought to retain within strict parameters. In some ways, it might be said that European governments were rather *too* cleverly Machiavellian in thinking they could neatly combine all these different hues and shades of geopolitics and institutional vehicles without major inconsistencies that would rebound against their own interests.

The chorus of opinion was that the EU had been inept in doing geopolitics and slow to adjust to a world more confrontationally at odds with its own liberal norms. By 2016 this standard assessment was pertinent in accounting for the persistent strategic uncertainties of the eastern crisis, but it also looked like a partial and simplistic diagnosis of the EU's shortcomings. The book reveals a more nuanced picture than that suggested by this now received wisdom on Europe's geopolitical denial – in terms of both the causes of the crisis and the EU's efforts to respond effectively to it.

The challenge remained of how to translate the EU's incipient geopolitical consciousness into fully effective action. As of late 2016, the eastern crisis was partially calmed, but far from over. In the Donbas region, separatist attacks continued to kill Ukrainians on a daily basis; many observers predicted major, outright conflict. Ukraine's reform process stuttered, while political trends in Armenia, Azerbaijan, Belarus, Georgia and Moldova were far from reassuring. Europe's relations with Russia remained fraught. Strategic threats from the Middle East were now competing for resources and space on the EU's foreign policy agenda. The intricate geopolitical balances that the EU delineated after 2013 were set to be severely stress-tested well into the future. This book reflects on both the strategic potential and limitations to the EU's emerging liberal-redux geopolitics, as the storm clouds of international tumult hovered menacingly over Europe's foreign policy horizons.

Map 1.1 Map showing the Six Eastern Partnership States

Map 1.2 Map of Ukraine

Map 1.3 Map of the Minsk Peace Deal

2 An Analytical Framework for European Union Crisis Responses

In order to orientate the book's empirical account of European Union (EU) responses to the eastern crisis, this chapter offers an analytical framework for assessing the EU's foreign policy actions. For many years, analysts have debated the EU's identity and effectiveness in foreign and security policy. Some writers argue that the EU has gradually found its voice in global affairs, based on a very particular understanding of international security and liberal order. Others are more sceptical, pointing to persistent differences between member states, the EU's power deficiencies and the cases where its professed approach to security has, in practice, not been fully implemented. These different points of view in part reflect varied ways of understanding and defining geopolitics. Taking on board these various strands of theoretical debate, this chapter maps a template for judging just how far and in what ways EU foreign policy changed in response to the post-2013 eastern crises. It suggests criteria for assessing how the EU's response should be characterised; how it should be explained; and how its effectiveness might be measured.

A Distinctive Foreign Policy?

Most theorists believe that European governments have incrementally solidified their cooperation and, consequently the EU as a whole has developed a distinctive foreign policy identity. Analysts typically conceptualise the EU as an actor wedded to cooperative rather than adversarial approaches to security, and one intrinsically drawn to positive-sum and holistic security policies. Both in policy and theoretical orientations, the eschewal of zero-sum power politics is seen as the almost quintessential pillar of the Union's common foreign and security policy. The standard descriptors of EU power – ethical, liberal, normative, post-modern – attest to the EU's widely supposed aversion to standard geopolitics.

The seminal 2003 European Security Strategy enshrined the notion that EU security is best pursued not through increasing relative power but by assisting other states to become stronger, more prosperous and more effectively governed.[1] The EU espouses a strategic philosophy based on the principle of cooperative inclusion. In its policy documents and statements, the EU fashions itself as a post-modern security actor. It insists that European interests are served not by preventing other states achieve their interests but by working with them to attain mutually beneficial advances in political and economic interests. Many theorists believe that the EU's narrative about itself shapes the substance of its foreign policy output.

The EU stresses that rules-based behaviour is the backbone of its geostrategic identity. Indeed, the EU has contributed greatly to expanding the definition of security beyond traditional notions. It insists that security cannot be reduced to defensive concepts but must be broadened to include soft security questions such as economic development, the combating of cross-border crime, counter-radicalisation, human security and environmental questions.[2] Member states often adopt the same narrative in their national security strategies and have increasingly sought to align these with such embedded EU-level norms.

Theorists point to an internal process of ideational socialisation around cooperative security norms very different from standard realpolitik. Constructivists argue that such common EU policy identities now outweigh realist national calculations of narrow self-interest. From a slightly different perspective, institutionalists emphasise how many years of regularised processes of coordination have bred common outlooks between member states around rule-based international action.[3]

[1] European Union, *European Security Strategy, A Strong Europe in a Safer World*, 2003.

[2] K. Smith, *European Union Foreign Policy in a Changing World*, 2nd edn, Cambridge: Polity, 2008; J. McCormick, *The European Superpower*, Basingstoke: Macmillan, 2007; M. Tèlo, *Europe: A Civilian Power? European Union, Global Governance, World Order*, Basingstoke: Palgrave Macmillan, 2007; S. Biscop and J. Andersson (eds) *The EU and the European Security Strategy: Forging a Global Europe*, London: Routledge, 2008; I. Manners, 'The normative ethics of the European Union', *International Affairs*, 84/1, 2008, 45–60; S. Lucarelli and I. Manners (eds) *Values and Principles in European Union Foreign Policy*, London: Routledge, 2006.

[3] For overviews of these different theoretical schools see T. Christiansen and B. Tonra (eds) *Rethinking European Union Foreign Policy*, Manchester: Manchester University Press, 2004; M. E. Smith, 'Toward a theory of EU foreign policy making: Multi-level governance, domestic politics, and

The standard theoretical approach towards the study of European security identity has been to stress the centrality of rules and governance norms, not of power. The mainstream view is that much of the EU's normative influence derives from the model it stands for as much as the purposive actions it undertakes through its traditional diplomacy. The EU wields its most notable influence through the formal or de facto extension of its own borders; it 'acts' beyond its borders by reproducing its own rules and norms more than in a classically geopolitical sense. Concepts like 'market-power Europe' (which holds that the 'EU most consequentially affects the international system by externalizing its internal market-related policies and regulatory measures')[4] and 'functional-power Europe'[5] convey the notion that the EU has found effective means to project influence that are conceptually distinct from traditional strategies of interest-maximisation.

The rationalist and instrumental use of EU rules is neither pure liberal interdependence nor classical geopolitics; it borrows some elements from each of these conceptual frameworks, but theorists commonly insist that it constitutes a distinctive category of international actorness. Some analysts argue that EU external action points towards a 'structural' rather than 'relational' foreign policy. It is concerned to develop rules and structures, between and within other states that could provide sustainable means of security and stability, rather than merely augmenting the Union's EU's power relative to other states. While EU foreign policy mostly includes a balance of the two logics, it clearly eschews a clear prioritisation of relational power. This foreign policy identity flows naturally from the internal logic of European integration and reflects the kind of rules that underpin cooperation between member states themselves.[6]

national adaptation to Europe's common foreign and security policy', *Journal of European Public Policy* 11, 2004, 740–45.

[4] C. Damro, 'Market power Europe: Exploring a dynamic conceptual framework', *Journal of European Public Policy*, 22/9, 2015, 1336–54; C. Damro, 'Market power Europe', *Journal of European Public Policy* 19/5, 2012, 682–99.

[5] S. Lavenex, 'The power of functionalist extension: How EU rules travel', *Journal of European Public Policy* 21/6, 2014, 885–903.

[6] S. Keukelaire and T. Delreux, *The Foreign Policy of the European Union*, Basingstoke: Palgrave Macmillan, 2nd edn, 2014. On the Eastern Partnership see pp. 256–57.

The EU is widely seen as uniquely wedded to a 'governance' approach to achieving international security. This denotes a distinct form of security management that flows from the EU's own structure as a deeply integrated security system. It reflects a less state-centric view of security than that adopted by other powers. It seeks the extension of a holistic security community, through policies involving different levels of actors and different sectors of action. It means that security policies emerge organically from a strongly rooted common European identity rather than taking shape as short-term interest-driven responses to external shocks.[7]

The EU's strategic ethos is, in principle, also informed by the concept of human security. The EU regularly commits itself to developing the notion of human security as a central part of its security policies in situations of fragility. Human security means a focus on the security of individuals as opposed to the prioritisation of traditionally defined state-centric power interests. It is widely argued that this notion has filtered into the EU's foreign policy culture, and that human security expressly pulls the EU away from what high-politics strategic interests might require.[8]

Such are the features of what most theorists see as signature EU approaches to foreign policy and the key processes through which European governments have united around distinctive approaches to international security. However, writers have increasingly pointed to the shortcomings of these approaches and to an apparent flagging of foreign policy commitment. The Eurozone crisis that hit the EU from 2009 led most member states to cut military and development budgets. It pushed governments to focus on more narrowly defined commercial interests in their external policies.[9] Observers note how governments have become more selective in their efforts to uphold multilateral rules

[7] J. Sperling and M. Webber, 'Security governance in Europe: A return to system', *European Security*, 23/2, 2014, 126–44.

[8] G. Christou, 'The European Union's human security discourse: Where are we now?', *European Security*, 23/3, 2014, 364–81.

[9] R. Youngs, *The Uncertain Legacy of Crisis: European Foreign Policy Faces the Future*, Washington DC: Carnegie Endowment for International Peace, 2014; R. Kempin and M. Overhaus, 'EU foreign policy in times of the financial and debt crisis', *European Foreign Affairs Review* 19/2, 2014, 179–94; F. Erixson, *How Trade and Security became Europe's Unhappy Couple*, Brussels: Carnegie Europe, March 2015.

and 'negotiated order'.[10] Critics lament that the EU has come to suffer serious consequences from its aversion to geopolitical engagement, while turmoil within Europe has undercut its appeal as a governance model to other countries.[11]

The 'standard' EU approach to the neighbourhood and to global affairs is to some extent an ideal-type, never fully implemented in practice and invariably diluted with tinges of traditional geopolitical actions. In the wake of economic crisis, unity between member states splintered and commentators talked of the 'renationalisation' of foreign policy.[12] Critics insist that the EU's ability to act geopolitically has been increasingly hampered by clashes between EU institutions and member state diplomacy.[13] Theorists observe a general drift back towards loose inter-governmentalism in European cooperation, cutting across EU-level foreign policy distinctiveness.[14] Some experts point out that member states increasingly seek international influence through various levels of agency, relying less on the EU as the central pillar holding up a liberal form of global governance.[15] In short, many writers have detected a general waning of EU strength, unity and distinctiveness in foreign policy in recent years. Before the eastern crisis erupted, internal and external trends were already asking searching questions of the EU's trademark foreign policy instruments and strategies.[16]

10 M. Smith, 'Beyond the comfort zone: Internal crisis and challenges in the EU's response to rising powers', *International Affairs*, 89/3, 2013, 653–71; O. Costa, 'A force for and because of multilateralism: When is the EU a multilateralist actor in world society?', *Journal of European Public Policy*, 20/8, 2013, 1213–28.

11 A. Menon, 'Divided and declining? Europe in a changing world', *Journal of Common Market Studies*, 52, Annual Review, 5–24.

12 C. Kupchan, 'Centrifugal Europe', *Survival*, 54/1, 2012, 111–18, pp. 111 and 115.

13 J. Wissel, 'The structure of the 'EU'ropean ensemble of state apparatuses and its geopolitical ambitions', *Geopolitics*, 19/3, 490–513, p. 505.

14 F. Schimmelfennig, 'Liberal intergovernmentalism and the euro area crisis', *Journal of European Public Policy*, 22/2, 2015, 177–95.

15 S. Keukeleire and H. Bruyninckx, 'The European Union, the BRICs and the Emerging New World Order'. In C. Hill and M. Smith (eds) *International Relations and the European Union*, Oxford: Oxford University Press, 2nd edn, 2012, p. 392.

16 For a particularly broad-ranging summary of theoretical interpretations of the ENP, see S. Gstöhl and S. Schunz (eds) *Theorizing the European Neighbourhood Policy*, London: Routledge, 2016.

Geopolitics: Conundrums and Options

In the aftermath of the Crimea crisis, politicians, journalists, bloggers, academics and civil society organisations frequently spoke of Europe facing a more 'geopolitical' environment. They commonly pushed the EU to adopt a more 'geopolitical' approach to its eastern neighbourhood. However, the term 'geopolitics' is itself contested: it means different things to different schools of analytical thought.

Academics have long struggled to agree a precise definition of geopolitics. Cassical geopolitics was initially associated with imperialism. It gradually became a broader synonym for balance-of-power politics; its central contention was that geography mattered in international relations. The concept saw power and influence as a matter of control over territory. International relations were a question of competitive struggle for hegemony over geographical spaces. Rudolph Kjellén's 1899 seminal volume, *Geopolitics* coined and defined the term as meaning the 'science of the state', understood mainly as the science of war. Halford Mackinder's 'Heartland' theory had enduring impact. It suggested that power rivalries in the contested geopolitical 'heartlands' or 'pivot areas' of Eurasia were the driving force in international relations.[17]

During the Cold War, the term geopolitics provided the conceptual umbrella for statecraft predicated on containment. Hard power was essential to maximise relative advantage over great power rivals. One state's security could only be achieved by holding the power of others in check. The concept was broadened to include a focus on relative economic gain, through the notion of geo-economic power. It was later associated with those insisting that modern international relations were a matter of adversarial struggle between cultural-religious blocs.[18] One influential work distinguished three types of geopolitics, shaped by civilisational, territorial and ideological competition respectively – distinctions with growing relevance to contemporary challenges.[19] While for some theorists geopolitics refers to the way

[17] H. J. Mackinder, 'The geographical pivot of history', *Geographical Society*, 23/4, 1904, 421–37.

[18] S. Huntingdon, *The Clash of Civilizations and the Remaking of World Order*, New York: Simon and Schuster, 1991.

[19] J. Agnew, *Geopolitics: Re-visioning World Politics*, London: Routledge, 1998.

geography determines foreign policy outcomes rather than a style of foreign policy as such, others questions this traditional understanding.

Within academia, geopolitics gave way to 'critical geopolitics'. This questioned some of the concept's core realist- and power-based premises. This 'anti-geopolitics' was highly normative, reflecting the fact that, by the late twentieth century, the very concept of geopolitics had acquired negative overtones of domination and seemed blind to the social, economic and environmental change unfolding across the world.[20] Critical geopolitics examined how the 'geopolitics' discourse was used to justify and legitimise political authority and certain political practices both domestically and internationally.[21] Geopolitics was widely seen to be a concept out of tune with contemporary global trends, running egregiously against the grain of a more liberal order. Western powers' conceptualisation of geopolitics prevented other states and societies from developing; it was a means of protecting a narrow set of elite power interests.

As the liberal order has encountered problems, so geopolitics has made a comeback. Some writers argue that international trends make a 'neo-classical geopolitics' necessary. This refers to a framework that recognises competitive rivalry over territorial space to be a potent driver of international politics – but that is shorn of geopolitics' unsavoury, imperial roots.[22] The notion of 'soft geopolitics' has taken root. If 'hard geopolitics' refers to states using military means to acquire political and territorial control over others, 'soft geopolitics' is the use of political, economic and socio-cultural tools in the competition among states: 'international great power war is marginalised, but territorial competition, and military balancing/hedging' is prominent.[23] The different notion of 'meta-geopolitics' captured the importance of power calculations and zero-sum threats, while seeing

[20] G. O'Tuathail, S. Dalby and P. Routledge (eds) *The Geopolitics Reader*, London: Routledge, 2003.

[21] A. Behnke, 'The politics of geopolitik in post Cold-War Germany', *Geopolitics*, 3, 2006, 396–419; G. O'Tuathail, *Critical Geopolitics*, St Paul Minneapolis: University of Minnesota Press, 1996.

[22] T. Haverluk, K. Beauchemin and A. Mueller, 'The three critical flaws of critical geopolitics: Towards a neo-classical geopolitics', *Geopolitics*, 19/1, 2004, 19–39.

[23] B. Buzan and G. Lawson, *The Global Transformation: History, Modernity and the Making of International Relations*, Cambridge: Cambridge University Press, 2015, p. 285.

these as conditioned by a far wider range of factors than traditional geopolitical models allowed for: as a consequence, 'multi-sum security' required a form of updated 'neo-statecraft'.[24]

Curiously, in the space of a few years, geopolitics has gone from being a rather out-dated concept of dubious heritage to being a more positively used term that is widely seen as capturing the need for Western powers to 'get real' about the way that their vital interests are now challenged by other, increasingly powerful states. The states of the Eastern Partnership (EaP) region are located in what geopolitical analysts have long referred to as the 'shatterbelt', an area fought over for centuries by the major powers – something apparently neglected by the EU's overly benign belief in liberal order.

Of crucial importance for this book is the question of how these debates over geopolitics relate to standard theoretical interpretations of EU foreign policy. The EU has commonly been seen as a counterpoint to classical geopolitics. The founding tenets of EU foreign policy saw classical geopolitics as anathema. Indeed, they appeared to correspond to the notion of 'anti-geopolitics'. Geopolitics has not fitted easily into mainstream conceptual accounts of EU foreign policy. The historical institutionalist perspective sees embedded EU identities exerting an influence that militates against instrumental geo-strategy.

In a more nuanced vein, some argue that the EU has never been entirely anti-geopolitics as much as geopolitical in a distinctive fashion. It is a competitive empire that exerts its control over neighbouring states by incorporating them into its own political system.[25] The EU ostensibly embraces Mackinder's notion of values being exported as a form of power projection, even if it rejects his notion of territorial ambition.[26] Post-structuralist critics see the EU's normative power narrative as a means of imposing a form of 'governmentality' on other states – a very securitised form of control over the periphery on the basis of norms and rules.[27] Some noted theorists insist that the EU is not entirely immune to

[24] N. Al-Rodhan, *Neo-statecraft and Meta-geopolitics*, Berlin: LIT Verlag, 2009.

[25] J. Zielonka, *Europe as Empire*, Oxford: Oxford University Press, 2006.

[26] G. Kearns, 'Beyond the legacy of Makinder', *Geopolitics*, 18/4, 2013, 917–32.

[27] Recent examples include R. Youngs, *Europe in the New Middle East: Opportunity or Exclusion?*, Oxford: Oxford University Press, 2014; R. del Sarto, 'Normative empire Europe: The European Union, its borderlands, and the "Arab Spring"', *Journal of Common Market Studies*, 54/2, 2016, 215–32.

the 'securitisation' logic of decision-makers using security issues to justify dramatic and exceptional policy responses.[28] Its ideal-type approach to geopolitics was, perhaps, always more aspiration than reality. Its implicit preference for 'soft geopolitics' might be seen as a distinctive point on the same spectrum as classical geopolitics rather than a qualitatively different, non-geopolitical approach to foreign policy.

Nevertheless, critics insist that while the EU might presume that its liberal, rules-based mode of action constitutes enlightened geo-strategy in a very generic sense, its foreign policy decisions often fail to embrace the kind of action needed to translate these into reality. The EU has rarely envisaged its distinctive geopolitics being neutralised by any serious counter-veiling powers or directly opposing influences in the neighbourhood. The analytical focus has been on the complex internal dynamics of bargaining between member states, leaving most articles on EU foreign policy strikingly bereft of any coverage of external geopolitical factors. Experts increasingly call for a more systematic focus on how EU instruments interrelate with other powers' foreign policies.[29] Critics say the EU may be good at focusing on the generic way it prefers to carry out international relations, but has failed to develop a 'grand strategy' in the more concrete sense of where and how its power resources are to be deployed with security interests in mind.[30] Recent work posits a useful advance: the broadly accepted view that collective identity underpins EU foreign policies needs greater precision in tracing how such an identity is operationalised in particular policy choices – given that a number of strategic choices may be compatible with the EU's embedded norms.[31]

The human security focus has, sceptics say, led the EU to pay more attention to the internal weaknesses of so-called fragile states than to

[28] O. Waever, 'Politics, security, theory' *Security Dialogue* 42/4, 2011, 465–80.

[29] L. Delcour, *The EU and Russia in their 'Contested Neighbourhood': Multiple External Influences, Policy Transfer and Domestic Change*, London: Routledge, 2017; E. Conceição-Heldt and S. Meunier, 'Speaking with a single voice: Internal cohesiveness and external effectiveness of the EU in global governance', *Journal of European Public Policy*, 21/7, 2014, 961–79.

[30] J. Rogers, *A New Geography of European Power?* Brussels: Egmont Institute, Egmont Paper 42, 2011; D. Stokes and R. Whitman, 'Transatlantic triage? European and UK 'grand strategy' after the US rebalance to Asia', *International Affairs*, 89/5, 2013, 1087–1107.

[31] K. Hebel and T. Lenz, 'The identity/policy nexus in European foreign policy', *Journal of European Public Policy*, 23/4, 2016, 473–91.

geopolitical rivalries *between* states. Member states' bandwagoning with the US still trumps efforts to develop an autonomous European geo-strategy tailored to specific EU interests.[32] In the run up to the 2013 eastern crisis, the chorus of criticism that the EU had been naively blind to revanchist geopolitics grew louder.[33]

In sum, the definition of geopolitics remains contested – and this is reflected in debates over EU foreign policy identities. The focus on *sui generis* EU policy-making processes and rules has distracted analysts from developing more eclectic mid-range theory capable of explaining the EU's role in international security.[34] The central question is whether the crisis in the east changed the way the EU sought to influence the Eastern Partnership region – and if so, precisely how did it understand the new 'geopolitical' imperative.

Conceptualising EU Responses

This analytical context helps direct our conceptual gaze at the most relevant questions for assessing the EU's reaction to the post-2013 eastern crises. Building from these evolving debates about EU foreign policy identities and different understandings of geopolitics, the book has three aims: First, to arrive at a conceptual categorisation of the way in which the EU responded to the eastern crisis; second, to examine how far this response had an impact on the underlying policy-making dynamics of EU foreign and security policy cooperation; and third, to assess the effectiveness of the EU's particular type of geopolitical response.

Characterising the European Response

The book seeks to disaggregate the elements of change and continuity in European foreign policies and to classify EU strategy in terms of

32 L. Cladi and A. Locatelli, 'Worth a shot: On the explanatory power of bandwagoning in transatlantic relations', *Contemporary Security Policy*, 34/2, 2013, 374–81.

33 L. Delcour and E. Tulmets (eds) *Pioneer Europe? Testing EU Foreign Policy in the Neighbourhood*, Baden-Baden: Nomos, 2008; R. Whitman and S. Wolff (eds) *The European Neighbourhood Policy in Perspective*, Basingstoke: Palgrave Macmillan, 2010.

34 A. Rodt, R. Whitman and S. Wolff, 'The EU as an international security provider: The need for a mid-range theory', *Global Society*, 29/2, 2015, 149–55.

several analytical metrics. These have to do with the EU's preferred mix of hard and soft diplomatic tools, its relations with both EaP states and Russia, and how the EU relates norms to interests. While the metrics inevitably overlap, unpacking the different areas of inquiry facilitates a multi-layered categorisation of European responses to the eastern crisis.

A first crucial question is how far the crisis caused the EU to increase its *level of engagement* with Eastern Partnership countries. Did diplomatic commitment and political will intensify, and were additional resources made available to the six EaP partners? There was much rhetoric suggesting that the crisis represented a watershed moment and one of the EU's most existential threats for many years. Yet, it must be asked whether governments really accorded the eastern crisis priority, compared to other areas of foreign or domestic policy. It is necessary to examine whether the EU sought to gain more direct 'control' over the EaP 'rimlands' as a means of holding Russia in check – and whether it sought to do this through the deeper inclusion of EaP states within a Euro-governance sphere.

In essence, this relates to the question of what combination of defensive and offensive strategies the EU favoured. A defensive geopolitical logic would predict that the EU should have 'retreated' from the eastern region, lowering its exposure to a crisis that did not have a bearing upon the core aspects of its own security and well-being. This was the strategy that many prominent experts favoured, as they called for Western strategic retreat from the EaP region and an end to EU efforts to promote transformative norms.[35] In contrast, a more offensive geopolitical option would involve the EU acting assertively to pre-empt a rival power encroaching upon its own would-be sphere of influence.

So, which approach did member states pursue? Did the EU calculate that it needed to push harder for control over the 'middle lands' lying

[35] H. Kissinger, *World Order*, London: Penguin, 2014; J. Mearsheimer, 'Why the Ukraine crisis is the West's fault', *Foreign Affairs*, September/October 2014; R. Haass, 'The unraveling: How to respond to a disordered world', *Foreign Affairs*, November/December 2014; I. Krasetv and M. Leonard, *The New European Order*, London: European Council on Foreign Relations, 2014; R. Sakwa, *Frontline Ukraine: Crisis in the Borderlands*, London: I. B. Tauris, 2015; H. Strachan, 'Europe, Geopolitics and Strategy', Egmont Lecture, 9 January 2015.

between it and Russia? Or had the EU already pushed too intrusively into this region, heedlessly awakening Russian irredentism; did the EU now need to backtrack to a policy that assuaged Russia? Did EU states bend to the logic of treating EaP states more as 'buffers' between themselves and an increasingly hostile Russia?

A second dimension relates to the use of *hard-security* instruments. Did EU governments complement the use of low-politics, technocratic policy tools with a strengthening of high politics security instruments? Did they believe that harder-edged security policy required some role for enhanced military capabilities, with more of an emphasis on NATO cooperation than before the crisis? Did an assessment of hard-security strategy enter into the EaP's rubric or remain institutionally separate, as a matter for NATO and national governments rather than EU institutional roles? Prior to 2013, the EaP had no hard-security component; the EU did not see any role for a defence or military dimension to its Eastern strategy. It is necessary to examine how far this situation changed after 2013. Classifying the European response to the eastern crisis requires a careful unpacking of debates over hard-security capacities, including military instruments and the complex relationship between national NATO and EU initiatives.

A third metric requires us to examine the balance between *isolation of and engagement with Russia*. A crucial issue was whether the EU made a fundamental switch towards the logic of excluding Russia from forums of cooperation. Conversely, it must be examined whether, in line with the tenets of cooperative inclusion, member states in fact judged that the crisis required a redoubling of efforts to tie Russia into more inclusive security and economic arrangements.

A key assessment deployed through the book's empirical chapters is the precise balance in EU responses between pressure and engagement. On the one hand, the crisis might have killed any notion of a liberal EU-EaP-Russia triangle. Some experts foresaw unavoidable confrontation with Russia and feared that attempts at compromise fundamentally misread the nature of Russian geo-strategy.[36] On the other hand, EU self-interest might require some baseline of common norms with Russia in the new management of the post-Soviet space. Exactly what

36 K. Giles, P. Hanson, R. Lyne, J. Nixey, J. Sherr and A. Woord, *The Russian Challenge*, London: Chatham House, 2015.

form this balance between pressure and engagement took is central to categorising what type of 'geopolitical' turn European governments sought to map out.

A fourth question was the role of *norms and values* in the European response. It is necessary to chart how far the EU shifted to a greater focus on relational, to the detriment of structural, foreign policy. Did the crisis change the terms on which the EU's member states engaged with EaP partners? Was support for democratic reform downgraded relative to geopolitical imperatives? Or did the EU judge democracy support to be its best form of geopolitical response? What was the balance between two contending strategic visions: security-though-inclusion versus security-through-resilient-governance? That is, was the EU's priority now to include EaP partners within firmly embedded institutionalised partnerships as allies against Russia? Or was it to use support for democracy and good governance as the best means of undercutting Russian influence in the region? As compliance with EU rules had proven so patchy, did the EU change the *way* it sought to further reform?

Using these four variables – degree of commitment to EaP partners; hard-security components; isolation of or engagement with Russia; and degree of commitment to democratic and other liberal values – an operational template for assessing EU strategic responses to the eastern crisis can be defined. This can be represented in the form of a matrix of geopolitical options, as shown in Table 1.

The four variables can combine in different permutations. For schematic purposes, these combinations can be grouped into different kinds of strategic response:

- A *standard EU approach* under which we would see a large degree of continuity in EU policy, a moderate degree of commitment to the EaP, no hard-security dimension, low-politics engagement with Russia, efforts to foster regional cooperation and modest support for liberal norms. Even if this 'standard' approach was not, in practice, implemented in pristine form prior to the 2013 crisis, it serves as a benchmark of the EU's self-identity in strategic affairs, against which we can measure new directions in strategic thinking after 2013.
- An *offensive geopolitical response* that would prompt European governments into a stronger commitment to the EaP, enhanced military capabilities (both nationally and through NATO commitments)

Table 1: *A Matrix of Geopolitical Implications*

'Standard' EU Approach	Offensive Geopolitics	Defensive Geopolitics	Liberal-Redux Geopolitics
Moderate commitment, at level of low-politics, expansion of technocratic rules.	Significant increase in commitment to EaP states: more aid, more incentives, accession perspectives.	Pull-back from EaP space.	Modest increase in commitment, but no far-reaching promises.
No hard-security dimensions.	Strengthened hard-security engagement and military capabilities. Stronger NATO role.	No military response. NATO retracts.	Modest (only) boost to defensive capabilities and deployment.
Partnership efforts with Russia, mainly though low-politics cooperation.	Punitive sanctions against Russia. Less dialogue with Russia. Efforts to reduce dependency on Russia.	Dialogue with Russia; shared problem-solving.	Reduced engagement with Russia, but open to dialogue
Modest efforts to support political reforms, mainly through technocratic, 'external governance' approach.	Transformational or non-transformational forms: enhanced focus on values, as best geo-strategic advantage; or engagement less conditional on democratic reform.	Lower interest in helping political values.	Sharper support for democracy; both more instrumental and more variation
EU institutions play lead role.	Member states assume greater role compared to EU institutions.	Low-key role of national diplomacy; EU technocratic, governance approach.	More balanced combination of member states and EU institutions/tools.

and wide-ranging punitive measures against Russia, all backed up by more engaged member state diplomacy and targeted bilateral policies in individual EaP states.

- A *defensive geopolitical response* that would see the EU pull back from the EaP space, eschew hard-security approaches and seek a new strategic accommodation with Russia.
- What might be labelled a hybrid or *liberal-redux geopolitics*. This conveys the idea of an upgraded EU diplomacy mixing assertive and defensive tactics and using its distinctive tools aimed at deepening inclusion, interdependence and political transformation more instrumentally and more variably to further immediate-term security interests.

As we will see in the following chapters, this concept of liberal-redux geopolitics helps categorise many elements of the EU response to the eastern crisis. It is a concept that is similar to that of soft geopolitics, adapted for the specificities of EU external relations. It might be thought of as a kind of 'liberal power politics' that lies somewhere between the assertive expansion of liberal values and defensive retraction.[37] It denotes geo-strategy that contains a hybrid mix of offensive and defensive strategies, and a combination of national, EU and NATO instruments. While some might object that to combine liberal and geopolitical concepts is oxymoronic, the idea is to capture how the EU sought to harness many of its *sui generis* EaP policy instruments for more purposively defined geopolitical near-term objectives.

EU Foreign Policy Dynamics

On the basis of its categorisation of these different types of geopolitical strategy, the book's second concern is to explore how far the eastern crisis changed the internal dynamics of EU foreign policy cooperation – measured against the theoretical reflections outlined above. One of the most important questions was whether there was now an external variable – Russian assertiveness – powerfully driving an upgrade in EU foreign policy cooperation. Was the external shock of the crisis severe enough to push member states towards a more united

[37] S. Rynning, 'The false promise of continental concert: Russia, the West and the necessary balance of power', *International Affairs*, 91/3, 2015, 539–52.

foreign policy? In structural realist terms, was the need to balance against Russia the motive for renewed EU cooperation, echoing the logic of Cold War days? Was the external variable of Russia's challenge a cause of greater unity or disunity?

While the book charts whether there was a drift from internal to external variables as the primary determinants of EU policies, it also explores the complex meshing of analytical drivers. Did any one level of causal variable clearly predominate over others or were EU foreign policy outcomes the result of a more balanced inter-linking of three levels: international, regional and domestic? Was this really a purely Russia-driven crisis or was the best explanatory framework one that saw external structural constraints being mediated through embedded EU institutional identities and, in turn, EaP domestic political structures?

A closely associated question is whether member states' diplomacy gained in prominence relative to the more technocratic policies of the EU institutions. Did the institutional balance shift from the actors of 'technocratic Europe' to those of 'power Europe'?[38] Did some member states gain more prominence in striking out on a bilateral course to circumvent shortcomings in a joint EU-level strategy? If certain European governments became more influential did they shift the focus away from the EaP to other organisational forums, such as NATO, where governments more clearly controlled policy outputs? After the Georgia crisis in 2008, France and Russia colluded as 'great powers' to patch up a deal over the country's contested territories: was there even more of a definitive switch to this kind of high politics approach from 2013?

In turn, did the EU tilt away from the constructivist logic of appropriateness towards more rationalised self-interest? Conversely, did embedded processes of institutionalisation keep EU approaches to an identity-based approach, limiting a switch to high geopolitical assertiveness? Did a new language of securitisation frame a lead role for member state governments adopting more antagonistic policies? Or was this an episode of failed securitisation: an attempt to define the crisis as one of grave seriousness that, in fact, did not lead to any revised or upgraded policies?

[38] European Council on Foreign Relations, *Foreign Policy Scorecard 2014*, London: ECFR, 2014.

Impact and Effectiveness

The book's third aim is to use these analytical categorisations and explorations to move towards an overall assessment of the effectiveness of different EU responses. It asks whether the EU response was a success in preventing instability and containing a new threat from Russia, or whether it was placed on the back foot, emerging as a far more constricted and defensive force across the EaP. The book seeks to distinguish between those EaP countries where the EU appeared to lose influence and those where the crisis led to increased European presence. It also looks for thematic variation: the sectors of policy in which the EU upgraded its policy commitments are contrasted with others where it failed to make appreciable improvement. A more sharply geopolitical environment made it more challenging to account for the variation in policy outcomes. It was important better to understand when the EU's vaunted 'transformative power' worked and when it did not. The bumpy evolution of the EaP heightened this crucial dilemma: under what conditions did the EU's transformative power still wield influence and what variables rendered it a much weakened force? As outlined in the first section of this chapter, analysts were beginning to ask these questions about Europe's apparently declining leverage as the eastern crisis erupted in late 2013; clearly, an assessment of the EU's response to the crisis needs to revisit such questions in measuring how far its emerging liberal-redux geopolitics did the job is was designed for.

Conclusion

In sum, these are the crucial analytical questions that the following chapters address in their empirical account of EU policy in the EaP region. This chapter has given a flavour of the ongoing debates that exist about the nature of European foreign policies. These debates provide a baseline of what could be expected of the EU in terms of its approach to the crisis and the kinds of power it was likely to wield. The chapter also cautions that the widespread references to 'geopolitics' since the 2013 crisis surfaced require careful investigation and some detailed conceptual unpacking. While politicians, diplomats and analysts insisted that geopolitics had returned to European affairs and many governments talked of their new geopolitical intent, it was far from clear what this meant analytically and in terms of specific policy choices.

The suggested typology of geopolitical options – standard EU, offensive, defensive and liberal-redux – is designed to move the book towards an overarching categorisation of the European response to the crisis. The analytical categories are somewhat idealised and schematic; in practice they overlap and European policy is likely to include elements of each. The aim of distinguishing the categories from each other is to help disaggregate in granular detail the different dimensions of European policies, as expressed through national, EU, NATO and other policy instruments. This should enable a more nuanced conceptualisation of European strategy towards the eastern crisis than simply pronouncing on whether or not this strategy was 'geopolitical'. On the basis of this categorisation, the book sets out to examine a number of pertinent questions related to the internal policy-making dynamics of EU cooperation. These conceptual questions in turn lead to an in-depth assessment of the impact of European strategy. In what follows, these three levels of analysis – categorisation, foreign policy dynamics and impact – are applied in turn to the different components of the eastern crisis.

3 *The Return of Geopolitics*

As prelude to the book's empirical chapters, it is necessary to dissect the nature of the geopolitical challenge that the eastern crisis has presented to the European Union (EU). As Russia sought to prevent a change of regime in Ukraine and then moved effortlessly to assume control of Crimea, many observers spoke of a fundamental redrawing of the whole post-Cold War order. Geopolitical rivalry was back, and threatened some basic tenets upon which European security had been predicated for over a generation. Others believed that the crisis was of less far-reaching magnitude. This short scene-setting chapter outlines the factors that upset the strategic scenario in the EU's eastern neighbourhood and challenged European foreign policy. It outlines different perspectives on the scale of the crisis and what precisely was at stake for European strategic interests.

From Crimea to Eastern Ukraine

The crisis developed incrementally. From mid-2013, Russia began imposing economic measures against Georgia, Moldova and Ukraine. It threatened punitive sanctions and the withdrawal of other forms of cooperation as several EaP states neared signing association agreements (AAs) with the EU. The region's geopolitics seemed to awaken from a slumber when Armenia made the shock announcement in September 2013 that it was pulling out of its new EU agreement to join Russia's embryonic Eurasian Economic Union (hereafter, Eurasian Union). This was followed by Russia's success in pushing President Viktor Yanukovich to announce that Ukraine would also reject its EU agreement.

This opened the way to a second stage of Russian involvement in Ukraine's domestic affairs. As later chapters will examine in detail, Russia used multiple instruments in an effort to keep Yanukovich in power against pro-European civic protests. When this failed, Russia executed an apparent masterstroke. In March 2014, within a few weeks of the regime falling in Kiev Russia annexed Crimea. The world stood aghast at the temerity and apparent ease with which Russia redrew Ukraine's borders. The referendum that followed to legitimise the annexation was patently manipulated; it returned what most saw as an improbably high 'yes' vote given that much of the population was either Tartar or Ukrainian.

This presaged a graver escalation to the crisis, as violence spread into parts of eastern Ukraine. During the spring and summer of 2014, pro-Russian separatist rebels launched a series of attacks on the region's main cities. They took control of city administrations in Kramatorsk, Slavyansk and a series of smaller towns, and then Donetsk and Luhansk. The rebel forces were supplied with advanced weaponry from Russia.

The interim Ukrainian government adopted measures that initially aggravated tensions in parts of the east. It deployed the army, attempted (unsuccessfully) to downgrade the status of the Russian language and appointed supportive oligarchs as governors in a number of eastern cities. The support of these oligarchs gave the new interim government important ballast against Russian tactics. Views differed on how much anti-Kiev feeling in the east had been stirred up by Russian intervention and how much was genuinely rooted in society.

An apparent pattern emerged. Russia provoked just enough trouble to keep Ukraine politically unsettled and to prevent Kiev regaining control over the east. One of Russia's aims was to ensure that its supporters secured key political posts in the eastern Donbas region, so that even though it was formally within Ukraine, the region would be loyal to Moscow. Russia moved tens of thousands of troops to its border with Ukraine.

The Ukrainian government failed to re-establish order. The weakness of Ukraine's armed forces became increasingly apparent; they were defeated as they attempted to move eastwards in August 2014. Ukrainian forces fighting against the Russians were an uneasy mix of oligarch-funded militia, the rump Ukrainian army, volunteer forces from the Maidan protests and far-right agitators from the so-called 'Right Sector'. Separatist attacks intensified and the rebels gained ground. Russia laid out claims to a wider swathe of 'Novorossiya' territory in eight regions of eastern Ukraine, stirred revolts in cities like Kharkiv and talked of establishing a land corridor through to Crimea and Transnistria.

The shooting down of Malaysian Airlines flight MH17 over eastern Ukraine in July 2014 dramatically aggravated the situation. The tragedy cost the lives of 298 people, with Dutch citizens accounting for the largest loss of life. It was widely suspected that pro-Russian rebels were responsible. The missiles that brought the flight down were generally agreed to have come from launchers provided by Russia. Instead of having a salutary effect on the combatants, the disaster unleashed even more intensive fighting.

Russia increased support for rebel fighters and stationed more troops at the Ukrainian border. Ukrainian forces mobilised. By August, as Ukrainian security operations made further inroads to rebel-held strongholds, Russia carried out large-scale military exercises just over the border and readied additional troops to intervene as 'peacekeepers'. The involvement of regular Russian troops became more blatant and extensive. Satellite imagery suggested that over 1,000 Russian troops had entered south-east Ukraine to shore up rebel forces.

This involvement worked. Russian troops and arms helped push back Ukrainian troops and reverse rebel losses. It was now more difficult to deny that Russia had *de facto* invaded Ukraine. Ukrainian troops lost much of the ground they had retaken. President Petro Poroshenko accused Russia of overt and direct aggression. President Vladimir Putin then proposed a ceasefire and peace plan; these would lock-in Russia's territorial gains and represent a notable victory for the Kremlin as Ukrainian forces had appeared to be on the brink of victory.

A ceasefire for east Ukraine was agreed during talks in Minsk on 5 September 2014, between Ukrainian government representatives and separatist leaders. The Minsk accord put in place a new deal for the occupied parts of Donbas. This included self-government for rebel-held areas; an amnesty for rebel fighters; protected status for the Russian language; local elections; funds from Kiev to help reconstruction; and a separate, locally controlled police force. Ukrainian foreign and defence policy was to remain unified at the national level. Ukrainian authorities and Russian-backed rebels agreed to create a buffer zone between the two side's forces; to withdraw heavy weapons; and to send foreign fighters home.

Many details were still hazy. It was not clear whether political arrangements were such that a pro-Russia bloc could wield significant power in the parliament in Kiev. Border control was still contested.

Ukrainian authorities proceeded with plans to install a properly functioning border between Russia and Ukraine as a prerequisite to exercising effective sovereignty. Russia stonewalled these plans. Poroshenko came under strong domestic attack for the deal; the government had to rely on murky internal parliamentary dealings to get it through.

The ceasefire gradually collapsed over the course of the winter. The death toll returned to pre-Minsk levels. Russian military cooperation with the separatists soon developed into permanent structures that gave Donbas its own *de facto* security forces. In an effort to calm the spiralling violence, a second Minsk accord was signed in early 2015. This reinstated the ceasefire and reconfirmed the core political commitment to grant the Donbas territories some kind of autonomous 'special status'. If anything, this second Minsk accord gave the separatists more favourable terms than the first agreement.

While the new ceasefire held temporarily, during the course of 2015, rebel forces gradually scaled up the intensity of their attacks. A UN report released in June 2015 reported that 6,417 people had perished in the conflict and that over 16,000 people had been seriously injured.[1] The report accused both pro-Russian militias and Ukrainian forces of committing human rights abuses and failing to desist from violent attacks. This situation of persistent, low-level violence continued into 2016. The Ukrainian government accused Russia and the separatists of preparing for outright war and of being unwilling to hand Kiev control over its national borders. Russia accused Kiev of failing to progress with its side of the Minsk deal, as the Poroshenko government stalled on legislation providing for Donbas' 'autonomous status' and for elections in the region. Few expected the uneasy and partial ceasefire to hold indefinitely. The conflict reached a new peak of intensity in the summer of 2016, and threatened to revert to full-scale violence during the final months of the year. A resolution to the conflict remains elusive.

A Deeper Strategic Challenge

While the conflict dragged on in eastern Ukraine, other Russian actions presented a much broader strategic challenge. Russian violations of European countries' national airspace induced emergency

[1] *New York Times*, 1 June 2016.

military aircraft scrambles with narrowly avoided mid-air collisions and close encounters at sea. Russia stationed ballistic missiles in Crimea. In response, the US talked of redeploying nuclear warheads in Europe. Russia signed treaties with the Georgian breakaway regions of Abkhazia and South Ossetia under which these territories committed themselves to effective integration into Russian security forces. Russia also tried to frustrate Western policies in the Balkans. Moscow voted against the extension of the EU mission in Bosnia-Herzegovina and talked more openly of turning western Balkan states back from moves towards EU accession. President Putin stoked a renewed challenge to Bosnia's territorial integrity from nationalist Serbian leaders.

Russia's armed forces tripled in size between the 2008 Georgian war and 2016, by when military expenditure assumed a third of the state budget. The Russian government launched a vast programme of military modernisation. President Putin talked of limited nuclear strikes as a means of pushing the West back from Russia's natural sphere of influence. As part of its ten-year re-armament programme, in July 2015 the Russian government announced that it was adding forty new inter-continental ballistic missiles to its nuclear arsenal. A growing number of cyber attacks on European governmental installations were traced to Russia. Russian naval activity in the Black Sea and Mediterranean increased dramatically, reaching an intensity not seen since the Cold War.

Russia funded European lobbyists campaigning against shale gas fracking, seeking to divert the search for a new energy source that would increase the EU's independence from Russian supplies of oil and gas. Moscow began financing both far-right and far-left anti-EU parties across Europe, gaining allies at both extremes of the European political spectrum. As Russian forces killed thousands in Ukraine, European parties lined up to accept funds from or express support for Russia – from far-left Syriza in Greece and Podemos in Spain to France's far-right Front National and Hungary's Jobbik. Moscow aspired to create a new 'conservative international' against Western liberal values. In 2016, there were signs that Russia intervened on the back of the EU's refugee crisis to foment both radical Islamist and populist groups in Europe, in particular as a means to unsettle the German government.[2]

[2] *The Guardian*, 4 March 2016.

In the Cold War the Soviet Union was essentially a status quo power, interested in maintaining the rules of bipolarity. Now it was a resentful and unpredictable revisionist power. Putin was intent on (re)creating a whole narrative of Russian identity and power. The challenge came not merely from the degree of Russian assertiveness, but also from the use of so-called 'hybrid' tactics that stoked instability and uncertainty but fell short of outright and conventional military threats. Russia was the purveyor of a whole new art of covert destabilisation within east and west European states, through criminal networks, information technology, propaganda tools and the corrupt influencing of elites. This required EU governments to reassess their conceptualisation of security threats.

The End of an Order?

The most common argument was that Russia's actions were a threat to peace and stability on the wider European continent. They demonstrated that visceral might was now dominant, that hard power was no longer effectively held in check by the rule of liberal order and that uncertainty had returned as the most potent geo-strategic dynamic. There was much speculation about the crisis reversing the whole thrust of economic interdependence across the wider European space.

Russia acted in violation of the UN Charter, the 1994 Budapest memorandum on Security Assurances, the Bilateral Treaty on Friendship, Cooperation and Partnership between Ukraine and Russia, the OSCE Helsinki Final Act and the EU–Russia Partnership Agreement. For many, the crisis foretold the return of a bipolar Europe, together with the Brezhnev-era doctrine of 'limited sovereignty' in Eastern Europe. Some analysts described an emergent 'Putin doctrine'. This involved a reconstitution of the 'Russian world', within which Ukraine and Belarus represented pillars of a single Russian nation; an explicit willingness to act outside the confines of international law; and a more overtly confrontational stance towards the West, now defined unequivocally as the main opponent to Russian interests.[3] In Ukraine,

[3] M. Menkiszak, *The Putin Doctrine: The Formation of a Conceptual Framework for Russian Dominance in the Post-Soviet Area*, Centre for Eastern Studies (OSW), 2014.

Russia had upended its own defence of national sovereignty against Western interventionism.

For President Putin's supporters in Moscow this was not narrowly about Crimea but about Russia offering a vision for international politics that would rally Asian powers in alliance against the declining West.[4] Russia's actions were driven by a sense of the country having been humiliated after 1991, but were also a calculated adjustment to the emerging post-Western order. For Putin's inner team, the competitive nature of this order needed to be met with a neo-Hobbesian focus on 'great power-ness'. The strategic aim was a polycentrism in global order that accommodated both balancing behaviour and the promotion of civilisational identity. Russia was responding not so much to EU assertiveness in the EaP area but to its apparent weakness – the Ukraine crisis was an opportunity to strike home a strategic advantage over an economically crippled Western Europe. A side effect would be to establish Russia as the key balancer and bridge between west and east, between the US and China.[5]

The action in Crimea was of a piece with Russia's efforts from 2011 to develop a 'grand strategy'. The Russian government published its 'Strategy 2020' in March 2012, along with a series of similar documents that developed a purported aim of mobilising Russian power resources around the long-term vision of the country being the 'heartland' power of a rising Eurasian region.[6] Russian plans to situate large amounts of offensive military capabilities in Crimea suggested an aim to project power into the wider Black Sea region.[7]

The Crimea annexation represented a more serious challenge than Russia's invasion of Georgia in 2008. While the status of South Ossetia and Abkhazia had been left in limbo, Crimea was incorporated wholesale into the Russian Federation. President Putin's speeches were a number of notches higher in their adversarial antipathy to the prevailing international order than they had been in 2008. After reincorporating Crimea, Putin promised to 'unite the Russian world'. He

[4] V. Ryzhkov, 'The new Putin doctrine', *Moscow Times*, 3 April 2014.

[5] B. Lo, *Russia and the New World Disorder*. London: Chatham House, 2015, chapter 2.

[6] A. Monaghan, 'Putin's Russia: Shaping a "grand strategy"?', *International Affairs*, 89/5, 2013, 1221–1236.

[7] R. Allison, 'Russian "deniable" intervention in Ukraine: How and why Russia broke the rules', *International Affairs*, 90/6, 2014, 1255–1297.

increasingly spoke of Novorussiya, a classically geopolitical concept concerned with according Russia territorial control over the belt of land extending from southern Ukraine through to Moldova and the Danube river. This was the most irredentist form of geopolitics: Russia as a unilateral arbiter of borders.

Putin did not even pretend that Russia should seek its identity as a Western state. Observers detected the contours of an emergent civilisational battle, waged by Putin on behalf of an imagined 'Eurasian Slavic-Orthodox space' against the West. This was not simply a matter of Putin's individual leadership, but was consonant with and firmly rooted in Russian society's drift towards conservative social values, with the Orthodox church assuming a more powerful and Kremlin-sponsored role in distinguishing a Russian national identity from the ills of Western liberalism.

Many noted the influence of political philosopher Alexander Dugin's neo-Eurasianism, which saw Russia controlling a sphere of conservative tradition pitted in geopolitical battle with liberal Atlanticism. There were debates about whether Dugin was capturing the essence of Putin's project or whether the president opportunistically harnessed neo-Eurasianism to give intellectual ballast to his largely *ad hoc* responses to international events.[8] Either way, these were the aggressive thrashings of an unhappy declining power. Many believed that they rendered null all prospects of Western cooperation with Russia on questions of 'global order maintenance'.

Many prominent writers concurred on the game-changing significance of the events in 2014. Dmitri Trenin wrote that the crisis marked the return of 'great power rivalry'. A quarter of a century of 'half-hearted rapprochement' between Russia and the West was firmly over; mistrust was now dominant on both sides. Trenin believed that the EU was just as much to blame as Russia in this breakdown, for neither treating nor understanding Russia well enough and for encroaching upon Russia's interest in the 'middle lands'. This new epoch would last a long time, with the prospect of enduring instability within eastern states and tense strategic rivalry.[9]

[8] A. Tolstoy and E. McCaffray, 'Mind games: Alexander Dugin and Russia's war of ideas', *World Affairs*, March/April, 2015.

[9] D. Trenin, *The Ukraine Crisis and the Resumption of Great Power Rivalry*, Washington DC: Carnegie Endowment for International Peace, 2014.

Most experts agreed that Europe had woken up to a fundamentally changed geopolitical context. Michael McFaul argued that the Crimea annexation 'ended the post-Cold War era in Europe'. Policy could no longer be based on the assumption that, for all the ups and downs in its relations with the West, 'Russia was gradually joining the international order'.[10] Sabine Fischer stressed that Russia was now 'claiming unrestricted hegemony in its immediate neighbourhood'.[11] Jonathan Eyal argued that the crisis represented a 'systemic threat ... not just a blip in east–west relations': Russia had showed its determination to undermine state cohesion in eastern states to keep this region as a controlled buffer between it and the EU.[12] Others noted that the Russian government even seemed to be thinking in terms of its pre-1917 lands, promising a direct threat to EU member states.[13] Ivan Krastev insisted that the West was now 'living in Putin's world', with the future of 'the European order' hinging on how far the Russian president chose further to unsettle Ukraine.[14]

In all this lay a fundamental change in the challenges facing Eastern European states. Even if President Putin stopped short of seeking to annex eastern Ukraine, some insisted he was set to destabilise the country sufficiently to ensure that Kiev would be unable to pivot towards the EU and away from Russian influence.[15] Precisely because affinities and linkages were increasingly apparent between Putin's coterie and rightist, illiberal parties within EU member states, Timothy Snyder went as far as asserting that: 'Ukraine has no future without Europe, but Europe also has no future without Ukraine' – in the sense that the crisis was about holding at bay the rise of illiberal political ideas in both Russia and the West.[16]

Domestic factors compounded the depth and gravity of the shift in Russian foreign policy. Putin's truculence towards the West and

[10] M. McFaul, 'Confronting Putin's Russia', *New York Times*, 23 March 2014.

[11] S. Fischer, *Escalation in Ukraine*, Berlin: SWP, SWP Comments, 2014, p. 2.

[12] J. Eyal, *Russia's Ukraine Srategy Ends Europe's Dream*, London: Royal United Services Institute, 2014.

[13] I. Bond, *Europe and Russia: Continental Divide?*, London: Centre for European Reform, 2014.

[14] I. Krastev, 'Putin's world', *Project Syndicate*, 2 April 2014.

[15] S Meister, *Putin's Plan*, London: European Council for Foreign Relations, 2014.

[16] T. Snyder, 'The battle in Ukraine means everything', *New Republic*, 11 May 2014.

risk-taking assertiveness was necessary to keep himself in power. His governing style changed fundamentally after the protests against his manipulation of elections in 2011. While the president successfully put down the protests, he could no longer claim to govern in the name of all Russians. He now relied on a more combative and divisive political ideology to underpin his regime. Putin focused on opposition to democratic and liberal European values as far more of a guiding narrative than in his earlier presidential terms. The annexation of Crimea was the expression of the regime's altered domestic political foundation.[17] Russia had never been through a process of definitively consolidating its borders; the origins of the Ukraine crisis lay deep within the unfinished process of Russian state-formation.

For some writers, all this denoted a patrimonial deification of the leader that had deep roots in Russian history and was as much about Russians' relationship with power as about Putin himself. Putin was not a natural or instinctively assertive nationalist but found himself dependent on the loyalty of those who were. His populism had confronted so many vested interests within the dysfunctional state that he needed to rebuild his own support base. He struggled to rebuild some form of communitarian identity, as Russian society had become more atomised and less collectively minded.[18] Further to this, for a system based on the political economy of rent-seeking, the Russian elite needed to assert its economic control and dominance over the countries of Eastern Europe. Ethnic and linguistic nationalism fused with kleptocratic political economy across the post-Soviet space.

There were broader aftershocks of the Ukraine violence. NATO gained a new lease of life. Disarmament processes ground to a halt. Mark Leonard believed that Putin's challenge to Western-designed rules was one with broader resonance amongst emerging powers across the world, making this a decisive tipping-point against the liberal international order far beyond Eastern Europe.[19] Many predicted that Russia's irredentism would encourage others also to reassert claims over lost territory, in particular China. Russia's actions undermined

[17] I. Krastev, *Democracy Disrupted*, Philadelphia, PA: University of Pennsylvania Press, 2014, p. 50.

[18] A. Arutunyan, *The Putin Mystique: Inside Russia's Power Cult*, Warks: Skyscraper, 2014.

[19] M. Leonard, 'Why Crimea matters', *Reuters*, 10 April 2014.

the carefully constructed balance between territorial integrity and self-determination that international organisations had crafted over many decades. A large number of non-Western countries refused to support a United Nations resolution condemning Russian's annexation of Crimea. They were keen to use the crisis to challenge Western tutelage over international norms.[20]

Analysts foresaw a range of apocalyptic ramifications of the eastern crisis, from the wholesale weakening of international law; the shift of non-Western states to Russia's side and away from partnership with Europe; a global rise of spheres of influence dynamics; and the possibility of non-Western powers creating their own economic and financial systems against the West.[21] The Ukraine conflict was part of a broader shift in international relations: Russia was moving into a Chinese camp in preparation for the ensuing rivalry between Beijing and the United States.[22] Some saw the crisis as a practice run for future challenges to the Western liberal order; China would watch and learn.

Walter Russell Mead painted a broader picture of geopolitical change enshrined within the Ukraine events: Russia's actions were, in fact, just one part of a growing tide of actions in the Middle East, Asia and other regions that were 'chipping away' at the very foundations of liberal world order and unavoidably bringing back an era of zero-sum geopolitics. This undercut the most basic premises of post-Cold War Western foreign policy. Maximising influence in Eurasia had returned as the key geopolitical stake. Unavoidable conflict in the 'rimlands' was one outcome of the broader demise of the Western liberal order.[23]

The 100th anniversary of the start of World War I hung in the air during the fraught months of 2014. Many saw parallels with the fateful period prior to World War I, as peace disintegrated in Europe. Historians cautioned that a repeat looked increasingly possible, and even likely. The Great War was not just caused by the well-known stories of individual political miscalculations. It was more structurally driven by a nationalist backlash against fast-deepening interdependence

[20] W. Burke-White, 'Crimea and the international legal order', *Survival*, 56/4, 2014, 65–80.

[21] European Council for Foreign Relations, *Annual meeting memorandum*, 12–13 June 2014.

[22] D. Trenin, 'Russia's great power problem', *National Interest*, 28 October 2014.

[23] W. Russell Mead, 'The return of geopolitics', *Foreign Affairs*, May/June 2014.

and against the whole assumption that cooperation and integration were good – a trend eerily present in the fretful European politics of 2014–16. One hundred years on, debates over the right level of engagement with Russia once more disturbed the heart of German politics, again in similar ways to 1914.[24]

Or Not?

In contrast to such warnings, some felt the direst prognostics might prove to be exaggerated. These voices insisted that the widespread talk of a 'new Cold War' was misplaced. They pointed out that Crimea was not the first incident of annexation: other post-World War II examples include Tibet, East Jerusalem and the Golan Heights, East Timor and Western Sahara. As Russian troops desisted from outright intervention in Ukraine's eastern borders, some observers speculated that the crisis might fall short of fundamentally challenging the European order. They cautioned that overreaction and hyperbole might provoke a more serious crisis than was strictly necessary.

Noted realists argued that President Putin's actions posed no serious threat to European security. Russia might be 'a regional spoiler and a local troublemaker', but it was not a 'true peer competitor' to Western powers. The crisis was nowhere near serious enough to draw EU states together in effective unity, because it simply did not matter that much to them – unlike to Ukrainians. Sceptics thought that Western governments misleadingly played up talk of a systemic threat, in part because they were keen to give NATO some purpose, when it now had none.[25] In a similar vein to this line of thought, analysts suggested that Putin did not plan the stages of the crisis as a fundamental and premeditated challenge to liberal order. Rather, he anticipated an international response to the conflict in Ukraine similar to that of Georgia in 2008: Western complaints but limited tangible pushback, then a brief period of tension leading into a situation where Western disinterest would leave Russia the dominant external player in Ukraine.

Francois Heisbourg insisted that Russia was not 'a challenge to the global order as a whole, because it is not a broad-based superpower'.

[24] M. Macmillan, *The War that Ended Peace*, London: Profile Books, 2013.
[25] S. Walt, 'NATO owes Putin a big thank you', *Foreign Policy*, 4 September 2014.

Additionally, Putin's foreign policy was not really driven by ethnic ties; he simply used these to make life strategically complicated for the West.[26] Lilia Shevtsova offered nuance in suggesting that Putin still wanted international rules, but simply needed to show that Russia had the right to revise those rules imposed during its decade of weakness after the collapse of the Soviet Union.[27] Russian observers closely following the texts of Putin's speeches noted that the president was not overtly against international cooperation but argued in favour of 'informal understandings' taking precedence over formal international law – which he insisted was unfairly tilted to the West's advantage.[28]

Russia dressed its interventions in legal language, claiming a right to 'armed humanitarianism' at the invitation of an endangered Russian minority. As Ukraine's new government came to power illegally, Russia insisted, all formal agreements respecting the country's territorial integrity were void. However unconvincing such arguments were to most international lawyers, the aim was to give the impression that Russia was maintaining certain legal norms of global order. Moscow's argument was that it was simply following the way in which Western states had intervened in other states in support of minorities' self-determination. The Kremlin insisted it was doing no more that supporting civic society and political parties abroad in the same way that Western governments did. Russia claimed success in making this case: only half the world's states supported a March 2014 UN resolution confirming Ukraine's territorial integrity. If the eastern crisis had revealed weaknesses in legal rules, then Russia suggested a conference to reboot international law – far from discarding the need for global norms.[29]

Some perceived Russia's actions in Ukraine to be the panicky nationalist impulse of a weakened power, not of a dangerous new strategic design. Putin reacted reflexively to the collapse of the Yanukovich regime rather than harbouring a wholesale geopolitical project. Sven Biscop argued that this crisis simply reinforced the challenge the EU

[26] F. Heisbourg, 'Preserving post-Cold War Europe', *Survival*, 57/1, 2015, 31–48, p. 34.

[27] L. Shevtsova, 'Don't be fooled, the Kremlin isn't back pedalling', *The American Interest*, 8 May 2014.

[28] A. Arutunyan, 'Putin's new foreign policy rulebook', *Open Democracy*, 3 November 2014.

[29] Allison, n. 7 above.

already faced in its neighbourhood and that Putin had reacted in an *ad hoc* way, rather than initiating a fundamentally new approach that required wholesale change in Europe foreign policy.[30]

By 2016, fears that the crisis constituted a systemic threat looked overblown as Russia had clearly not yet pursued territorial ambitions anywhere else in the region.[31] Eastern Ukraine did not fall uniformly under Russia's sway; in contrast to the self-proclaimed Donetsk and Luhansk People's Republics the region's two other main cities Dnipropetrovsk and Kharkiv remained loyal to Ukraine – partly due to the contrasting actions of local elites, to different popular sentiments and to a selective concentration of Russian agitation tactics.[32]

Some analysts suggested that the domestic roots of President Putin's actions lent them a degree of expediency. Rather than confidently riding a desire to pick apart the European order, Putin had to work hard to co-opt nationalists who criticised him for over-extending Russia's international reach. If one strand of Russian nationalism was aggressively expansionist, another was more inward-looking and parochial. Resurgent nationalism in part reflected the need for Russia still to form a state project and identity after losing its status as a great empire. The driving dynamic in Russia, many observers insisted, was not about imperialism, but about both state and nation formation. Putinism included an uneasy mix of illiberal isolationism and expansive neo-imperialism; these two internal factions battled constantly. The West may not have liked the former strand of illiberal isolationism but it did not represent a systemic strategic threat to Western interests. One common interpretation was that the Ukraine conflict was a kind of shadow war that Russia saw as useful to regain leverage over the West; once unleashed, the Kremlin could not control it in quite the manner it believed was possible.[33]

From a contrasting liberal perspective, John Ikenberry also warned against over-stating the severity of the crisis. Because Russia was only

30 S. Biscop, *Game of Zones: The Quest for Influence in Europe's Neighbourhood*, Brussels: Egmont Institute, Egmont Paper 67, 2014.
31 M. Korfman, 'How to start a proxy war with Russia', *National Interest*, 5 February 2015.
32 A. Portnov, 'How 'eastern Ukraine' was lost', *Open Democracy*, 14 January 2016.
33 Arutunyan, *The Putin Mystique*, above n. 18.

a 'part time spoiler', and actually rather weak in terms of effective power and alliances, the West could and should manage tensions through strengthening forms of cooperative inclusion – rather than pushing Putin further into a corner that obliged him to adopt confrontational policies. Russia's power would be checked by China, which was a far less aggressively revisionist power than Russia, for all its desire to reconfigure parts of the global order. While China led on economic issues, it had almost sub-contracted the lead on global security debates to Russia. This now looked increasingly risky and – this argument ran – some of the latent tensions between China and Russia would increasingly complicate their strategic relationship.[34]

More broadly, there were conflicting views on where Europe's main geopolitical priority lay. Some geo-strategists argued that, for all Russia's menace to the rules of European order, the EU's most pressing geopolitical priority was to build a common front with Russia and the United States to contain the rise of certain Asian powers and protect key supply routes from and through that region.[35] In the broader scheme of a new world order, Ukraine was only a local squabble, a distraction from impending US–China rivalry and the need for both the EU and Russia to assume firmer positions on this. Some concluded that Western attitudes reflected instinctive 'Russophobia' rather than reasonable geopolitical calculation – or that western governments used the discourse of geopolitical threat while in practice feeling relatively sanguine about a future of normal relations with Russia.[36]

Russia's surprise military intervention in Syria prompted cooperation between Moscow and the West, now in the context of efforts to degrade the insurgent terrorist organisation, Islamic State. This development in 2016 showed how strongly Putin sought a global concert of great powers to manage international affairs – and many intuited that he was willing to compromise on Ukraine in pursuit of cooperation with the United States and Europe to this end. Russian foreign minister Sergei Lavrov argued in March 2016 that the emergence of new global strategic threats meant it was more necessary than ever for Russia and European governments to create a security architecture – and that Russia was closer to achieving

[34] J. Ikenberry, 'The illusion of geopolitics', *Foreign Affairs*, May–June 2014.
[35] L. Simon, 'Post-European world', *European Geostrategy*, 7 June 2015.
[36] D. Wedgwood Benn, 'On re-examining Western attitudes towards Russia', *International Affairs*, 90/6, 2014, 1319–1328.

this overarching strategic objective as it became clear that the EU and Russia could not achieve their goals without cooperating.[37]

Conclusion

The eastern crisis combined some elements of internal civil conflict within Ukraine with inter-state conflict between Russia and many of its neighbours. The crisis was manifest in a mix of orthodox and unorthodox tactics. A number of factors played some role in explaining Russian actions: opportunism as events unfolded on the ground; geostrategic expansionism; a broader agenda of contesting the liberal global order; a genuine sense of defending 'the Russian world'; and Putin's domestic power calculations. Russia was part aggressor, part paranoid declining power salvaging a modicum of bygone influence.

While the Ukraine crisis brought with it a tragedy of alarming magnitude, it remained uncertain how far this crisis was the expression of a deeper and broader challenge to global geopolitics. Some feared that events in Ukraine and elsewhere in the EaP region might unleash wider international tension and insecurity. Yet there were different views on what Russia's ultimate aims were and also on whether its meddling in Ukraine really represented a major threat to Western interests. For some, the striking factor was that the conflict remained confined to one small area of Ukraine. As will become evident in the chapters that follow, EU governments found themselves with the dilemma of understanding exactly what the crisis amounted to: a conflict that was deadly and vicious but specific to Ukraine; a redrawing of regional power balances; or one element of emerging global political rivalry. The challenge presented by this definitional uncertainty fed into the book's three areas of concern: the shape of European responses; the shift in EU foreign policy dynamics; and the impact of European strategies. There was a broad consensus that 'geopolitics was back'. But doubts remained over the form that such geopolitics would assume and in consequence over what was the most appropriate form of riposte.

[37] S. Lavrov, 'Russia's foreign policy: Historical background', *Russia in Global Affairs*, 2016, English version available at: www.mid.ru/en/foreign_policy/news/-/asset_publisher/cKNonkJE02Bw/content/id/2124391.

4 *Pre-Crisis European Union Eastern Policy*

It is first necessary to understand the evolution of European strategy in the period preceding the eastern crisis. European Union policy towards Eastern Europe and the Southern Caucasus was not overtly geopolitical prior to the crisis that began in 2013–2014. Analysts overwhelmingly studied the European Neighbourhood Policy (ENP) through the lens of a supposed extension eastwards of EU governance, functionalist and institutionalist dynamics. While European policy-makers did not think of the Eastern Partnership (EaP) in terms of geopolitical rivalry, Russia increasingly perceived the initiative as a strategic threat. This mismatch sowed the seeds of the subsequent crisis in Ukraine and the broader region.

This chapter examines this dearth of geopolitical deliberation at both the policy and analytical levels prior to 2014. It assesses the record of the EaP after its creation in 2009 up to the explosive crisis of late 2013 and 2014. This provides the background necessary for identifying and explaining changes to EU policies after 2013. In the period before 2013, most foreign policy activity centred on the development of the EaP; that is the focus of this chapter. Later chapters will reveal how, after 2013, the centre of gravity in EU policy-making shifted to a select number of national capitals and the importance of member states policies increased alongside the EaP. The assessment of the EaP's early years offered here speaks systematically to each of the book's three core analytical concerns: it categorises the baseline 'standard' EU approach to geopolitics; points to strongly embedded internal-institutionalised EU policy-making dynamics; and details the varied and in some senses perverse impact of EU policies.

The Eastern Partnership up to 2013

The Eastern Partnership began as a relatively low-level initiative in 2009. Sponsored initially by Poland and Sweden, it did not engender either great enthusiasm or attention from most other member states – indeed, their separate national foreign policy engagement in the region remained strikingly modest. In its origins, the EaP was in part a trade-off against the newly formed Euro-Mediterranean Union, not primarily an externally or strategically driven initiative. In the aftermath of Russia's 2008 invasion of Georgia, geopolitical concerns were certainly present. But, the policy initiatives launched under the EaP rubric were focused on trade, aid and low-level societal engagement. While the six EaP partners – Armenia, Azerbaijan, Belarus, Georgia, Moldova and Ukraine – welcomed the new framework, they principally noted that the EU was not willing to use the offer of enlargement to underwrite and prompt economic and political reform. The EaP seemed to them more like a poor substitute than an important new umbrella for geo-political protection.

Eastern partners were offered association agreements (AAs), under whose terms Deep and Comprehensive Free Trade Areas (DCFTAs) would be negotiated. The long process of negotiating these agreements began, moving slowly and without any apparent urgency. A beefed-up Comprehensive Institution Building Programme and 'Structured Approximation Process' commenced. A new set of AAs required more in terms of legislative transposition and approximation than several of the stabilisation and AAs in the Balkans – that of course came with the offer of membership.

Prior to 2014, even where the EU did bring about approximation and prompt technical level reforms the processes were opaque with little civil society awareness or engagement. This compounded the feeling that the EaP was a low-level technocratic exercise rather than a high-level political project.[1] EaP partner states routinely stated that the EU's offer of visa liberalisation was the most powerful incentive. However, talks on visa liberalisation proceeded slowly; the EU required sixty benchmarks to be met, covering security of border management and travel documents. This conditionality went beyond that attached to visa liberalisation in the Balkans.

Commission aid available to the eastern Neighbourhood doubled between 2009 and 2013. A range of new aid initiatives was launched.

[1] Eurasia Partnership Foundation, *Alternative Assessment Report, Implementation of the ENP Action Plan and EaP bilateral and Multilateral Roadmaps of 2013*, Tbilsi, 2014.

By 2013, over fifty EaP twinning arrangements existed with various ministries and regulatory agencies. Armenia, Georgia and Moldova won additional funds for commitments to political reform. Aid targeted civil society for greater support, although in overall terms most funding continued to go to governments and was increasingly in the form of direct budget support, which gave regimes greater freedom on how to use the aid.[2] In some sectors where they were not too vulnerable to Russian pressure, EaP states used European funds to take on board EU regulations as a means of giving themselves a greater degree of manoeuvrability over Moscow.[3]

EaP initiatives were framed in an almost expressly un-geopolitical fashion. Detailed empirical accounts found that prior to 2014, EU policies were aimed at supporting very specific sectors of reform in Armenia, Georgia and Azerbaijan and failed to take any account of Russia's rising role as a 'democracy blocker' – that is, the EU failed to adjust its own strategies to take this gradually more apparent geopolitical reality into account.[4] Officials admitted that the focus was on incubating the conditions for eventual reform, more than on immediate, tangible democratic advances across the eastern region. Central and Eastern European member states pushed not only to raise the EaP's profile but also to place democracy support at its heart. Support for democracy was central to these new member states' strategic vision for the region. They had only limited resources available and mainly confined their policies to non-intrusive means such as sharing their own transitions lessons and best practice.[5]

The EU's efforts to help resolve or de-escalate conflicts were modest. Its approach to the Moldova-Transnistria conflict was focused on trying to get the two sides committed to an inclusive process of integration and cooperation, especially at the level of local civil society actors. This was preferred to any attempt to favour one side over the other or

[2] N. Shapovalova and R. Youngs, *Civil Society Support in the Eastern Neighbourhood*, Madrid: Fride, 2013.

[3] E. Ademmer, 'Interdependence and EU-demanded policy change in a shared neighbourhood', *Journal of European Public Policy*, 2015, 22/5, 671–89.

[4] N. Babayan, *Democratic Transformation and Obstruction: The European Union, United States and Russia in the South Caucasus*, London: Routledge, 2014.

[5] T. Petrova, *From Solidarity to Geopolitics: Support for Democracy among Postcommunist States*, Cambridge: Cambridge University Press, 2014.

directly confront Moscow's involvement.[6] The EU ostensibly adhered to a similar approach in Georgia and funded civil society initiatives in Abkhazia and South Ossetia to improve local governance capacity – although critics charged the EU with being too supportive of the Georgian government and not flexible enough in contemplating the territories' case for more autonomy.[7]

Policy towards Belarus veered between isolation and engagement. Pressure was stepped up through targeted sanctions imposed against members of the Belarusian regime, diplomatic support for opposition leaders and the removal of trade preferences in 2007. In the late 2000s, sanctions were diluted, travel restrictions eased and aid increased. In the wake of Russia's invasion of Georgia, President Alexander Lukashenka was seen as a potential ally to be courted against Russian expansionism. A 2006 'shadow' action plan declared 'What the EU could bring to Belarus'. Belarus was included in the Eastern Partnership and a new Commission aid package was made available to the country in June 2009. However, when the regime clamped down hard on the opposition in the 2010 election, tougher sanctions were imposed and cooperation stalled once again.

Cooperation with Russia was a declared a priority during this period. NATO undertook a 'reset' in 2009 to support cooperation with Russia. Some thought the EU failed to engage seriously with President Dimitry Medvedev's proposal for a new security treaty, based on Russia having a 'zone of privileged interests'. Yet the official EU position was to cooperate with Moscow on such questions of security architecture. France and Germany ensured that NATO expansion was effectively taken off the table after 2008.

In the years prior to 2013, France tightened strategic relations with Russia in response to the US's declining commitment to Europe, Asia's rise, German predominance within the EU and turmoil in the Middle East.[8] The Baltic states felt obliged to accept EaP initiatives, but stood

[6] V. Dias, 'The EU's post-liberal approach to peace: Framing EUBAM's contribution to the Moldova–Transnistria conflict transformation', *European Security*, 22/3, 2013, 338–54.

[7] S. Pogodda, O. Richmond, N. Tocci, R. MacGinty and B. Vogel, 'Assessing the impact of EU governmentality in post-conflict countries: Pacification or reconciliation?', *European Security*, 23/3, 2014, 227–49.

[8] L. Simon, 'The spider in Europe's web? French grand strategy from Iraq to Libya', *Geopolitics*, 18/2, 2013, 403–34.

fundamentally at odds with the EU mainstream precisely because these policies eschewed any kind of geopolitical projection or calculation of possible difficulties coming from Russia.[9] When President Putin launched his new Eurasian Union, the EU spoke of positive cooperation between this and its various trade arrangements. There were tensions in energy policy; Gazprom was obliged to reduce prices to EU customers from 2012 as the EU pushed back against the company's monopoly position. Yet, most member states increased their imports from Russia and saw the Eastern space as one where cooperative solutions over energy security could be negotiated.

The Vilnius Turning Point

European governments hoped the EaP Vilnius summit in November 2013 would end with the signing of a raft of AAs designed to lock the EU's Eastern partners into a sphere of European influence and ensure progressive political and economic liberalisation. The EU's high representative for foreign affairs and security policy, Catherine Ashton, promised that the Vilnius summit would 'open a new chapter' in the EU's relations with its Eastern partners.

The summit awoke much interest across Europe. Germany in particular worked to raise the meeting's profile; Sweden, Finland, and the Benelux countries intensified their diplomacy in the region. However, there was still little evidence of any precise assessment of where the EU's strategic interests lay. Member states undoubtedly claimed that they cared about the Eastern dimension, but the EaP effort still felt like a lobbying exercise undertaken by a small minority of Central and Eastern European member states. The Southern dimension of the ENP generated more priority interest across the totality of member states in a way that was still to be seen in the EaP.

However, as the summit approached, the EaP's process of non-dramatic, gradual 'approximation' began to unravel. The run-up to the summit was fraught; the meeting becoming a defensive exercise in damage limitation. What looked set to be a relatively smooth summit was suddenly front-page news. European Union foreign-policy meetings that had been focused on the Middle East and on strengthening EU

[9] K. Raik. 'Liberalism and geopolitics in EU–Russia relations: Rereading the Baltic factor', *European Security*, 25/2, 2016, 237–55.

relations with cash-rich Asia in the shadow of the Eurozone crisis, now made room for more in-depth discussion of the Eastern Partnership.

Alarms bells rang in September 2013, when Armenia announced it was joining the Eurasian customs union (that preceded the Eurasian Union proper) and pulling out of the AA talks. With the economic value of the high-tariff customs union on Armenia's economy far from obvious, it was clear that political dynamics lay squarely behind this decision.[2] Russia intensified tensions as it imposed sanctions against Ukraine, Georgia and Moldova to dissuade them from signing their AAs. Commissioner Stefan Füle sent signals that the EU and Russia could work towards a broader free-trade area and regulatory cooperation that would guarantee Eastern partners a notable rapprochement with the Eurasian customs union. The EU promised to open the European market fully to compensate for Russian sanctions on Moldovan wine.

However, at the summit, only Georgia and Moldova initialled their AAs. Ukraine dramatically pulled out at the last minute. The EU and Azerbaijan did not sign a proposed Modernisation Pact, as an alternative to the AA that Baku had rejected. Belarus resisted any kind of pressure or inducements, and did not engage seriously in the summit. Mention of Article 49 – which stipulates that any European state is eligible to apply for EU membership – was excised from the summit's conclusions. The EU's eastern policy suddenly seemed to be falling apart: Russia pushed assertively to neuter many of its key policy instruments and EaP states complained vociferously that the EaP lacked content and strategic bite.

An Analytical Mainstream

Prior to the crisis, the analytical framework for studying EU neighbourhood policy was dominated by several assumptions. The staple focus of analytical work was on neighbourhood countries' compliance with EU rules. The conceptual framework of 'external governance' gained in prominence and was applied to those parts of the neighbourhood outside the scope of enlargement. Analysts held that the EU enjoyed a unique ability to offer grades of inclusion into its own 'governance space'. They stressed that EU external policy was qualitatively different to standard foreign policy by exporting the governance rules that guided relations between member states within the EU itself. EU external action in the Eastern Partnership states was imbued with the tenor of public policy analysis, distinct from high-politics foreign policy. The EU's approach to the east bore some resemblance to the 'critical geopolitics' described in Chapter 2: cooperation was sought through shaping the norms and identities of belongingness and was nominally bereft of the calculation of relative power gains.[10]

Theorists termed the EU a functionalist power in its neighbourhood. It exerted influence by offering other states a share in the benefits of EU policies.[11] Analysts argued that the ENP was essentially about normative ends being pursued through value-shaping persuasion and rules-based influence.[12] The EU aimed to support more accountable governance mainly through technical areas of sectoral cooperation based on its own internal legal rules.[13] Non-prescriptive and cooperative mediation characterised the EU's core approach to the neighbourhood.[14] External governance proceeded primarily through participatory networks, mixed with a more hierarchically functionalist logic of rules-transfer to non-EU states.[15] Analysts saw EU foreign policy as being infused with an ethos of joint community building, based on cooperative rather than competitive bargaining.[16]

ENP dynamics were not about geopolitical rivalry but the way that governments weighed up the costs and benefits of adopting certain EU rules. The analytical focus was on the way that non-EU governments tended to accept these rules in sectors that did not threaten their domestic political power, but resisted those that did.[17] Analysts

[10] A. Makarychev and A. Devyatkov, *The EU in Eastern Europe: Has Normative Power become Geopolitical?*, Eurasia Policy memo 310, George Washington University, February 2014.

[11] J. Zielonka, 'The EU as an international actor: Unique or ordinary?', *European Foreign Affairs Review*, 16, 2011, 281–301.

[12] T. Forsberg, 'Normative power Europe, once again: A conceptual analysis of an ideal type', *Journal of Common Market Studies*, 49/6, 2011, 1183–204.

[13] F. Schimmelfennig, 'How substantial is substance? Concluding reflections on the study of substance in EU democracy promotion', *European Foreign Affairs Review*, 16/4, 2011, 727–34.

[14] K. Raik, 'The EU and mass protests in the neighbourhood: Models of normative (in)action', *European Foreign Affairs Review*, 17/4, 2012, 553–76.

[15] S. Lavenex and F. Schimmelfennig, 'EU rules beyond EU borders: Theorizing external governance in European politics', *Journal of European Public Policy*, 16/6, 2011, 791–812.

[16] D. Thomas (ed.) *Making EU Foreign Policy*, Basingstoke: Macmillan, 2011.

[17] C. Hagemann, 'External governance on the terms of the partner? The EU, Russia and the Republic of Moldova in the European neighbourhood policy', *Journal of European Integration*, 35/7, 2013, 767–83.

argued that, in this sense, the EaP was predicated on the EU's 'structural power', its own rules being used as a means to bring about a convergence of other states' political and economic systems around European norms.[18] All this conformed to a particular theoretical way of interpreting EU external action, namely that such action flowed from the core, 'transnational institutionalist' forms that were constitutive of the EU's own integration model.[19] In short, most experts saw the EU's neighbourhood policy as driven by the logic of 'governance' rather than the traditional forms of foreign policy 'leverage' or national governments' engagement.[20]

Such analytical prisms for studying the ENP and EaP most commonly celebrated the novel strengths of EU external actions – modes of action that were widely seen to mobilise the best features of the European integration model and avoid the shortcomings of traditional geopolitical thinking. However, as it became patently clear that the EaP was struggling to advance many of its declared objectives analysts began to take a more critical line.

Gradually a consensus emerged in the academic literature that the ENP and EaP were failing to gain traction, either because they declined to offer a membership perspective or because they focused on getting governments to adopt formal EU rules and regulations without building up genuinely mutual partnerships with eastern societies.[21] In practice, the EU was willing to support reforms only where EaP states were already implementing such reforms. The extensive literature on EU international regulatory influence evolved: studies pointed to areas where the EU's famed 'regulatory power' increasingly suffered effective pushback from others.[22]

[18] S. Keukalaire, 'The European Union as a Diplomatic Actor: Internal, Traditional and Structural Diplomacy'. In W. Rees and M. Smith (eds) *The International Relations of the European Union*, London: Sage, 2008.

[19] V. Birchfield 'A normative power Europe framework of transnational policy formation', *Journal of European Public Policy*, 20/6, 2013, 907–22.

[20] S. Lavenex and F. Schimmelfennig, 'EU democracy promotion in the neighbourhood: From leverage to governance?', *Democratization* 18/4, 2011, 885–909.

[21] F. Melo, 'Perspectives on the European Neighbourhood Policy failure', *Journal of European Integration*, 36/2, 2014, 189–93.

[22] A. Young, 'The European Union as a global regulator? Context and comparison', *Journal of European Public Policy*, 22/9, 2015, 1233–52 and others in this special edition.

It was striking that the standard accounts of the ENP and EaP made no reference to Russia at all, being almost entirely focused on variables internal to EU deliberations, institutional competences and inter-state trade-offs.[23] Until 2014, the EaP was judged to have more of a functionalist logic and less of a strategic tint than many other areas of EU policy. In Central Asia, the EU made a shift towards security engagement, a change enshrined in the five-year review of its regional Central Asia Strategy.[24] In the Middle East, the Arab Spring pushed the EU towards more geopolitical deliberation, reflected in the greater variation in European policies and presence across different Middle Eastern states.[25] A similar shift was still absent from the EU's eastern policy.

A view spread that the external governance focus was becoming a handicap to the EaP, diverting the EU from considering what partners really wanted, broadening partnerships beyond governments and bringing in hard power. Two writers quipped that the EU had made a strategic choice simply 'to be attractive' – but without considering to what end and by what means, or what the attractiveness might consist of in particular circumstances.[26] The EaP was commonly assessed as if it were subject to a set of self-perpetuating functionalist-institutionalist dynamics, hermetically sealed off from geopolitical influences. This approach had worked in the Central and Eastern European states that joined the EU in 2004. However, that was in a context where the core elements of democratic transition had already occurred and where the EU seemed to be the clearly preponderant external reference point.

Critical Assessments

In this period, analysts argued that the EaP was neither sufficiently geo-political nor developed enough to provide a positive-sum form of inclusion. Critics accused the EU of lazy assumptions that its

[23] T. Techau, S. Keukalaire and V. van Hüllen, 'One voice, one message, but conflicting goals: Cohesiveness and consistency in the European Neighbourhood Policy', *Journal of European Public Policy*, 21/7, 2015, 1033–1049.

[24] A-S. Gast, *A Shift in the EU Strategy for Central Asia*, Carnegie Moscow Centre, 2014.

[25] R. Youngs, *Europe in the New Middle East: Opportunity or Exclusion?*, Oxford: Oxford University Press, 2014.

[26] K. Nielsen and M. Vilson, 'The Eastern Partnership: Soft power strategy or policy failure?', *European Foreign Affairs Review* 19/2, 2014, 243–62, p. 261.

anti-geopolitical liberal principles would, in fact, deliver all kinds of security gains. The EaP was left stranded as an ineffectual half-way house – neither geopolitical nor offering full inclusion. Amidst encroaching strategic tensions, the EU rejected an overtly realpolitik approach. However, it did little to put meat on the bones of its professed cooperative approach or to support transformations in the east that would benefit both the EU and EaP countries. Indeed, it showed signs of being tempted at least a few steps along the path of mutually exclusive binary strategic choice. Some feared that the EU implicitly turned the EaP into a mechanism for 'keeping EaP partners away from Russia'.

The EaP was predicated on an agenda of transformative power. The EU would work to reform the economic and governance structures of eastern partners; this was assumed to be synonymous with the latter drawing closer and embedding themselves within an EU-centred security community. The results of this approach were disappointing. While the increased density of economic, social and diplomatic linkages with the EU contributed to some degree of political change in EaP states, these links were filtered through domestic processes of contested 'stateness' – resulting from regional cleavages and ethno-territorial conflicts – in a way that failed to consolidate far-reaching democratic gains. Moreover, linkages between EaP states and Russia increased in some cases by an equal magnitude to those with the EU.[27]

Academic assessments concurred that the EU's approach to supporting reform and building deeper networks of effective socialisation had been of only modest impact. One argument was that while the EU formally shifted towards a policy based more on partnership and networked relations at all levels of society, in practice most elements of the EaP were based on more top-down rules transfer – and thus increasingly resisted.[28] Experts argued that the EU had limited success in bringing about regulatory convergence because it did not put enough resources into empowering non-state actors to overcome

[27] G. Sasse, 'Linkages and the promotion of democracy: The EU's eastern neighbourhood', *Democratization*, 20/4, 2013, 553–91.

[28] E. Korosteleva, 'Evaluating the role of partnership in the European Neighbourhood Policy: The Eastern neighbourhood', *Eastern Journal of European Studies*, 4/2, 2013, 11–36; E. Korosteleva, *The European Union and its Eastern Neighbours: Towards A More Ambitious Partnership?*, London: Routledge, 2012.

opposition to reform, nor did it offer governments sufficient rewards where adaptation costs were high.[29] EaP civil society cooperation brought about only a limited degree of socialisation.[30] Administrative and financial conditions prevented most EaP funds from being spent, or from helping reforms.[31]

The logic of attraction was at least partly supplanted by that of 'transactional' instrumentalism. The 2013 EaP Integration Index, which recorded the EaP countries' progress in converging with EU norms, uncovered a mismatch between partners' incremental administrative and managerial alignment with the EU, on the one hand, and the increasingly acute high-politics impediments to reform, on the other. EU policies were not able to cope with the incipient return of very old-style politics. By early 2014, EaP states had not, as a bloc, moved conspicuously closer to the EU and European diplomats had failed to recognise that the enlargement-lite framework could only work where elites had an interest in approximation with it.[32] There was clearly greater domestic variation amongst EaP partners than there has been among Central European candidates; critics regularly berated the EU for adhering to one-size-fits-all policies.

In some cases, certain sectoral governance initiatives had a positive effect on democratic reform, while in others they inadvertently shored up regime power structures. The EU did much to ensure that civil society actors were consulted on EU matters, but these actors still often complained that the EU itself was opaque. It engaged mainly with pro-European parties; it was, one insider noted, guilty of 'confirmation bias'. Critics charged European donors with fostering an 'engineered civil society' that had few local organic roots.[33] Through

[29] J. Langbein, 'European Union governance towards the Eastern Neighbourhood: Transcending or redrawing Europe's East–West divide?', *Journal of Common Market Studies*, 52/1, 2014, 157–74.

[30] H. Kostanyan and B. Vandecasteele, 'The socialization potential of the Eastern Partnership Civil Society Forum', *Eastern Journal of European Studies*, 4/2, 2013, 95–110.

[31] Polish Institute of International Affairs, *Learning from Past Experience: Ways to Improve EU Aid on Reforms in the Eastern Partnership*, Warsaw: PISM, 2014.

[32] S. Lehne, *Time to Reset the European Neighbourhood Policy*, Brussels: Carnegie Europe, 2015.

[33] A. Ishkanian, 'Engineered Civil Society: The Impact of 20 Years of Democracy Promotion on Civil Society Development in Former Soviet Countries'. In T.

its 'network Russia' initiatives, Russia seemed to be more effective in building soft-power-type links.

There was a tendency towards regulatory overload. No roadmap was provided to help EaP states achieve the required harmonisation of around 80 per cent of the EU *acquis*. The policy was designed in terms of what was best for the functioning of the EU's own internal market rules, not what was best geopolitically for the EaP as a whole.[34] The EU was fixated with exporting formal rules in a region where informal politics predominated. The External Action Service – the EU's new foreign policy directorate - struggled to gain overall strategic direction, as the lead role in DCFTA negotiations was played by DG Trade officials.[35]

These shortcomings were especially significant in the case of Armenia's decision to favour the Eurasian customs union. One local civic partner observed that the EU delegation in Yerevan still preferred 'project management to [seeking] political influence'. Armenia underwent all the preparations for technical approximation to EU rules, but then politically tilted to Russia. Some also detected an incipient democratic backslide in Armenia. Part of the Armenian administration still hoped for some kind of accord with the EU. But these officials felt the EU still believed it could run its initiatives somehow disconnected from the country's overall political situation. One EU politician drew the lesson from Armenia: 'we need to shape views before setting such high conditions'.

The most serious charge was that most in the EU simply did not see the Russian threat approaching when the signs should have been visible. Russian assertiveness had begun to surface before 2013. Western cooperation with Russia did not suffice to assuage the latter's feeling of vulnerability. European governments should have seen that liberal cooperation and interdependence were not working as intended. The EU erred in not fully realising how Russia was beginning to interpret ostensibly innocuous EaP policies as far more threatening than

Beichelt, I. Hahn-Fuhr, F. Schimmelfennig and S. Worschech (eds), *Civil Society and Democracy Promotion*, Basingstoke: Palgrave Macmillan, 2014.

34 K. Wolczuk, *Ukraine and the EU: Turning the Association Agreement into a Success Story*, European Policy Centre, 2014.

35 H. Kostanyan, 'Examining the Discretion of the EEAS: What Power to Act in the EU-Moldova Association Agreement?', *European Foreign Affairs Review* 19/3, 2014, 373–92.

had been intended.[36] It was also slow to wake up to the impending collision between its DCFTA offers and the new Eurasian customs union, and remiss in not quickly appreciating that, for President Putin, this initiative was to be a vehicle of strategic pushback not just customs harmonisation. European governments also failed to realise that Russia could not be a helpful mediator in the region's frozen conflicts as it was committed to fomenting those conflicts to consolidate its own power.[37]

The EaP was not without geopolitical impact. The problem was that the EaP had strategic weight sufficient to awaken Russian ire, but then did not know how to deal with it. The EU's positive incentives aimed to extend the sphere of Euro-governance; but these incentives increasingly hit obstacles and the EU was unwilling or unable to acknowledge that this required a fully strategic response. Russia saw the EaP as a threat, but also saw it as limited in its reach; it noted that a crisis-hit EU was constrained in what it was willing to offer under the EaP in terms of resources and incentives. The EaP paradoxically gave Russia both the need and opportunity to begin a more concerted pushback against European influence.

The EU got the worst of both worlds: while it eschewed overt geopolitics, Russia now treated it as a geopolitical rival in the region. Many European diplomats remained sanguine, with the oft-repeated line that the EU was winning the hearts and minds of people in the east. This line began to look a little too relaxed. The EU claimed the EaP was not about creating a sphere of influence. But this was not what Russia perceived. At this stage, the EU did not see any major danger coming from Russia's territorial and civilisational understanding of security. It confidently assumed that it could rebut Russian tactics, offering EaP states solidarity without direct bribe-like compensation. The EU did not see any need to bring a withdrawn US back into the region's politics.

[36] T. Forsberg and H. Haukkala, 'Could It Have Been Different? The Evolution of the EU-Russian Conflict and Its Alternatives'. In C. Nitoiu (ed.) *Avoiding a New 'Cold War': The Future of EU–Russia Relations in the Context of the Ukraine Crisis*, London: LSE Ideas Report, 2016, p. 12.

[37] S. Cornell, 'European Union: Eastern Partnership vs Eurasian Union'. In S. Starr and S. Cornell (eds), *Putin's Grand Strategy: The Eurasian Union and Its Discontents*, Washington DC: Central Asia-Caucasus Institute, Johns Hopkins University, and Stockholm: Silk Road Studies Program, 2014.

Conclusion

This chapter provides background for our assessment of how the EU responded to the eastern crisis that bubbled menacingly to the top of its foreign policy agenda at the end of 2013. It shows that elements of that crisis had been in slow gestation for some time. It has addressed the book's three core areas of concern in the period before 2013: how to categorise European approaches to geopolitics; the nature of EU foreign-policy dynamics; and the results of EU strategies.

Categorisation

The chapter shows how EU policies within the EaP up to 2013 corresponded to the standard and distinctive form of European foreign policy outlined as the first of four geopolitical categories in Chapter 2. The EaP was imbued with a significant degree of anti-geopolitics. It was based on a series of generic assumptions about EU interests and cooperative inclusion, but lacked any carefully calibrated strategic instrumentality. The incremental return of geopolitical rivalry in the eastern borderlands had begun to make itself felt before late 2013. While the EU insisted that it began to fine-tune its policies in reply to this change, there was widespread agreement among both analysts and policy-makers that the EaP's whole structure was largely devoid of geopolitical adjustment in this period.

Foreign Policy Dynamics

EU policies were dominated by a policy-making dynamic centred on the role of EU institutions and internal European Union rules and norms rather than on incipient geopolitical or external strategic factors. Member states' engagement in the EaP was modest in this period. Both policy deliberation and mainstream analytical models largely failed to identify the countervailing geopolitical influences beginning to take shape. While many analysts pointed to the gradual emergence of more geopolitical factors, both in the neighbourhood and in the broader international system, EU policy-dynamics were not strongly driven by any rationalised, interest-based response to the geopolitical strategies of other actors. Rather, the EU focused mainly on reproducing itself in quasi-technocratic fashion on its own periphery. Analytical work saw the EU as subject but rarely object – the focus was invariably on how far the EU influenced others, far less on how it was conditioned by other actors' power. Policy-making dynamics were more self-referential to EU internal norms and processes than they were tailored to specific elements of external geopolitical change.

Impact

If analysts and diplomats saw in the EaP the contours of a far-sighted, reform-oriented approach to the eastern periphery, this approach was evidently not working in practice. The EU's ability to influence outcomes in its immediate neighbourhood appeared increasingly weakened. The EU's low-politics approach to sectoral reform gained traction only in some areas of policy. The paradox was that the EU's self-consciously non-geopolitical approach stirred up fiercely geopolitical reactions from Russia and hard-security concerns inside EaP states. If the EaP had an impact, it was the opposite of what the EU had intended.

All this left the EaP in uncertain limbo, both in terms of policy options and analytical ramifications. If it was clear by 2013 that all was not well in the east, the urgency and difficulty of rectifying this situation would now become much greater.

5 *Eastern Policy from Low to High Politics*

From mid-2013, the dynamics of the Europe's eastern policies changed. The Eastern Partnership (EaP) became more high profile and occupied priority attention within European Union (EU) foreign policy deliberations. Russian attempts to neuter the EaP, civic protests in Ukraine and the annexation of Crimea combined to sharpen EU foreign policy. As armed conflict in eastern Ukraine intensified then followed many twists and turns into 2015 and 2016, European governments mapped out a multi-pronged response – nationally, through EU instruments and within NATO.

In this period, upgrades to the common framework of the EaP were accompanied by more intense member state engagement too; in contrast to the pre-crisis period described in the previous chapter, the post-crisis response involved a more balanced combination of joint EU-level and national diplomatic initiatives; European foreign policy coordination in the east became a different kind of enterprise. The chapter outlines the principal strands of this overarching European response to the crisis: sanctions against Russia; defensive security measures; an increased commitment to the Eastern Partnership; and changes to energy policy. Together, these added up to a multi-faceted form of geopolitical reaction and a notable change of gear in the EU's eastern policies. European policies brought in new elements of a more offensive geopolitics, while EU governments flanked these with more defensive geopolitical options. This chapter focuses on those elements of change that opened the EU to a new category of geopolitical action and different forms of foreign-policy dynamics; the subsequent chapter sets these off against the elements of continuity in post-2013 European strategy and works towards a rounded assessment of EU responses to the eastern crisis.

Russia: From Partner to Problem

Many EU and member state proclamations insisted that the crisis terminated the European commitment to strong partnership with Russia. The crisis changed European governments' basic strategic perceptions of Russia. Arguably the most striking change was in German positions. German politicians and diplomats gradually lost trust in President Putin, as at each stage in the crisis the Russian president acted in a way that contradicted what he had promised privately to Chancellor Angela Merkel. This basic break between Berlin and Moscow was perhaps the most significant strategic change to flow from the conflict.[1] One German diplomat insisted that, 'we no longer plan on the basis of Russia being a partner in any meaningful way – and people have not realised the scope of this change'.

Germany suspended many of the high-level dialogue forums that it had commenced with Russia in the preceding years. Key German politicians and diplomats were now not being received in Moscow; indeed several German diplomats were expelled. The Russian government talked of blocking Germany's quest for UN Security Council membership. Chancellor Merkel was reputedly forthright in her dissatisfaction with the 'soft' positions adopted by EU high representative Federica Mogherini towards Russia.

Merkel expressed her toughened view that Russia was increasingly an adversary with whom partnership was impossible, warning that: '[T]he Ukraine crisis is in no way a regional issue ... It affects all of us.' Accommodation with Russia was increasingly unthinkable: 'Otherwise, one would have to say: We are too weak, we can't accept any others, we have to first ask Moscow if it is possible. That's how things were for 40 years; I never really wanted to return to that situation ... And that doesn't just apply to Ukraine. It applies to Moldova, it applies to Georgia.'[2] At the Munich security conference in early 2015, Merkel developed her reasoning that Europe faced a long drawn-out battle, akin to the moment when the Berlin Wall was constructed; the West did not react militarily, but exerted determined pressure on the Soviet bloc over a long period of time. One analyst

[1] A. Rinke, 'How Putin lost Berlin', *IPG Journal*, 29 September 2014. Available at: www.ipg-journal.de.

[2] *Speigel Online*, 17 November 2014.

described Germany's new approach as a 'frostpolitik'; this retained a belief in diplomatic engagement but was no longer based on an assumption that Russia could be a benign partner.[3]

French president François Hollande also called for a robust response, as the Ukraine–Russian conflict risked 'total war' that could ensnare the whole of Europe. The UK government was adamant that there could be no 'great power' cooperation deciding peoples' fates in the EaP region over their own heads; until Russia accepted EaP partners' territorial integrity and free will there could be no new formal EU–Russia dialogue on the area.[4] British foreign secretary Phillip Hammond stated in September 2014: 'For more than two decades since the collapse of the Soviet Union, the west has opened a door to Russia and sought to draw her into the international rules-based system, offering partnership, trade, investment and openness. By its illegal annexation of Crimea and its aggressive destabilisation of eastern Ukraine, the Russian leadership has slammed that door shut. It has chosen the role of pariah rather than partner, and in doing so it has undermined the long-term security architecture of Europe.'[5]

The Polish perspective was that the EU had been remiss in continuing to offer Russia too much inclusive, rule-shaping cooperation well past the stage at which Putin had become entirely derisive of such Western liberal notions. Polish foreign minister Radek Sikorski insisted: 'we must drop the idea that we can organise European order in a way that everyone's interests are advanced at the same time'.[6] Taking office in August 2015, Poland's new president Andrzej Duda indicated a shift towards an apparently even more hawkish foreign policy against Russia, calling for EU governments more firmly to resist Russian military incursions with the use of assertive hard power. Concerned at weakening EU resolve on Russia as counter-terrorism became top priority, the new Polish foreign minister said in April 2016: 'Russia is an existential threat, terrorists can make damage but are not an existential threat.'[7]

[3] T. Forsberg, 'From ostpolitk to frostpolitik? Merkel, Putin and German foreign policy towards Russia', *International Affairs* 92/1, 2016, 21–42.

[4] House of Lords European Committee, *The EU and Russia: Before and Beyond the Ukraine Crisis*, London: EU External Affairs Select Committee, 2015 p. 49.

[5] *Hansard*, 10 September 2014, col. 920.

[6] Wroclaw Global Forum, 6 June 2014.

[7] GlobaSec Conference, Bratislava, 15 April 2016.

For several Central European states there was no merit in now seeking dialogue with Russia, or finding specific items on the global agenda where the EU and Russia shared common interests. They argued that more fundamental and irreconcilable differences in threat perceptions underlay the crisis. Even if the Cold War analogy was not entirely accurate, Central European and Baltic diplomats routinely warned that the EU response would need to mimic elements of pre-1989 policies. The challenge was not dialogue with Russia on specifics of the Ukraine conflict, but deciding what was needed to address the even more serious dangers of escalation that would fundamentally threaten Europe – amongst these, the need to get arms control agreements back on track was paramount. These member states certainly began to deploy the terminology of a bygone era: they talked of cold peace, deterrence, détente, the balance of forces, appeasement and arms control.[8] One senior Finnish diplomat justified a tough response and rejected the 'Finlandisation' doctrine of neutrality that carried his country's name.

The appointment in 2014 of Donald Tusk as president of the European Council in part reflected the drift towards a tougher stance towards Russia. Insiders said this was balanced by the choice of Federica Mogherini as high representative – although they also pointed to the fact that her new powers to cohere the positions of all external relations commissioners reflected a strong consensus that the EU needed to be more geopolitical. On the day he took over as Council president in December 2014, Tusk warned: 'Politics has returned to Europe. History is back.'[9] One senior EU diplomat reported that partnership on a global non-proliferation regime was also now taken off the agenda, as Russia simply could not be trusted as a partner.

The EU worked hard to build a much more geo-strategically directed alliance with Turkey to help contain Russia. This effort had mixed results. Turkey was critical of Russian actions, pushed hard for the protection of Crimean Tartars and wound down cooperation with Russia in the Black Sea. Trilateral dialogue advanced between Poland, Romania and Turkey. Yet Turkey refused to impose sanctions, and

[8] L. Kulesa (ed.) *Is a New Cold War Inevitable? Central European Views on Rebuilding Trust in the Euro-Atlantic Region*, Warsaw: PISM, 2014.

[9] A. Rettman, 'The year history returned to Europe', *EU Observer*, 22 December 2014.

indeed benefited by selling more to the Russian market after the EU introduced its sanctions. The Turkish government was not so highly concerned with a revisionist Russia as many EU member states. It doubted that an EU counterweight was necessary to outside influences in the Black Sea region. Turkey recoiled from improving relations with South Caucasus states in the name of weakening Russia, at the EU's behest. When Turkey's relations with Russia fractured in 2015 it was because of specific differences related to Syria and not because of Ukraine or Russia's general disregard for global norms.

Those pressing for a more assertive line tended to stress how far Western power exceeded that of the Russian federation. It was not true that Russia was better equipped for zero-sum geopolitics, they argued. The EU and US economies together were eight times the size of the Russian economy. NATO military expenditure was well over ten times the Russian defence budget; during the Cold War, western and eastern defence budgets had been more evenly matched. Also unlike the Cold War period, Russia could now count on few allies. Rising powers may not have enthusiastically backed the West over Crimea, but neither were they keen to ally with Russia. If President Putin wanted a confrontation, the more hawkish member states implied that the EU should not recoil from such a prospect for fear of Russia's supposed geopolitical prowess.

Sanctions

The most high-profile element of the EU response was the imposition of sanctions against Russia. At each stage in the debate over sanctions, many member states expressed a reluctance to use punitive measures against Russia. As the crisis worsened, however, the EU gradually extended its range of sanctions and member states agreed to measures they had initially ruled out. Sanctions were costly for Europe, unlike for the United States. The EU conducted 10 per cent of its trade with Russia in 2013; the US only 1 per cent. The Netherlands, Germany and Italy were the largest traders with the Russian Federation. Russia did around 50 per cent of its trade with the EU. Russian GDP plummeted by around 40 per cent between 2013 and 2016; while most of this fall was the result of lower oil prices and depreciation of the rouble, sanctions also contributed. The economic battlefield between the EU and Russia involved high stakes.

After Russia took control of Crimea, European governments agreed the template for a three-stage sanctions ratchet. Punitive measures would be imposed incrementally. At each turn, clear and realistic conditions would be stipulated. The first stage was to interrupt talks on visa liberalisation and a new partnership and cooperation agreement; these measures were taken immediately in response to the Crimea incursion. The second stage would be to impose asset freezes and visa bans. The third stage would entail a broad range of economic sanctions, the suspension of military cooperation and an arms embargo.

After stage one measures were adopted, governments made a tentative move into stage two in connection with the astonishingly fast-moving events in Crimea. Officials drew up a list of names to be subject to visa bans and asset freezes. Spain, Greece, Cyprus and Portugal were initially hesitant to agree the measures.[10] After internal debate, however, the EU imposed asset freezes and visa bans on 21 Russians and Ukrainians, including eight Crimean politicians, ten Russian politicians, and three Russian military chiefs. Separately, Western leaders discontinued the G8 format, reconvening as the G7 for the first time in sixteen years, without Russia.

Leaders agreed that the red line for stage three measures was any Russian encroachment into mainland Ukraine. As they contemplated tougher sanctions, there was debate on 'burden sharing' of the impact among EU countries. The French government opposed measures that would endanger its €1.25 billion order to supply Russia with two warships. Germany insisted that energy policy be left untouched. The UK was reluctant for the burden to fall on Russian business at the London stock exchange. Each member state advocated sanctions that would be most costly to other EU economies.

It was notable then that despite these misgivings, EU positions gradually shifted in late 2014. Violent separatist activity in eastern Ukraine brought forth more toughly worded EU statements. The Commission and External Action Service drew up proposals for targeting Russian companies linked to the aggression in Ukraine. These sanctions were defined as 'stage 2-plus'. The idea was to extend punitive measures to Russian individuals and companies 'benefiting from' Russian support to separatists in Ukraine. The Commission, European Investment

[10] *EU Observer*, 14 March 2014.

Bank (EIB) and European Bank for Reconstruction and Development (EBRD) suspended aid projects they were preparing in Russia.

After the MH17 plane tragedy in July 2014, the EU endorsed the first raft of stage three sanctions. These measures included an arms embargo (although only for new contracts); measures to close Russian banks out of international capital markets (serious when Russia needed to service $16 billion of debt); and a ban on sales of technology needed in the Russian energy sector (although only the oil, not gas sector). These steps were taken in the face of opposition from domestic lobbies such as the financial sector in the UK and the powerful German Committee on Eastern European Economic Relations. The US followed suit with a similar package of tougher measures.

The *Financial Times* defined the decision to impose these measures as 'the end of a 25 year chapter' in the West's effort to develop positive, engagement-based relations with Russia.[11] Those member states that had long argued against sanctions changed position. The UK accepted the measure for which it would bear the highest cost: closing Russian state banks out of international markets would have a big impact on the City of London. Germany even scrapped a €135 million contract to provide Russia with a military training centre –stopping a contract already signed even though the sanctions formally were not retroactive. Finland and Lithuania suffered particularly heavily from this round of sanctions.[12] Russia retaliated by banning the import of a range of EU agricultural produce, worth €12 billion to EU exporters. The EU held talks with Latin American states to dissuade them from stepping in to replace Europe's banned agricultural exports to Russia.[13]

In the autumn of 2014, leaders instructed the Commission to draw up options for the further tightening of sanctions in response to the involvement of Russian troops in fighting in several east Ukrainian cities. France announced it would, after all, halt the sale of two Mistral warships to Russia. The EU added restrictions to the export of dual-use goods and further limits were placed on Russian institutions' access to international capital markets. German exports to Russia had plummeted by nearly 20 per cent by the end of 2014. As oil prices

[11] 'Closing a 25-year chapter with Russia', *Financial Times*, editorial, 30 July 2014.

[12] NATO, *Sanctions after Crimea: Have They Worked?* Brussels: NATO, 2015.

[13] *Financial Times*, 12 August 2014.

tumbled, inflicting great pain on Russia's economy, many European governments were increasingly convinced that this economic track offered the best chance of tempering Russian aggression.

Differences briefly widened between member states after Russia signed the Minsk peace deal. Matteo Renzi, François Hollande and Federica Mogherini spoke of positive developments on the ground and a more flexible Russian attitude, and advocated a possible easing of sanctions. Hollande said in January 2015: 'I think the sanctions must stop now … Mr Putin does not want to annex eastern Ukraine.'[14] Federica Mogherini commissioned a paper from her officials to look at areas where cooperation with Russia might now be restarted – a move that caused much controversy with many member states.

However, events on the ground soon pulled governments away from any leniency towards Russia.[15] After a series of lethal attacks in Mariupol and other locations, member states instructed the high representative to prepare additional restrictive measures. Even Greece signed up to this, after some doubts that it's new, more Russia-leaning Syriza government would agree to do so. Angela Merkel was the pivotal player, as she insisted that sanctions be maintained. While insisting they sought deeper economic cooperation over the long term, in practice both the EU and Russia began diversifying away from each other and limiting sectoral-technical working contacts.[16]

Member states needed to renew sanctions each six months. They agreed such extensions in July 2015, at the start of 2016 and again in July 2016 and December 2016. On each occasion a number of member states (including Italy, Hungary, Slovakia and the Czech Republic) argued for an easing of sanctions. However, a consensus was maintained on the grounds that Russia had yet to comply with the conditions of the Minsk II peace accord and continued to support separatist attacks in Donbas. Council president Donald Tusk, Poland and Lithuania were particularly robust in pushing for tough sanctions to be maintained.

[14] *EU Observer*, 6 January 2015.

[15] J. Ćwiek-Karpowicz and S. Secrieru (eds) *Russia and Sanctions*, Warsaw: PISM, 2015, p. 37.

[16] T. Romanova, 'Sanctions and the future of EU–Russian economic relations', *Europe-Asia Studies*, 68/4, 2016, 774–96.

Defensive Security

There was also a defence and military dimension to the aftermath of the crisis –this brought national policies and NATO cooperation to the forefront. A key and sobering point was that much of the European reaction centred on bolstering the defence of European territory. Some European governments were increasingly concerned with neutering Russian threats to their own territory, perhaps more so than aspiring to be 'security providers' to EaP states. This represented a return to something akin to the NATO alliance's Cold War rationale. Even if the prospect of Russia intervening in the Baltic states seemed an overheated and fanciful notion to many, the fact that deliberations ran in this direction reflected how far the security panorama had changed.

Officials argued that NATO's collective defence commitments were now of the utmost importance. Surveillance flights were stepped up over Baltic states to dissuade any Russian action in supposed defence of these countries' Russian minorities. A new NATO Baltic Air Policing mission scrambled hundreds of times; it doubled in size during 2015. NATO also beefed up border defences, for instance in Romania. The US deployed 600 troops to Poland and the Baltic states. Backing such measures, German defence minister, Ursula von der Leyen, said: 'Vladimir Putin has destroyed an enormous amount of trust with his conduct ... Currently, Russia is not a partner. Partners adhere to joint agreements.'[17]

Working meetings under NATO's 2010 strategic partnership with Russia were stopped. The deployment of NATO troops to Central European states was significant as it reversed a 1990s agreement to keep troops away from Russia's borders. In June 2014, President Barack Obama visited Poland and launched a $1 billion US European Reassurance Initiative. This promised more NATO drills in the region, US warship patrols in the Baltic and Black Seas and military aid to Ukraine, Georgia and Moldova. Poland wanted even more commitment, in the form of a permanent NATO base on its soil. Romania and Poland led an initiative for NATO 'eastern flank' states to deepen cooperation amongst themselves. According to their diplomats, Central and Eastern European member states began to feel that NATO's Article 5

[17] *EU Observer*, 13 June 2015.

commitment (to joint territorial defence) had some real meaning and prospect of being used to protect their territory.

At a NATO summit in September 2014 leaders pledged a 2 per cent of GDP target for defence expenditure. They agreed to ensure that 20 per cent of their defence spend went on equipment, to move funds away from simply keeping soldiers in uniform. The NATO Response Force was to expand from 13,000. to 25,000 troops. In addition, a 5,000-strong Very High Readiness Joint Task Force (VJTF) would be created to be deployable within 48 hours. Until the VJTF was launched in 2016, a Spearhead Force was deployed in mid-2015. The new force would ensure the forward positioning of assets in Baltic states and set up skeleton command-and-control facilities. The force would be trained in unconventional actions, to deal with Russia's funding of separatist groups. More exercises would be carried out and situational awareness would be enhanced.

A June 2015 Spearhead exercise was NATO's first-ever mock mass mobilisation. A British-led 10,000-strong joint expeditionary force was also set up, with a broader peacekeeping remit and contributions from seven nations. In early 2016, the US announced it would increase the rotating deployment of heavy weapons, armoured vehicles and troops in Central and Eastern Europe. Taking a step further, at their July 2016 summit in Warsaw, NATO leaders agreed to deploy so-called Battlegroups in the three Baltic states and Poland. They also injected stronger momentum behind the defence spending target, the VJTF and Spearhead Force. At another NATO summit in October 2016 leaders further increased the planned scale of deployments for Central and Eastern Europe.

NATO increased training and capacity building for Ukrainian armed forces. Ukraine received training on civil emergency response. NATO reinforced support to Ukraine through programmes to build capacity in command, control, communications, cyber defence and medical rehabilitation. Four trust funds were created to upgrade Ukraine's logistics, cyber warfare, command and control and medical services, respectively. Twenty-six member states contributed €4 million over two years.[18]

The crisis changed German attitudes to defence. Germany pledged to reinforce air-policing capacities in the Baltic states and sent a vessel

[18] A. Gatmanchuk, *Ukraine-NATO: A Hidden Integration or Undeclared Neutrality?*, Kiev: Institute for World Policy, June 2015.

for NATO's naval task force in the Baltic Sea. It also doubled its presence in the alliance's Northeast headquarters in Poland, from 60 to 120 staff officers. Germany, Poland and Denmark committed to upgrading military readiness at this facility. The German government published a new foreign policy strategy in February 2015; this committed Germany to playing a more active international security role, in terms of conflict resolution and upholding global rules; the eastern crisis was the main impulse behind this upgrade.

The French armed forces switched their core planning from an assumption that the Middle East was the most likely theatre of conflict to force planning oriented toward a crisis in the east. In late 2014, the UK deployed weapons systems to Poland. In the autumn of 2015, the British government announced that further cuts in its defence budget would not be made and that it would retain military spending at 2 per cent of GDP, with both the Russia–Ukraine and Middle East theatres cited as justification. The UK defence and security review published at the beginning of 2016 identified the risk of an attack by another state as a priority, in contrast to previous reviews; Russia was the perceived risk, and this was a major reason why the government committed to halting half a decade of defence cuts and to increase military spending up to 2020.[19]

Sweden promised significant increases in its defence budgets and the Nordic states committed to a reinforced defence pact. Sweden and Finland signed host-nation support agreements with NATO. Beyond even this, the Swedish and Finnish governments both established commissions to study the possibility of NATO membership. The Russian ambassador in Stockholm threatened 'retaliatory measures'. Sweden responded by reaffirming its promise to increase defence spending by 11 per cent over five years.

Reversing a trend in place since the beginning of Europe's economic troubles nearly a decade previously, in 2016 defence budgets were set to rise in all EU states except Italy, Greece and Luxembourg – with especially large hikes in Central and Eastern Europe.[20] The largest planned increases for 2015–2016 were from Lithuania (50 per cent),

[19] HM Government, *National Security Strategy and Strategic Defence and Security Review 2015 A Secure and Prosperous United Kingdom*, London: Stationery Office, 2015.

[20] A. Marrone, O. De France and D. Fattibene (eds) *Defence Budgets and Cooperation in Europe: Developments, Trends and Drivers*, IAI, IRIS, SWP, RUSI, 2016.

Poland (20 per cent), Latvia (15 per cent) and Estonia (7 per cent). Despite Hungarian premier Viktor Orban's avowed admiration for President Putin, Hungary supported and participated in the NATO Spearhead Force, and increased its defence budget by 17 per cent in 2015. Romania for the first time met the 2 per cent defence expenditure commitment. A new joint Polish-Lithuanian-Ukrainian battalion starred in the parade celebrating the twenty-fifth anniversary of Ukraine's independence in August 2016. [21] In October 2016, the defence ministers of France, Germany, Italy and Spain issued a joint letter to push forward plans for a European military command, concerned that 'Euro-Atlantic security is [being] challenged in a way that was not the case for decades'.[22] By the end of 2016, plans were afoot for a new European Defence Fund to help boost and coordinate EU military power.

New Commitment to the EaP

On a separate track from such defence initiatives, European leaders regularly committed to strengthening the EaP in response to the crisis. The limited success of the 2013 Vilnius summit was a sobering wake-up call. Russia's more assertive attempts to undercut the EaP jolted EU institutions into action. Many policy-makers feared that the whole EaP was in danger of collapsing. Loosely floated ideas for a more political focus that had been voiced before the Vilnius summit were now expressed in formal EU proposals. Crucially, the EU began to distinguish more systematically between the three states – Georgia, Moldova and Ukraine – that were keen to move ahead with deeper partnership and those – Armenia, Azerbaijan and Belarus – that were more ambivalent. This so-called 'differentiation' became a key means of unlocking the EaP's strategic potential and flexibility.

Officials insisted that the Crimea crisis engendered a geopolitical shift in the whole nature of the EaP. Diplomats talked of the EaP needing to address the 'political origins' of the crisis. Some experts claimed that the Ukraine crisis had engendered a wholesale change

[21] Stockholm International Peace Research Institute, *SIPRI Yearbook 2015: Armaments, Disarmaments and International Security*, Oxford: Oxford University Press, 2015.

[22] *EU Observer*, 13 October 2016.

in EU policy in the region towards long-term and more geopolitical thinking.[23] One Polish diplomat opined: 'We must no longer be blind to geopolitics … our whole method in the EaP has been fundamentally flawed.' One Czech ambassador angrily disagreed with the suggestion that the EU had caused the crisis by too assertively moving into the post-Soviet space; indeed, the problem was that it had left a vacuum there, and 'like a rule of nature, Russia filled the vacuum'.

The Commission presented a paper on the EaP to the foreign affairs council in February 2014, which gained widespread support from member states. The paper promised more high-level commitment, inducements, funds and public diplomacy campaigns; a more strategic use of conditionality; a European package of tangible benefits beyond the association agreements (AAs); consideration of a Common Economic Area to include the eastern region; a new type of accord for Armenia and those rejecting an AA; more strategic coordination with EaP states; and more effort on the EaP's multilateral track.[24]

In a March 2014 communication, the EU adopted a different tone to its previous annual ENP reviews. It stressed that the ENP must now be harnessed more systematically as a means for 'defending the EU's strategic interests'. The EU would do more to promote itself as 'a diplomatic actor and provider of security'. The communication promised 'more action based on diplomacy, conflict prevention and mediation'. The EU's central aim would be to ensure 'greater consistency between overall strategic and political bilateral objectives'.[25]

The EU accelerated the signing of the AAs with Ukraine, Georgia and Moldova. These agreements were brought forward to June 2014, ahead of their originally estimated dates. The EU did this, policy-makers noted, without worrying about the minutiae of outstanding elements of conditionality. To address Russia's concerns, the EU agreed to delay full implementation of Ukraine's DCFTA for 18 months up to the end of 2015. Despite much pressure from Russia

[23] J. Techau, 'Ukraine: Birthplace of strategic Europe', Carnegie Strategic Europe blog, 18 March 2014.

[24] Leaked extracts of the paper were posted by the *Financial Times*. Available at: http://blogs.ft.com/brusselsblog/files/2014/02/20-points-on-Eastern-Partnership.pdf.

[25] European Commission and High Representative for Foreign and Security Policy, *Neighbourhood at the Crossroads: Implementation of the European Neighbourhood Policy in 2013*, JOIN(2014)12. Quotes from pp. 2 and 17.

and some member states' preference for a further delay, implementation of the DCFTA was then unfrozen and moved steadily ahead through the course of 2016. Ukraine began to adopt liberalisation measures, the EU having already opened its market unilaterally. The EU offered Ukraine a generous seven-year transition period and entry into the Euro-Mediterranean rules of origin system. Russia suspended its free trade area with Ukraine. The EU and member states offered more help through a plethora of projects to assist Ukrainian exports into the EU market. These policy moves had an impact on the ground: in 2012, Russia took 25 per cent of Ukraine's exports; in 2015 it took only 12 per cent.

The EU added a 'Common Security and Defence Policy panel' to the EaP's multilateral track, to deepen security partnerships. It also beefed up an EaP Police Cooperation Programme. EU diplomats explained the driving aim: the ENP needed more than a minor change; the security dimension needed to be brought to the forefront; this was what partners now most wanted from the Union. Separate from but relevant for the EaP, the EU fleshed out its 'Comprehensive approach' to conflict resolution. The EU began signing 'state-building contracts' to strengthen help for fragile states. The External Action Service's new mediation support team extended its range of action. A new inter-agency coordinating committee was set up in Brussels to provide security input to the use of development aid – with Ukraine in particular in mind. Several member states also promised a tighter focus on the 'drivers of conflict'.

The EU promised to make the €15 billion allocated under the European Neighbourhood Instrument (ENI) for the 2014–2020 period available on terms that were 'more flexible' and 'incentive-based', with lighter forms of conditionality. It granted EaP states longer transition periods to ease the process of regulatory harmonisation with the EU; some approximation requirements were made more optional than legally binding. The AAs included over 2,000 pages of detailed commitments to cooperation based on the application of EU law in EaP states; forty-six annexes offered flexibility and variation within different sectors.[26] The EU's Agreement on Certification and Accreditation introduced greater flexibility, allowing partners a gradual and piecemeal adoption of EU standards. In the event of EaP states not implementing

[26] Ibid, p. 9.

their AA commitments, the EU did not threaten suspension. It framed conditionality in a softer tone, reiterating that the politics of inclusion would prevail over any prospect of punitive exclusion.

One aspect of the more strategic flavour was that member state engagement increased in the region, through a web of bilateral relations alongside the EaP. France re-engaged. Insiders insisted an informal deal was struck, under which France would back Germany in the east, and Germany would help France in the Sahel. The Weimer triangle took on a new life, in some senses returning to its very original rationale of coordination between France, Germany and Poland. Member state representatives agreed in private that they had to play a heavier role in driving strategy in the region in order to inject geostrategic effectiveness.

Poland increased funding levels, with a particular focus on new democratic reform initiatives in the EaP states. The Czech government organised a consultation on the EaP in Prague in April 2014. At this event, a number of European ministers opined that the EaP needed to be qualitatively upgraded.[27] Romania proposed a 'Security Trust', a series of thematic security dialogues to serve as platforms for diplomatic coordination with EaP partners. Italy pushed for mechanisms that would allow the ENP to draw more readily on EU crisis management instruments – so that the management of security emergencies fed more coherently into the long-term reform focus of the ENP toolbox.

EaP work plans detailed commitments to intensify cooperation on economic integration; energy policy; democracy and good governance; security sector reforms; and educational and youth exchanges.[28] The EU drew up 'Civil society roadmaps' as vehicles for enhancing support to local civic actors, around their own priorities. The Conference of the Regional and Local Authorities for the Eastern Partnership launched a new initiative on devolution, as a means of 'addressing growing tensions, instability and security challenges in the region.'[29] In mid-2015

[27] Czech Association for International Affairs, *Conference Report: The International Conference 'Eastern Partnership Five Years On: Time For a New Strategy?'*, Prague: 2014.

[28] See website of the External Action Service, under ENP for the four platform working programmes.

[29] EU Committee of Regions, *CORLEAP: Looking Forward to Democratic Reform in the Eastern Partnership Countries*, Brussels, 2014.

the European Commission launched a DCFTA Facility for Small and Medium Enterprises (SMEs), offering €200 million in grants each year and aiming to unlock over €2 billion for investment. These measures reinforced the strategic use of the EaP's low-politics approach.[30] Away from the media headlines, EaP initiatives were gaining momentum.

Funding levels increased. Most dramatically, the EU promised €11 billion to Ukraine. Much of this amount was made up of EBRD and EIB loans, but also included the largest package of macro-economic assistance the EU had ever offered to a third country. Eighty per cent of ENI funds would go direct to governments through budget support, to improve dispersal rates and local ownership. The Neighbourhood Civil Society Facility was increased from €90 million for 2011–2014 to €150 million for 2015–2018. The UK set up a £20 million Good Governance Fund covering Ukraine, Moldova and Georgia in particular. It promised to double this to £40 million per year by 2019. One EU senior diplomat explained these upgrades to reform-orientated funding mechanisms: 'supporting better governance is the only we can do geopolitics'.

Several initiatives began to work on countering Russian propaganda. A so-called East Stratcom team was established in the External Action Service to monitor Russian news and correct misinformation; governments agreed to expand the team in October 2016. The European Endowment for Democracy (EED) launched a more assertive alternative to run a new 'content factory' unit aimed at countering Russian propaganda. By 2016, European donors were funding dozens of media projects aimed at Russian speakers in EaP states and inside the EU itself – they were now taking the phenomenon of Russian information warfare seriously. Follow-up to an EED study into this issue was supported by the Dutch, Polish, British and Latvian governments and involved a cluster of media work against Russian propaganda and 'misinformation warfare'. At the end of November 2016, Finland announced it was planning to set up a new centre in Helsinki dedicated to fighting 'hybrid' threats and the use of misinformation; other EU states planned to cooperate.[31]

[30] L. Delcour and H. Kostanyan, *Towards a Fragmented Neighbourhood: Policies of the EU and Russia and their Consequences for the Area that Lies in between Brussels*, CEPS Policy Brief 17, 2014.

[31] *Euractiv*, 22 November 2016.

The EU stepped up its offers of visa liberalisation. By mid-2015, five of the six EaP states had some kind of visa accord with the EU, while the sixth, Belarus, was almost ready to sign an agreement. Four EaP states had also signed mobility partnerships. This was a significant choice made by European governments, given the broader political context. After the Charlie Hebdo attacks in Paris in early 2015, some member states suggested that restrictions of visa-free travel were necessary on security grounds. Yet a restrictive approach did not entirely prevail and visa talks advanced even as the EU grappled with the arrival of over 1 million refugees from the Middle East in 2015 and 2016. EU officials insisted that this demonstrated how the Union's notion of geopolitics was (still) to encourage contacts across borders not 'protect territory'.

Several institutional changes facilitated the political impulse. New EU institutional structures clustered together external relations commissioners and the high representatives to improve coherence – a change motivated explicitly by turmoil in the neighbourhood. A new Directorate General for Neighbourhood and Enlargement Negotiations (NEAR) was designed to improve strategic direction and get financial resources contributing more directly to overarching foreign and security policy imperatives.

Many member state diplomats saw the EaP's Riga summit in May 2015 as a particularly important moment. A Swedish diplomat defined it as a step towards a firmer defence of EaP states' sovereign right to choose a deeper partnership with the EU. The Latvian secretary of state believed the Riga summit was a 'crossroads' in resisting Russian threats to retaliate against new EaP commitments. The Riga summit declaration reaffirmed 'the sovereign right of each partner freely to choose the level of ambition and the goals to which it aspires in its relations with the European Union'.

The EU undertook a review of the ENP that was strongly influenced by the eastern crisis. EU diplomats spoke of the logic driving the review: EU policy could no longer be based on the assumption that neighbouring states would smoothly align themselves with and into an EU sphere of governance. The EU had to start from a clear and disaggregated understanding of its geopolitical interests and build tailor-made strategies with each individual state from such an assessment.[32]

[32] European Commission and High Representative for Foreign Affairs and Security Policy, *Joint Consultation Paper: Towards a New Neighbourhood Policy*, JOIN (2015)6 March 2015, p. 8.

EU commissioner Johannes Hahn explained: 'Until now the ENP has relied almost exclusively on community instruments. This review offers the possibility to bring all our instruments together, to attempt a much more coherent approach to the key security challenges in the region.'[33] Several member state officials involved in the review pushed for what they saw as a more geostrategic logic to EU policy. Strategy could no longer be based on an assumption of 'benign convergence' and this was 'reason for a new realism'. Ten member states compiled a non-paper that stressed the need for a more 'transactional' approach.

The resulting ENP Review document was published in November 2015. It promised 'new ways of working' and indicated that security and 'stabilisation' would now be the EU's highest priorities. To allow deeper cooperation the principles of 'differentiation and greater mutual ownership' would be encouraged. The EU would search for 'more effective ways to support democratic, accountable and good governance'. There would be increased engagement 'with partners in the security sector' and on conflict prevention. Member states would be more fully involved in selecting priorities and more ministerial meetings would be held. The EU would modernise its funding instruments, like twinning and technical assistance programmes to make these more strategic and targeted. A 'flexibility cushion' would allow for quick funding in response to changes on the ground. The document again mentioned the possibility of a common economic area for EaP states.[34] The EU Global Strategy published in June 2016 took the geopolitical logic of the ENP review a step further, stating that the EU would 'support different paths to resilience to its east and south, focusing on the most acute dimensions of fragility and targeting those where we can make a meaningful difference'.[35]

Re-orientating Energy Security

A fourth prong to the European response was in the area of energy security. As a longer-term strategy, plans were launched to move

[33] Speech to the European Parliament, 10 March 2015. Available at: http://europa.eu/rapid/press-release_SPEECH-15-4591_en.htm.

[34] European Commission and High Representative, *Review of the European Neighbourhood Policy*, JOIN(2015) 50 final, November 2015.

[35] European Union High Representative for Foreign and Security Policy, *Shared Vision, Common Action: A Stronger Europe: A Global Strategy for the European Union's Foreign and Security Policy*, June 2016, p. 17.

European countries away from their dependence on Russian energy supplies. In May 2014, the Commission produced an EU Energy Security Strategy that had an explicitly geopolitical tone. This was followed in March 2015 by an even more important strategy for an Energy Union. In both these watershed documents the imperative of reducing reliance on and vulnerability to Russian oil and gas supplies was now presented as a primary goal of energy policy. The Energy Union was driven forward by Polish and other leaders as a direct strategic response to Russian foreign policy actions.

The Energy Union promised that the EU would develop new energy partnerships with a raft of alternative suppliers to decrease dependence on Russia. The EU committed to a whole battery of policy moves designed to bolster energy resilience against Russia: completion of the internal energy market; increased storage capacity; strengthened solidarity mechanisms, to provide concrete protection especially for those half-dozen states still entirely dependent on Russia for energy imports; coordination on pipeline projects so that one member state did not decide on a project that undermined the security of another; an eventual enlargement of the Southern Gas Corridor through the inclusion of Iraq, Iran and Turkmenistan; an extension of the Energy Community through the EU's neighbourhood; more External Action Service involvement in energy policy to ensure that geopolitical aims were fully incorporated; and €27 billion of investment in renewal energy sources.[36]

After the Nabucco pipeline project collapsed, European commitments to a reconfigured Southern Gas Corridor intensified. By 2016 these plans were beginning to gain momentum and had an increasingly geopolitical tint. While the Nabucco line would have rested heavily on applying EU rules and market regulations, arrangements for the Southern Gas Corridor were more flexible and more political. Diplomats recognised that the new plans required an approach based on geopolitical engagement and diplomacy, rather than on the extension of EU energy market rules. While Azerbaijani supplies only accounted for 2 per cent of overall EU imports, they were of some significance for Italy, Greece and Bulgaria.

[36] European Union, *A Framework Strategy for a Resilient Energy Union with a Forward-Looking Climate Change Policy*, COM (2015), 80 final; S. Far and R. Youngs, *Energy Union and EU Global Strategy*, Stockholm: Swedish Institute for European Policy Studies, 2015.

The EU stepped up legal pressure on Gazprom. This pressure proved enough to end the South Stream project, the Russian-led initiative to bring supplies into European markets on a route circumventing Ukraine. In December 2013, the Commission found that the contracts signed by the six member state governments involved in South Stream contravened EU competition law, as they helped Gazprom to maintain anti-competitive practices. In December 2014, President Putin announced Russia would no longer pursue South Stream, citing EU opposition as the reason for this apparently momentous decision.

A wider Commission investigation against Gazprom was frozen in April 2014, to give diplomacy a chance after Crimea's annexation. In 2015, the Commission restarted the case – as the emollient approach had clearly not worked. The charges related to the contracts Gazprom struck with eight Central and Eastern European countries: Bulgaria, the Czech Republic, Estonia, Hungary, Latvia, Lithuania, Poland and Slovakia. The aim was to remove restrictive destination clauses in Gazprom contracts with EU purchasers.

In this way, the EU managed to put Gazprom on the back foot. The company's exports dipped by more than 5 per cent in 2015. It accepted the extension of the EU-mediated deal providing low gas prices for Ukraine. The Ukraine crisis stiffened EU unity on many such energy matters. President Putin on several occasions contacted select member states individually in relation to gas issues; each time, member states authorised the EU to respond on behalf of them all. Facing a possible fine of 10 per cent of its revenues, Gazprom changed its approach. It sought a negotiated settlement and a more cooperative approach in Europe.

The EU also pushed back against the substitute project of Turkish Stream, insisting that European strategic aims would not be served by the EU supporting this new Russian proposal for a pipeline route across Turkey. The EU stressed that any extension of Turkish Stream into Greece would need to comply with EU competition rules; the EU would not fund infrastructure to collect gas at the Turkish border. The project was downsized and then seemed to grind to a halt, partly due to EU coolness and partly due to the deterioration in Russian-Turkish relations.

The EU offered Ukraine protection through 'reverse flow' connections. The European Commission supported an Eastring gas line for connecting gas infrastructures between Slovakia, Romania and Bulgaria with the goal of running reverse supplies. Slovak pipeline operator Eustream built a pipeline for Western European gas to be channelled back to Ukraine. From September 2014, this line supplied up to 10 bcm of gas a year. Together with existing connections from Hungary and Poland, Ukraine was now able to obtain up to 16–17 bcm of gas from Western Europe.

The European Commission provided between €800 million and €1 billion for Ukraine's gas purchases. The European Bank for Reconstruction and Development extended a loan to Ukraine to help make the gas purchases. The EU launched a Central East South Europe Gas Connectivity High Level Group in February 2015 and opened this initiative to non-EU members of the Energy Community. All such initiatives aimed to strengthen the energy and geopolitical resilience of Eastern European states in relation to Russia.

The EU had increasing leeway to take these steps. By 2014 its dependency on Russian gas had decreased to only 6 per cent of Europe's total energy mix. Gas storage levels were high, the shale gas revolution had fundamentally changed the strategic calculus; the EU's internal energy market was now more integrated; and less Russian gas was transported across Ukraine than in 2009. A more indirect, energy-related impact of the crisis was that both the EU and the US declared they would make the compromises necessary to free up energy trade. The prospect of the US agreeing to export shale gas supplies to the EU would help significantly to prize European economies away from their reliance on Russian gas. The US began oil exports to Europe in 2016, in part because its shale industry needed a fillip against falling oil prices, but also to help EU states wean themselves off Russian gas.

Conclusion

While this chapter's account is partial, in focusing only on the ways in which European policies were altered, upgraded or intensified in response to the eastern crisis, it is nevertheless instructive to reflect on what it contributes to the book's core analytical aims:

Categorisation

The various strands of the European response resonate with the variables suggested in Chapter 2 for categorising different geopolitical options. European governments' degree of commitment to the east in general and the EaP in particular intensified through a range of concrete initiatives and new resources. They exerted pressure on Russia through a range of sanctions that had seemed unlikely to win support from many member states at the beginning of the crisis. Partnership with Russia atrophied and a logic of exclusion crept into EU policy for the first time since the Cold War era. On a separate track, most European governments pushed for a hard-security dimension to the response through NATO commitments, both within EU territory and in some EaP partners. European support for political and economic reform within EaP states was enhanced as a geopolitical tool, mainly through EU instruments although also through some national member state initiatives. Such support was also framed in more flexible ways, so that it was capable of assisting concrete strategic aims in the near term. Hiski Haukkala believed that the crisis ended the EU's strategic logic of seeking to embrace Russia within an EU-centred unipolar European order and ushered in a bipolarism of the wider European continent.[37]

Foreign Policy Dynamics

Member states became more active. The crisis became *chefsache*, with prime ministers and presidents seeking tighter hold on strategy, relative to the influence of EU institutions. Noted and well-respected experts on the region detected in all this a meaningful shift towards an EU policy that was more strategic, more assertive and more coordinated. Timothy Garton Ash was impressed with how Angela Merkel engaged in a robust enough fashion to push President Putin back into a defensive corner – her Mercury of patient, solid pushback gaining the upper hand over his Mars of impetuous conflict.[38] In addition, European governments pursued part of their response through upgraded NATO commitments, not entirely dovetailed with EU institutional frameworks. A more equal balance of institutional levels and pathways was

[37] H. Haukkala, 'From cooperative to contested Europe? The conflict in Ukraine as a culmination of a long-term crisis in EU–Russia relations', *Journal of Contemporary European Studies*, 23/1, 2015, 25–40.

[38] T. Garton Ash, 'Angela Merkel has faced down the Russian bear in the battle for Europe', *The Guardian*, 22 December 2014.

evident in the forms through which European governments sought to map out a response to the crisis.

Yet the measures outlined in this chapter were only one part of the equation – the more notable ways in which European governments responded with apparently significant changes to the eastern crisis. We need a properly rounded picture that also traces the *limits* to these responses in order to reach a full categorisation of European geopolitical tactics, understand the full range of EU foreign-policy dynamics and evaluate the impact of European strategies. This is the subject of the next chapter.

6 *Limits to the European Union Response*

Change and bolder geopolitical commitments were offset by a heavy dose of continuity in Europe's eastern policies. While the responses outlined in the previous chapter were undoubtedly significant, each area of policy change displayed features that fell short of dramatic strategic repositioning. The European Union (EU) certainly exhibited a heavier measure of geopolitical awareness than before 2014. Yet, there were clear limits to the changes in European policies. The EU still shied away from classical geopolitical thinking and tried rather to shape an eastern policy that was strategic in a distinctive way. Its practical response belied much of its own rhetoric that the geopolitical context was now qualitatively different. Its aim was to sharpen existing policy tenets and instruments, rather than give a fundamentally different geopolitical hue to the Eastern Partnership (EaP) framework. This chapter outlines the ways in which the post-2013 changes to EU eastern policies were circumscribed and cautious. Taken together with the previous chapter, the analysis offered here shows how the European response corresponded to components of liberal-redux geopolitics conceptualised in Chapter 2.

Limits to Hard Security

A highly significant aspect of the European response was that offensive military measures were discounted early on, publicly and unequivocally. While US army chiefs were said to have at least prepared for the possibility of military action and insisted that 'all options are on the table', European leaders explicitly rejected 'out of area' military options in Ukraine or elsewhere in the post-Soviet space.[1] There was no serious discussion of military engagement by European forces to help stem armed conflict in eastern Ukraine. Such a use – or even threat – of

[1] *EU Observer*, 14 March 2014.

hard power formed no part of European governments' understanding of a geopolitical response. One 2015 opinion poll showed that only in the UK, Poland and Spain was the population favourable to using military force should Russia invade a NATO ally; strong majorities in France, Italy and Germany were against taking any action against Russia even in the event of such a direct attack.[2]

Many European governments expressed unease with the US move to increase NATO's profile. While there was much debate about NATO stationing bases in Central and Eastern Europe, most European governments did not support this option. German officials were particularly adamant in insisting that 'permanent bases' were neither appropriate nor necessary in Central and Eastern Europe. When in June 2015 the US talked to Poland about permanently stationing tanks and other heavy weaponry in Central Europe and the Baltics as part of the Spearhead Force, most European governments opposed this move. Symbolising hard power limits, NATO's 'Steadfast Jazz' training exercise in Poland and the Baltic states was relatively modest in scale, while Russia's much larger live exercise, 'West 2013', coordinated with Belarus, revealed a much higher level of military preparedness.[3]

By 2016, the NATO rapid reaction force was still not fully ready to be deployable within 48 hours, as promised. There was no European equivalent of the US's new 'Offset Strategy' that spurred military advances specifically to neuter the enhanced military capabilities of Russia (and other powers, like China). In June 2016, German foreign minister Frank-Walter Steinmeier criticised NATO's just-starting Anaconda exercises in Eastern Europe and called instead for dialogue with Russia.[4] At the July 2016 Warsaw summit, NATO states again rejected the option of permanently stationing troops in Central and Eastern Europe.

In December 2014, Ukraine's parliament voted overwhelmingly to drop the country's non-aligned status. Frank-Walter Stienmeier responded by pointedly ruling out support for Ukraine's entry into NATO.[5] European governments tried to rein back President Poroshenko,

[2] Pew Research Centre, *Global Attitudes Survey*, Spring 2015, p. 52.

[3] L. Kulesa (ed.) *Is a New Cold War Inevitable? Central European Views on Rebuilding Trust in the Euro-Atlantic Region*, Warsaw: PISM, 2014.

[4] BBC News, 18 June 2016.

[5] *EU Observer*, 27 December 2014.

arguing that his plea for NATO membership was self-defeating and counter-productive. When Georgia stepped up the pressure for a NATO membership action plan (MAP), France and Germany opposed such an offer, reinforcing their position from the years before the crisis; Georgia was consequently refused a MAP at the NATO summit in September 2014. European doubters won the battle against NATO expansion; they even got the US on board to lobby Ukrainian politicians not to push for NATO membership.

Limits to governments' responses through NATO were reinforced by their reluctance to bring hard-security issues into the separate – and not entirely congruent -track of EU policy instruments. The EaP remained some distance short of challenging Russia as the primary security player – both provider and spoiler – in the region. Its most serious security lacuna was its failure to offer really significant assistance in building up eastern states' border controls, needed to stiffen their resilience as sovereign territorial entities.[6] European governments did not back proposals for a new security forum that included EaP partners but not Russia – which might have circumvented the Organization for Security and Co-operation in Europe's (OSCE) stasis to provide strategic protection to the region. One EU official lamented: 'We cannot improve the EaP as a security forum because we still lack a common Russia policy.'

Policy-makers from the EaP states admonished European governments for this security deficit. One Georgian politician expressed a common view that: 'It is because the EU is still not giving us security guarantees, that we need the US back'. A Moldovan diplomat noted that: 'EU transformative power has worked but now the EU is not able to protect us from the security implications of this'. Ukrainians insisted that in limiting its security projection the EU confused cause and effect in the crisis: Russia annexed Crimea after the country had accepted de facto non-aligned neutrality; it was the annexation that turned Ukrainian opinion against neutrality and made external support necessary.

Revealing a discrepancy with NATO's revived agenda, EU diplomats acknowledged the uncertainty over what 'securitising' the EaP meant in practice. Their common observation was that everyone now

[6] N. Popescu, 'First Lessons from the Ukrainian Crisis', *ISS Issue Alert*, Paris: EU Institute for Security Studies, October 2014.

accepted that the EaP must be more geopolitical, and not 'just about trade and aid', but they were not sure how exactly to add a security dimension to sector cooperation. They also insisted on the need for continuity: the EU could not jettison the whole EaP framework each time a crisis erupted. The EaP and the European Neighbourhood Policy (ENP) should not become crisis management tools, diplomats commonly insisted. By 2016, most diplomats acknowledged that the EU's basic strategic aims were relatively modest. As one minister lamented: 'Even after such a sobering crisis, member states are still not willing to unblock a genuinely common European security and defence policy.' One Western security official summarised: 'Putin seeks escalation, we avoid escalation.'

While most European governments promised increases for 2015 and 2016, these came after a 3 per cent decrease in European allies' defence spend in 2014 and even bigger reductions in 2013.[7] Beyond the NATO 2 per cent commitment, there was little progress on the modernisation of capabilities. While the UK halted military cuts in 2015, its capabilities remained much diminished. From the end of the Cold War to 2015, NATO per capita defence expenditure had halved, with the UK reducing armed personnel from 300,000 to 80,000, and its stock of tanks from 1,300 to 200. While European governments dramatically boosted their intelligence capabilities to deal with Islamist jihadism, they did not significantly strengthen capabilities relating to Russia.

While European governments began some – both national and EU – initiatives to defend against the Russian offensive in cyber warfare using social media and propaganda, they held back from any direct attack against Russian power in this sphere. They did not resurrect their Cold War information warfare and use of irregular tactics. Europe was open to Russian media and cyber companies, while Russia increasingly impeded European media and information technology access. While the Kremlin funded over fifty organisations in the EU with a budget of over $1 billion as part of its information warfare, the East Stratcom team consisted of only ten people –only one of these tracked 'misinformation', while the other nine worked on a 'positive

[7] Stockholm International Peace Research Institute, *SIPRI Yearbook 2015: Armaments, Disarmaments and International Security*, Oxford: Oxford University Press, 2015.

agenda' of disseminating a more upbeat and accessible image of the EU. In November 2016, member states did not agree to a request for funds significantly to upgrade this team. European donors kept their anti-misinformation projects at a low level in order, they said, not to over-politicise the media sphere as a confrontational tool towards Russia. The general EU view was that Russia's use of misinformation was an annoyance not an existential threat. High representative Federica Mogherini had her immediate team dilute East StratCom statements on Russia propaganda so as to lessen friction with Moscow. The view was that copying Russia in this sphere was not a way to exert effective power. The EU also declined to devise policies specifically to tackle Russia's counter-democracy policies in the EaP.[8]

Limits to Russia's Zero-sum Exclusion

While many EU leaders alluded to the end of partnership with Russia, the basic ethos of searching for positive cooperation in the relationship did not entirely disappear. Many European diplomats insisted there were still positive-sum possibilities in the link between the EaP and EU-Russia policy. Many privately accepted the thesis that the EU had been too dismissive of Russian ideas and projects, and that this was, in part, the cause of the Ukraine conflagration. One External Action Service director suggested: 'We should have talked more to Russia. We underestimated how seriously Putin would push the Eurasian Union for geopolitical gain.' Many policy-makers felt that Russia's actions grew out of the absence of an adequate post-Soviet Eurasian security architecture.

Russia was the only country to which the EU had offered two annual summits. One senior diplomat summarised the general view: we have had more dialogue with Russia than with any other big power, and yet most governments insist we need more, not less engagement. When the crisis broke it was the EU that was pushing for a new partnership and cooperation agreement and Russia that was indifferent to this offer. Officials pointed out that the EU had been proposing a common economic space with Russia and (what were now) Eurasian Union states since 1994. European officials suggested that the EU should have taken then-president Dimitri Medvedev's 2009 ideas for a

[8] N. Bouchet, *How to Counter Russia's Anti-Democratic Strategy*, Washington DC: German Marshall Fund, 2015.

security pact more seriously. Even if these were a thin basis for discussion, they were the last chance before Putin's return to the presidency when a reasonably constructive atmosphere existed for dialogue.

The EU still largely rejected the notion that the new geopolitical game was one of 'clashing billiard-balls' separate from states' internal politics. Commentators observed that most member states declined to accept that Russia was now an entirely adversarial strategic rival, committed to undermining EU influence in the EaP states.[9] One advisor to the Commission summed up the general reading: 'we have isolated Russia too much, now it is time to bring it back in from the cold'. It was common to hear European diplomats argue that the danger to security lay not so much in the Ukraine conflict but in the prospect of a new dividing line slicing through Europe. This was to be avoided at all costs. Some diplomats sympathised with Russia's claim that it was a necessary mediator of the region's intra-state conflicts. Downplaying the utility of hard-power confrontation, European Commission president Jean-Claude Juncker quipped that 'the EU cannot let its relations with Russia be dictated by the US'.[10]

One member state diplomat argued: 'We need to be geopolitical not in Russia's sense but in the sense of knowing what we want and how we get it.' Another concurred: 'We will lose if we play Putin's game.' Another diplomat framed the policy preference thus: 'We will not engage in direct confrontation with Russia, but can only hope through attrition to limit the extent of Putin's offensive across the region.' One senior diplomat in the region said the concern was to prevent the EU 'sleep-walking' its way into an 'us and them' rivalry with Russia. Many diplomats insisted that their concern was not so much with Russia being a direct threat in the east but it being emboldened to act as a spoke in the wheels of global order, and preventing the emergence of effective global governance to address long-term strategic challenges. One senior member of the German government opined: 'there can be no European order without Russia'.

Some charged eastern member states with pulling the whole EU towards drawing new battle lines in the east that it was never going

[9] I. Bond, *The EU and Russia: Uncommon Spaces*, London: Centre for European Reform, 2014.

[10] W. Jakobik, 'A return to business as usual', *New Eastern Europe*, 29 October 2015.

to be able to defend in a classically geopolitically fashion. For their part, Eastern European and Baltic diplomats felt that the EU failed to develop a firm geo-strategy or upgrade the EaP sufficiently to meet the magnitude of the crisis. One Polish official stressed the fundamental mismatch between Russia's strategy based on antagonism and an EU policy trying to avoid antagonising Moscow too much, beyond the sanctions.

The general EU line was that geopolitical riposte was essentially a question of making EaP states more resilient to fend off Russian pressure. Some member state diplomats still felt that Eastern European governments overplayed the Russian threat in order to strike a better deal for their own security protection. Many in the EU still believed that the long-term solution was positive cooperation to modernise the Russian economy.

While Germany became more critical towards Russia and agreed to stronger NATO defences in Eastern Europe, German ministers expressed the view that the EaP had been at fault for not taking Russian considerations sufficiently into account.[11] German diplomats insisted that while sanctions were in order, the EU would need to work with Russia to achieve its aims in Ukraine. Indeed, German media commentary routinely presented foreign minister Frank-Walter Steinmeier running a parallel foreign policy to that of the chancellor. There were differences within the Social Democratic Party with some younger politicians seeing it as still too drawn to the Ostpolitik philosophy of the Willy Brandt era. One German diplomat admitted that Germans still felt more empathy for Russia than for Ukrainians' plight. Another German diplomat summarised: 'We seek to contain the conflict, not contain Russia.' In the summer of 2015, Germany began pushing strongly for the NATO-Russia Council to be revived, to provide a forum for strategic dialogue and potential cooperation.[12]

Diplomats from southern member states, Germany and France suggested the EU needed to rein back the hawkish statements of the NATO secretary general, the Baltic states and Poland. The Spanish foreign minister insisted that the EU needed to 'fit [its policy] around

[11] R. Formuszewicz, *Germany's Policy towards Russia: Old Wine in New Wineskins*, Warsaw: Polish Institute for International Affairs, 2014, p. 4.

[12] *New Europe*, 3 August 2015.

the Eurasian Union'. Spain's September 2014 Foreign Policy Strategy defined Russia as a 'strategic partner'. Spanish diplomats highlighted that any solution must have Russia's 'acquiescence'. Portugal's outgoing secretary of state for Europe advocated a 'Eurasia geo-strategy' that returned to President Putin's original 'Lisbon to Valdivostock' proposal.[13] One EU diplomat revealed that most in the EU still believed, in practice, 'that Putin has some kind of right to rebuild Russia's influence in the post-Soviet space'.[14]

One French insider noted that France thought not in terms of EaP norms but great power deals and trade-offs. The Belgian foreign minister said: 'Russia must remain a partner.'[15] Even diplomats from relatively 'tough' or principled states like The Netherlands spoke of the need to keep offers of cooperation open with Russia. Slovakia, the Czech Republic and Hungary shifted towards more pro-Russian positions. In April 2016, in discussions about another imminent NATO summit, the Czech defence minister insisted that it was now more important than ever 'not to isolate Russia'.[16] One southern European diplomat admitted that the crisis in Ukraine was not especially 'uncomfortable for us' and did not merit a radical change in positions towards Russia. Early 2015 saw Hungary, Cyprus and Greece's new Syriza government all seal new political partnerships with Russia. By mid-2015, the leaders of France, Germany, Hungary, Italy and Slovakia had all held bilateral summits with Putin, discussing the general crisis but also areas of bilateral cooperation. Cyprus gave Russia's navy berthing rights, close to British bases on the island.

Both the far-right and far-left in Europe were apparently sympathetic to Putin's project: conservatives because of its focus on traditional values, the far-left because of its challenge to Western power interests. Many believed that Moscow simply wanted to be recognised as an equal power to the EU rather than the EU treating it as the equivalent of an aspirant state – with a partnership based on the expectation that Russia would align itself to EU rules. The EU had indeed offered Russia much dialogue; yet the Russian feeling was that they had been

[13] B. Maçães, 'We are all Eurasian now', *Financial Times*, 25 November 2015.
[14] Quoted in A. Rettman, 'Four fallacies of EU foreign policy', *EU Observer*, 13 March 2015.
[15] Brussels Forum, 21 March 2014.
[16] GlobaSec Conference, Bratislava, 15 April 2016, Debate reproduced on GlobSec.tv.

passive consumers of such dialogue offered on European terms, rather than shapers of the terms on which dialogue took place.

Finnish Prime Minister Alexander Stubb summed up a commonly heard assessment: 'We perhaps did not work hard enough to understand what Russia was truly like. We wanted Russia to become a rule-taker, while it has always seen itself as a rule-setter ... We do not do tit-for-tat ... mutually beneficial, still functioning business relations and people-to-people contacts; at the end of the day they can be our best guarantee for peace.'[17] Romania pushed an upgraded Black Sea security forum as a means of engaging Russia on regional geo-strategic issues. Italian diplomats argued that the EU should involve Russia in the redefining of the ENP, to avoid future recriminations.

Several European governments encouraged the OSCE to launch discussions over a new security arrangement. The OSCE's low-level Corfu process – designed to study new security arrangements – morphed into a 'Helsinki plus 40' initiative. German diplomats in particular urged consideration of new security forums that gave Russia fuller inclusion. Federica Mogherini moved further in this direction at the end of 2015, when she insisted that the OSCE needed to be strengthened as a forum for dialogue with Russia and the pursuit of 'cooperation that will build and safeguard our collective security'.[18] The OSCE's eminent persons panel reported in November 2015 and recommended a 'return to diplomacy', cooperation towards a new treaty on European security and dialogue on what kind of 'neutrality' might be acceptable to all parties with stakes in the eastern region. Most EU member states, and especially Germany, enthusiastically welcomed the report.[19] If Russia was searching for a 'Yalta 2', EaP states believed the EU was not explicit enough in unequivocally ruling this out.

Many commentators advocated backing away from criticism of Putin's domestic record in order to leave room for a deal on Ukraine; the EU's effort to foster democracy in Russia dwindled to almost

[17] A. Stubb, 'European Policy towards Russia', speech delivered in Berlin, 29 September 2014. Available at: http://vnk.fi/ajankohtaista/puheet/puhe/en.jsp?oid=426086.

[18] Statement by High Representative/Vice-President Federica Mogherini at the OSCE Ministerial Council in Belgrade, 3 December 2015.

[19] Organization for Security and Cooperation in Europe (OSCE), *Back to Diplomacy: Final Report and Recommendations of the Panel of Eminent Persons on European Security as a Common Project*, 2015.

nothing. The EU did not increase its support to opposition figures within Russia. EU support to civil society in Russia decreased dramatically, to only around €4 million a year. There was no favourable re-consideration of introducing a so-called 'Magnitsky list' of Russian regime figures against whom sanctions could be imposed; the US had availed itself of such legislation and the European Parliament had called for a European equivalent since 2009. There was no move to re-activate the dormant EU-Russian human rights dialogue; Russia insisted on such restrictive conditions that this had never gained momentum.

Views from the region generally saw the EU as too emollient towards Russia. One Georgian politician perceived that the EU had gone back to indulging Russia's claim that it had a 'back-yard' there. The Georgian foreign minister lamented there was still no robust EU pushback against Russian threats to national sovereignty in the region. The Ukrainian deputy foreign minister criticised the EU for being overly cautious and reactive: behind the curve in responding to Russian tactics.

Global geopolitical considerations to some extent counteracted regional calculations. For most states, Russian cooperation on Syria and Iran was a more crucial geopolitical imperative than Crimea. By 2016, international attention was focused on Syria more than Ukraine. The Syrian – and not the Donbas – conflict was the theatre where it seemed that the relationship between Russia and the West would be most decisively determined. By the end of 2016, sharper European criticism of Russian bombing raids in Syria co-existed uneasily with a shared concern with Moscow to weaken Islamic State. Ukraine and the EaP suddenly seemed like a by-product of Middle Eastern challenges and the kind of EU-Russian relationship that these might produce.

Several member states supported enhanced cooperation with Russia in Syria as the EU grappled for a response to the refugee surge in 2015 and 2016. Germany and Italy were prominent among those calling for a new counter-terrorism alliance with Russia. Italian Premier Matteo Renzi went to Moscow coveting Putin's help in stabilising Syria and Libya, and in taking on radical Islamist groups. While the UK and France were more sceptical, arguing that Putin's support for President Bashar Assad remained an obstacle to cooperation, they, too, suggested that Russian help in pushing back Islamic State was necessary.

Jean-Claude Juncker visited President Putin in June 2016 in an effort to revive EU–Russia strategic dialogue on these questions. The Finnish government welcomed President Putin in June 2016 to talk about possible security cooperation. In the same month, the Global Strategy called for cooperation with Russia on a range of international issues.[20]

More broadly, by the end of 2016, the French presidential campaign was shaping up to be between two candidates, François Fillon and Marine Le Pen, advocating warmer rapprochement with Russia, while President-elect Donald Trump's promise to move US policy in a similar direction during his upcoming presidency also began reshaping European debates.

Limits to Sanctions

While sanctions were significant, they were implemented incrementally and fell far short of entailing a complete rupture in economic relations. Oil and gas exports, accounting for around 70 per cent of Russian export earnings, continued almost untouched. Sanctions experts argued that the EU did not invest in the additional capacities needed to make sure that upgraded sanctions were implemented in a watertight way.[21] While Russian trade with the EU dropped by over a third during 2015, it dropped by a similar amount with both Eurasian Union countries and China. The general state of the economy was a weightier factor than the sanctions.

German business was a brake on sanctions, at several crucial junctures. This mattered because German trade with Russia was hugely in excess of the trade of any other member state. While many in the EU were seeking to tighten sanctions in 2014, the head of Siemens had a meeting with President Putin from which he emerged to declare that business would continue as normal. One gathering of European business leaders in Berlin berated the German government even for the limited sanctions imposed so far and pressed for limits to future additional measures.[22] While many German companies backed Chancellor Merkel on the need for some form of sanctions, they expressed growing

[20] European Union High Representative for Foreign and Security Policy, *Shared Vision, Common Action: A Stronger Europe: A Global Strategy for the European Union's Foreign and Security Policy*, June 2016, p. 21.

[21] A. de Vries, C. Portela and B. Guijarro-Usobiaga *Improving the Effectiveness of Sanctions: A Checklist for the EU*, Brussels: Centre for European Policy Studies, 2014.

[22] *EU Observer*, 11 April 2014.

unease as the conflict dragged on into 2015 and 2016, arguing that improvements on the ground in Donbas were sufficient for a gradual unwinding of punitive measures.

Polish and Baltic state diplomats complained frequently that sanctions were weak. As one diplomat lamented, early in the crisis: 'We are talking about a fundamentally changed order, and our reaction is to say that a few officials cannot come shopping in Europe!' Most of those on the EU sanctions list had, critics insisted, already moved most of their assets out of Europe, as these measures had been flagged up and debated in public for so many weeks prior to being adopted. The EU's widening of visa bans was constantly behind the US in excluding inner circle regime members from the list. The continuation of sanctions was increasingly uncertain: Italy, France and several other states pressed for a relaxation of sanctions through the early months of 2016, even as separatist violence spread in Donbas and Russian attacks intensified against moderate opposition strongholds in Syria.

During the Eurozone economic crisis, many member states had introduced new schemes to entice Russian investment into their recession-battered economies. They did not revoke these incentives after 2013. An increasing number of French firms (including Total, Danone, Renault and Safran) joined the Franco-Russian Observatory that lobbied against sanctions. Nearly all political parties, from the Socialist Party cadres through to the National Front, were critical of François Hollande for being too ready to support sanctions; one common argument in French debate was that being tough on Russia was too pro-American.[23] These domestic views meant that France constantly diluted the extent of proposed EU sanctions.

There were many possible punitive measures that were not included in the EU's understanding of a geopolitical response. Diplomats in some member states raised the possibility of ejecting Russia from the Council of Europe and the OSCE; there was negligible support for looking at such options at all seriously. Proposals to ban Russia from the Swift system of banking payments were on the table, but not taken forward. Moreover, according to insiders, the EU invested little effort in building support for sanctions from rising democratic

[23] N. Dufour, 'France's D-Day Diplomacy: Time for Paris to End its Hedging on Russia', *PISM Bulletin No. 84*, Warsaw: Polish Institute for International Affairs, 2014.

powers; the crisis became a tug-of-war between Russia and the West, when arguably it should have entailed a mobilisation of the global community against one state's contravention of a core principle of international order.

Limits to the European Partnership Upgrade

While the EU moved up a gear in its commitment to the EaP, after an initial flurry of ambitious rhetoric and new policy documents it did not implement radical change to the partnership. Many member states believed that the scope and ambition of the EaP should be reined back so as not to provoke Russia.

Most notably, the offer of EU membership was still not placed on the table as part of EaP commitments. One southern member state diplomat clarified: 'Accession is now off the table *because* of the crisis.' In private, diplomats complained that their governments still underestimated how vital the membership perspective was to EaP states. In the words of one Moldovan minister: 'Giving us a European future is the only thing that can keep Russia away.' Ukrainian leaders constantly pleaded that accession could make the decisive difference in their efforts to unite the country and rebuff Russian incursions. EU commissioner Stefan Füle pressed for membership perspectives to be offered, but he made little headway against member state opposition.[24]

The EaP declaration agreed at the Riga summit in May 2015 included only a non-specific and somewhat awkward reference to 'the European aspirations and the European choice of the partners'. This language represented no advance on the Vilnius declaration 18 months previously; many member states wanted to be even less forthcoming. Germany was influential in diluting the summit's deliverables. A senior EU official involved in Riga sent a blunt message to EaP states: 'forget accession, current cooperation is enough to be getting on with'. Civil society organisations in Riga submitted a symbolic membership application for Ukraine, Moldova and Georgia to Commissioner Hahn – registering their displeasure with the EU's denial of accession perspectives. Latvian diplomats involved in the summit revealed that

[24] S. Füle, 'New Europe and enlargement in a new political context', reprinted by European Commission, SPEECH/14/323, 11 April 2014.

many member states had wanted to use the meeting to close the accession door for good.

Governments habitually claimed their domestic populations were resolutely hostile to further enlargement. Some surveys showed that a clear majority of EU citizens in fact supported offering Ukraine membership.[25] Yet by late 2016 popular opposition to further enlargement was spiking to unprecedented levels. In Austria, Belgium, Finland, France, Germany and Luxembourg over 60 per cent of people said they were hostile to allowing in new members. Put off by this hostility, citizens in Georgia, Moldova and Ukraine were by this stage also losing their enthusiasm for cooperating with the EU.[26]

Even short of membership, the EU's offers were not generous enough to satisfy EaP states. While the EU offered visa accords, these offers were offset by tougher border management conditions. The border agency, Frontex reported in 2015 that migration flows into the EU were falling from the east while increasing from the south. The visa-free regime offered to Moldova was not that generous as many Moldovan citizens already had Romanian passports. Visa-free travel and access to EU labour markets remained anathema to a number of member states. In June 2016, in the midst of the EU refugee crisis, the EU quietly pushed back decisions on visa liberalisation for Georgia and Ukraine. France and Germany insisted on a 'snapback' mechanism that would enable liberalisation provisions to be revoked at short notice in order to contain surges of people into EU states. Ukrainian politicians, officials and civil society representatives angrily accused the EU of delaying visa-free travel in deference to Russia. EU officials retorted that Ukraine had not implemented promised anti-corruption preconditions. While the EU did finally agree to grant the visa accords to Georgia and Ukraine in November 2016, even then the EU still had to finalise details of the emergency brake and the long delay had soured the atmosphere.

The EU did not offer a customs union to EaP states as it had to Turkey – an option that would have given strategic protection and

[25] German Marshall Fund, *Transatlantic Trends 2014*, Washington DC: German Marshall Fund, 2014.

[26] L. Litra and I. Chkhikvadze, *EU Membership Perspective for Georgia, Moldova and Ukraine: Impossible, Forgotten or Hidden*? Kiev: Institute for World Policy, 2016, p. 6.

market access, without heavy regulatory imposition. Nor did member states follow though on opening the European Economic Area to EaP states. The EU offered asymmetrical access for some agricultural products but not complete trade liberalisation for this sector, still the most crucial area of activity for several EaP states. Deep and Comprehensive Free Trade Areas (DCFTAs) imposed over 1,000 pages of requirements, with the benefits accruing only in the long term. Arguably, more than tariff reductions, EaP states required huge amounts of investment to help modernise their economies; yet this investment was not forthcoming. Moreover, in April 2016, Dutch citizens voted against the Ukraine AA in a referendum, throwing the agreement into question once again. In December 2016 the EU offered the Dutch government clauses to specify that the AA did not give Ukraine the 'status of a candidate country' or involve 'security guarantees or military assistance' or give Ukrainians the right to live and work in the EU. These provisions still had to be approved by the Dutch parliament before ratification of the AA could be ensured.

The levels of EU funding available to EaP states increased only at the margins and not significantly. In mid-2013, before the outbreak of the crisis, the EU allocated €5 billion to EaP states for the 2014–2020 budget period – a freeze relative to the previous five-year budget cycle. The EU did not increase this core amount of funding after the crisis began; it only introduced a select number of new sector-specific initiatives. Southern member states pushed to ensure that the Ukraine crisis did not divert resources and attention away from the southern Mediterranean, and that the latter still received two-thirds of the €15 billion total ENP budget.

One EU director complained that member states continued to block any significant increases in resources as well as the creation of trust funds to provide long-term support in crisis situations like that of Ukraine. For all the rhetoric of the crisis constituting a watershed moment for the liberal order, member states did not invest significant resources in the region. No EaP state appeared in the top twenty recipients of German aid.[27] Poland also allocated very limited amounts of its own money. The amounts offered to Ukraine and other EaP states looked even more limited alongside Greece's €172 billion bail-out.

The upgrade in European democracy support across the EaP region was less than far-reaching. NGO forums in the various EaP partners

[27] See the online OECD development aid database. Available at: www2.compareyourcountry.org/aid-statistics?cr=5&lg=en&page=20.

made a familiar litany of criticisms: the crisis had not made the EU more attentive to local needs or more agile in its procedures. While member states rhetorically insisted that supporting democracy was one of their most powerful geopolitical tools, in practice their efforts to encourage political change did not dramatically intensify – a fact that will be demonstrated in detail with respect to each EaP state in the following chapters. Civil society activists complained that the EU's engagement with them did not appreciably improve. One ambassador admitted that the EU had 'no good response' to the intensified repression meted out against civil society organisations. One Georgian writer criticised the EU for treating values and geopolitics as a mutually exclusive trade-off, rather than more energetically prioritising efforts to embed democracy in the EaP as a profoundly geopolitical response.[28]

Several of the low-politics regional EaP initiatives, involving civil society, parliamentarians and businesses continued to be stymied by political differences.[29] Georgia's former ambassador to the EU saw it becoming less committed to these dimensions of the EaP.[30] One Polish commentator judged that the supposed EaP upgrade failed to the extent that minorities across the region were increasingly doubtful that the EU could offer them more than Russia.[31] Under tough questioning from a sceptical EaP Civil Society Forum, Commissioner Hahn insisted there was no contradiction between the 2015 ENP review's focus on stabilisation and the EU's ostensible commitment to democratic reform. Most civil society representatives were left unconvinced. They pointed out that the EU was committing itself to supporting 'security partners' in states where such actors were ecklessly dedicated to protecting the regime not protecting the security of society.

Some officials admitted that debates about the EaP as a pan-regional initiative were crowded out by the focus on Ukraine's emergency. Indeed, a new division opened up between the three states that signed

[28] G. Nodia, 'The revenge of geopolitics', *Journal of Democracy*, 25/4, 2014, 139–50.

[29] J. Boonstra and L. Delcour, *A Broken Region: Evaluating EU Polices in the South Caucasus*, Madrid: Fride, 2015, p. 4.

[30] S. Samadashvili, *Building a Lifeline for Freedom: Eastern Partnership 2.0*, Brussels: Wilfired Martens Centre for European Studies, 2014.

[31] P. Pieniazek 'Last chance for European values', *New Eastern Europe*, 22 March 2014.

DCFTAs – Georgia, Moldova and Ukraine – and the three that did not – Armenia, Azerbaijan and Belarus. This weakened the EaP's strategic unity vis-à-vis Russia. Moreover, in terms of ministerial effort and resources, eastern EU member states complained that too much attention was switching back to the Middle East, as the Islamic State threat intensified in 2015 and 2016. The EaP received less attention as conflict raged in Iraq, Syria, and Libya.

Trade as a Bridge

The EU intensified efforts to retain positive-sum economic linkages between the EaP and Russia. It offered a new series of technical dialogues with Russian officials to search for cooperative ways forward in trade relations. Officials said their aim was to help EaP states have free trade with both Russia and the European Union. Russia complained that under the DCFTAs, European goods would flood through EaP states into Russia tariff free. The EU insisted that World Trade Organization (WTO) rules of origin would prevent this from happening. EaP producers would not be obliged to adopt EU standards if they wished to focus sales on the Russian market.[32] The EU offered to draw up provisions more formally to ensure that Russian exports into Ukraine and other markets would not be penalised. To avoid friction, the EU declined to press for proceedings against Russia at the WTO in relation to the measures it imposed against EaP exports. Trade officials suggested that moves towards a common economic space between Russia and the EU would reduce regulatory tensions.[33] EU officials stepped up training of Eurasian Union officials.

In one of the most notable moves of the crisis, in September 2014 the EU agreed with Russia and Ukraine that the latter would delay implementation of its association agreement until the end of 2015. President Petro Poroshenko faced fierce criticism from within parliament and from civil society for agreeing to the delay. After so many people had given their lives to defend Ukraine's European future, to many this looked like a capitulation to Russia. The EU was effectively

[32] M. Emerson, *Russia's Economic Interests and the EU's DCFTA with Ukraine*, Brussels: Centre for European Policy Studies, 2014.

[33] I. Dreyer, 'EU Ukraine DCFTA versus Russia-sponsored Eurasian economic union: Flexibility on implementation in sight', *Borderlex*, 28 August 2014.

acknowledging that high politics complicated its low-politics policies. This link was enshrined in the Mink peace accord, which gave Russia a say over trade relations between eastern Ukraine and Russia.

EU officials insisted they were willing to compromise on standards and tariff questions under the Ukraine agreement. One idea was to oblige Russian producers to meet EU standards only over the very long term.[34] Trade commissioner Karl De Gucht suggested that the delay was in effect a 'peace clause', a 'time-out' for peace. The German government stated that while it would not contemplate fundamental change to the AA text, there could be 'technical adjustments' to avoid deleterious effects on Russian trade with Ukraine.[35] During 2015 and 2016, Germany frequently pressed the Commission to consider more generous concessions to meet Russian concerns on the DCFTAs.

The EU gave consideration to cooperation with the Eurasian Union. EU officials talked of the principle of mutual recognition helping positive-sum linkages. Mutual recognition would allow trade on the basis of parties recognising each other's regulations. This was suggested as a way of taking zero-sum politics out of the EU–Eurasian Union relationship. The EU institutions and member states showed a general willingness to explore such options, even though differences remained. Angela Merkel pressed new trade talks between the EU and Eurasian Union in November 2014. Russia's view was that EU–Eurasian Union cooperation could help solve the Ukraine crisis; the EU saw such cooperation as possible after Ukraine stabilised and as an incentive to moderate Russian actions. Member states were split on whether the EU should establish formal relations with the Eurasian Union when this formally came into existence on 1 January 2015.

A group of member states pushed for positive engagement against the technical advice of the European Commission. DG Trade Officials complained they were being pushed by French and German diplomats in particular to drop key EU rules in order to smooth political relations with Moscow. While some national capitals saw geopolitical value in resurrecting the 'Lisbon to Vladivostok' ideal, EU officials tended to point out that the Eurasian Union concept of economic integration simply would not allow for an EU–Eurasian Union free trade area. At member states' insistence, a series of 'trade trilaterals' began bringing together

[34] *Reuters.com*, 23 September 2014.
[35] *The Financial Times*, 29 September 2014.

EU, Ukrainian and Russian trade experts. EU trade officials insisted that Russia showed little willingness to engage on issues of technical convergence. They cautioned that the Eurasian Union was not yet fully compatible with WTO rules; that Belarus and Kazakhstan were not members of the WTO, a basic EU requirement for trade talks; and that cooperation with the Eurasian Union would in effect mean unfreezing trade talks with Russia and contravening the EU's sanctions.[36] More critical member states disliked the notion that relations with parts of the EaP zone would now be managed on a bloc-to-bloc basis, with Moscow effectively representing other sovereign states.[37] Yet, most governments sought ways to explore just such cooperation, even if it meant bending EU norms. In late 2016, German officials were reportedly re-examining the possibility of beginning talks about an EU–Eurasian Union free trade area.[38] Reactions from the EaP partners were varied. Many interlocutors in the region welcomed the EU's greater effort to avoid imposing zero-sum trade agreements. For many this was a belated recognition of a reality: Russia was still enormously important in economic terms to the region and could not be excised from trade arrangements. As one Armenian insider put it: 'the EU needs to avoid over-selling its AA provisions in a way that raises Russia's hackles'. Yet, as we will see in subsequent chapters, many others in the region complained that the EU erred too far in the positive-sum direction. They insisted it was naive to think that the EU could turn the EaP into a shared economic space with Russia. EU officials admitted that twenty rounds of trade dialogue produced nothing concrete and that Russia had not used the talks as a way of backing away from confrontation. As a consequence, these consultations were wound down in 2016.

Limits to New Energy Policies

While the EU promised diversification in its energy supplies, there was no major shift away from Russian oil and gas. Many policy-makers

[36] I. Dreyer, 'EU not yet ready to talk to Eurasian Economic Union as WTO cases mount', *Bordelex*, 7 December 2014.

[37] L. Delcour, H. Kostanyan, B. Vandecasteele and P. Van Elsuwege, 'The implications of Eurasian integration for the EU's relations with the countries in the post-Soviet space', *Studia Diplomatica*, LXVIII-1, 2015, 5–33, p. 14.

[38] Bertelsmann Stiftung, *Free Trade from Lisbon to Vladivostok A Tool for Peace and Prosperity: The Effects of a Free Trade Area between the EU and the Eurasian Region*, Gütersloh, 2016, p. 6.

admitted that the cost of diversifying significantly would be prohibitively high for many European countries. The realistic aim was not for the EU as a whole to switch away from Russian supplies, but to reduce the 100 per cent dependence of several Central European states. Russia seemed more concerned with sustained low gas prices due to structural conditions in international markets than the Energy Union's talk of diversification.

When the then Polish Prime Minister Donald Tusk pushed for an Energy Union, European Energy Commissioner Günther Oettinger said that diversification could not be the leading edge of the EU's response to the eastern crisis. EU sanctions on Russia did not target core operations in the energy sector, with the exception of some technological services. Many new energy deals were signed in 2015 and 2016. BP, Shell, Eni, Statoil and other European oil majors extended cooperation in Russia and with Gazprom. E.ON, BASF/Wintershall, OMV, the French company ENGIE and Royal Dutch Shell formed a new consortium to develop the Nord Stream 2 pipeline, which would double the capacity of Russian gas coming directly into Germany, bypassing Ukraine.

By 2016, this putative Nord Stream 2 initiative looked set to have major implications for EU eastern geopolitics. The new pipeline was slated to increase Russia's share of German gas imports from 40 to 60 per cent – the very opposite of the geopolitical aims set out in the Energy Union strategy. Italy and other states protested furiously that they could not be expected to bend to Angela Merkel's pressure for sanctions on Russia to be rolled over when Germany was embarking on a pipeline extension that would hand President Putin a major victory over Ukraine. The EU published a gas strategy in February 2016 that was silent on the vexed question of Nord Stream 2.[39] In August 2016, five European companies withdrew from the project. However, the Commission then cleared the project at the end of October, reaching a judgement that it was compatible with EU competition law. Debate sharpened between member states over whether or not the project should proceed.

Hungary announced an agreement with Russia to modernise the country's nuclear energy infrastructure. Euratom refused to approve

[39] S. De Jong, 'Why Europe should fight Nord Stream II', *EU Observer*, 23 February 2016.

Hungary's plans to import fuel exclusively from Russia. Prime Minister Viktor Orban modified the deal to open supplies up to competition after 20 years, but went ahead with enhanced cooperation with Russia. Lithuania used its LNG terminal to negotiate a better deal with Gazprom, not to cancel its cooperation with the latter. Indeed, a mooted Baltic energy cooperation scheme did not advance, despite the apparent security imperative behind it.

Several European governments and companies insisted that new deals with Gazprom should not be derailed by the Commission's strict interpretation of the third energy package – that required power generation and distribution to be separated. These differences emerged in particular during the fraught case of South Stream, in which the Italian, Austrian and Greek governments sided with Russia rather than with the Commission. Many member states worried more about inefficiencies in Russia's energy sector reducing the amount of gas available than about Russia's assertive use of the 'energy weapon'. Most member states were still unwilling to share information about their bilateral contracts with Russia, let alone give these contracts up for a common EU negotiation with Moscow. One member state's energy ambassador noted that several member states were still focused on obtaining cheaper, below-market prices from political deals with Russia and so didn't see the incentive to sign up to the ostensible market logic of the Energy Union. The Commission and Gazprom worked their way towards a negotiated settlement of the ongoing legal case outlined in the previous chapter.

The EU played its most productive role mediating dialogue between Ukraine and Russia. The EU used its power to avert an energy security crisis by setting itself up as an even-handed mediator between Ukraine and Russia, as Russia demanded that Ukraine pay its debts and accept a significantly higher gas price. The Commission encouraged Ukraine to reach successive deals with Moscow to prevent any disruption to supplies. Reverse flows into Ukraine were still made up mainly of Russian gas, simply transited through EU member states.

It was even suspected that the EU was cautious over sanctions against Russia because Crimea was thought to contain most of Ukraine's potential shale gas. A major new Russian gas deal with China engendered caution too, however unfavourable the terms of the agreement were to Moscow. And US uncertainty about allowing the export of shale gas and the apparent collapse of EU–US trade talks in late 2016 – after many had hoped that the prospective Transatlantic Trade and Investment Partnership would include an energy cooperation chapter – narrowed the EU's short-term alternatives to Russian gas. Combining all these factors together, most member states acted on the basis that, for all the talk of diversification, energy imperatives reflected the reality of a 'Russia first' policy that continued in the aftermath of the Ukraine crisis.

Conclusion

If the previous chapter outlined the bolder elements of EU responses to the eastern crisis, this chapter has shown their more cautious side. This points us towards an overall conceptual picture of the European response to the eastern crisis:

Categorisation

The chapter has unpacked European governments' reluctance to pursue a fully exclusionary or confrontational strategic logic against Russia. Most European governments were concerned not to over-securitise responses in the military sphere or to accord NATO a clear lead role. The chapter shows the limits to new EU engagement in the Eastern European region and the implicit ceiling that some member states placed on the EaP's level of ambition. The EU was doggedly determined to keep searching for forms of triangular coordination between member states, EaP partners and Russia. The EU clung to many elements of positive sum thinking – even when many doubted cooperative security could now put down any roots at all.

The EU tried to cooperate with Russia over the EaP and especially on trade relations. A common critique was that the EU erred in framing its offers to EaP states in a way that was incompatible with the Eurasian Economic Union.[40] European officials insisted this was an unfair and factually erroneous criticism: the EU's offers were

[40] For example, a line adopted by most chapters in C. Nitoiu (ed.) *Avoiding a New 'Cold War': The Future of EU-Russia Relations in the Context of the Ukraine Crisis*, London: LSE Ideas Report, 2016.

fashioned before Russia pushed forward the EEU explicitly to neuter EU cooperation; it was the way that the EEU was structured that ensured incompatibility between the two regional projects, not the EU's association agreements. The EU then offered dialogue on finding pathways towards compatibility, insisting that Russia refused to engage in these talks with any genuine intent

Germany led other member states towards a balance: continued strategic engagement with Russia, while ostensibly refusing to accept the notion that the latter had an exclusive and privileged sphere of influence.[41] The EU's position was to resurrect dialogue without accepting the notion that Russia had an intrinsic entitlement to infringe sovereignty and dismember former Soviet states.[42] Experts pointed out that in some ways it was ironic that Russia's most egregious move in annexing Crimea became less of a barrier to European strategic dialogue with Moscow than the murky and on-going operations in Donbas.[43]

Taking this and the previous chapter together we get a composite picture of the balance between change and continuity; between inclusionary and exclusionary logics; between the offensive and defensive approach to geopolitics; and between commitment and hesitancy in pressing for reforms in EaP states. It is through these permutations that the EU moulded its responses around the category of liberal-redux geopolitics.

The chapter shows that it would be empirically questionable to accuse European governments of being over-assertive. John Mearsheimer, Henry Kissinger, Zignew Zbresinski and other master strategic luminaries all called for Ukrainian neutrality and for the EU to pull back from direct encroachment into what should be treated as a buffer zone between the West and Russia. But they surely failed to

[41] C. Major and J. Puglierin, 'Europe's new (in)security order', *IPG Journal*, 25 November 2014. Available at: www.ipg-journal.de.

[42] R. Allison, 'Security Policy, Geopolitics and International Order in EU-Russian Relations during the Ukraine Crisis'. In C. Nitoiu (ed.) *Avoiding a New 'Cold War': The Future of EU-Russia Relations in the Context of the Ukraine Crisis*, London: LSE Ideas Report, 2016, p. 31.

[43] T. Caiser, 'Why the EU-Russia Strategic Partnership could not Prevent a Confrontation over Ukraine: EU just as Zero-Sum now as Russia'. In C. Nitoiu (ed.) *Avoiding a New 'Cold War': The Future of EU-Russia Relations in the Context of the Ukraine Crisis*, London: LSE Ideas Report, 2016, p. 24.

understand European governments' nuanced response to the crisis or the fact that what was on offer through the EaP was not remotely like the kind of NATO-centred geopolitical competition so redolent of Cold War days. Of course, it might be argued that if EU offers had been framed in a less-exclusivist fashion before 2013, tensions with Russia might well have been less sharp; the EU could undoubtedly have done more, earlier, to flag the positive-sum dimensions of its policies. But it was Russia that framed its actions and the EEU as directly confrontational. The crisis was marked by the growing *asymmetry* between EU positive-sum efforts and Russia zero-sum geopolitics.

Foreign Policy Dynamics

The previous chapter shed light on how the elements of change in European policies entailed different kinds of EU foreign-policy dynamics. Member states took over more initiative from EU institutions in an effort to shape higher-level and wider-ranging responses to the eastern crisis. In its turn, this chapter shows that member states engaged sometimes to rein back certain elements of EU policy, not always to spur EU initiatives to new levels of intensity. This reinforced an incipient dynamic of strategic adjustment to external factors, giving this logic greater weight relative to internally embedded EU processes and identities. In several important ways, the EU began approaching the eastern neighbourhood more explicitly as a zone of consultation and compromise, an area where policy was reformulated in a way that was more heavily conditioned by Russia than prior to the Ukraine crisis. This was not an entirely new feature of EU policy – it was evident at crucial moments before 2013 – but it was now pursued more openly and with apparently more ordered strategic intent.

At the same time, this chapter demonstrates that the crisis did not entirely sweep away the EU's embedded foreign policy identities or long-standing institutional processes. Many in Brussels and member states continued to have faith in traditional EU low-politics cooperation. If the reliance on low-politics and positive-sum areas of cooperation persisted, this demonstrated the enduring force of pre-crisis institutional patterns. Many member states did not, in practice, seem to attach such overwhelming importance to the eastern crisis so as to drive exceptional, overtly securitised responses outside the scope of existing EU foreign-policy patterns. While they sought to upgrade security protection through NATO, European governments did not choose the NATO track as the primary institutional route through which to respond to the crisis. Rules-based EU-level activity continued to represent a significant part of overall European foreign policy efforts – indeed, in a way that did not sit entirely comfortably with the separate NATO track. Institutionally set rules often acted as a counterpoint to geopolitical expediency, even as member states sometimes sought to circumvent such rules for gains in immediate strategic crisis-control. In sum, the chapter reveals a subtle mix of institutional refinement and constancy – a mix that fed into the geopolitical balances that defined European liberal-redux geopolitics.

Impact

Many European diplomats celebrated the success of these carefully moderated responses in containing a crisis that could easily have descended into a far more tragic, explosive and structural threat. If some of the most alarmist predictions of systemic meltdown outlined in Chapter 3 did not come to fruition, it is reasonable to suggest that European responses were one of many geopolitical factors that helped dampen the eastern region's flammable volatility. However, European geo-strategic caution bred discontent and a feeling of vulnerability in EaP states. Surveys showed that EaP states' populations increasingly worried that the AAs would leave them exposed to Russian intimidation – with European governments unwilling to protect these states from the strategic consequences of a pro-European choice.[44] Sanctions against Russia were not without bite, but their ambition was incrementally diluted: their ostensible goal shifted from stopping Russian intrusions beyond Crimea to dissuading Russian meddling in Ukraine's national politics. Diplomats often insisted that sanctions were less about 'saving' eastern Ukraine than they were about limiting further Russian actions in other places across the EaP region. They were too

[44] A. Inayeh, D. Schwarzer and J. Forbrig (eds) *Regional Repercussions of the Ukraine Crisis: Challenges for the Six Eastern Partnership Countries*, Berlin: GMF Europe, 2014.

weak to entail really significant constraint on the Kremlin or to prize the moneyed elite away from Putin's inner circle.

In sum, European responses at best contributed to a fragile holding operation. By the end of 2016, the eastern crisis was calmer than many had predicted, but the geopolitical situation remained febrile enough that it could easily take a major turn for the worse. This fragility, and the distinctly uneven effects of European foreign policy responses, will become evident in the following chapters, as we now move to examine EU policies in each individual EaP state in turn.

7 *Ukraine I: Shepherding Revolution?*

Having examined the nature of over-arching European Union responses to the crisis, the next three chapters more specifically detail what support the EU offered to Ukraine: first, in the Maidan revolution; second, in trying to resolve violent conflict in eastern Ukraine; and third, in setting Ukraine on a longer-term path towards political and economic modernisation. This chapter chronicles EU involvement in the popular uprising that removed the Yanukovich government from power in early 2014. It notes that EU support for the uprising and revolution came about almost by accident. The EU may modestly have helped pave the way for Ukraine's 2013–2014 revolt, but it was in no way the prime agitator for the dramatic political rupture that occurred. European support was undoubtedly of some influence, but was also seen by Ukrainian democrats as insufficient and behind-the-curve of fast-moving events. In light of what transpired after President Yanukovich fled from office, the EU's search for consensual change was not without merit. Yet the EU was circumspect in its efforts to shore up the 2004 Orange revolution and then to avert the violence that preceded the opening of Ukraine's next window of democratic opportunity in the spring of 2014.

The Run-up to Revolution

In the 2004 Orange revolution, the EU supported pro-democracy civil society organisations, but was generally caught in reactive, catch-up mode. It did not push proactively for democratic breakthrough during the 1990s or early 2000s. Member states had reached an accommodation with the Leonid Kuchma regime that they saw as a bridge with Russia and as being capable of allaying possible instability in Ukraine. After the dramatic events of December 2004, when protestors succeeded in ensuring election results were scrutinised and respected, the EU offered the new, formally democratic Ukrainian government a package of long-term assistance for institution building. This was largely government-orientated aid, apparently on the grounds that the 'good democrats' now held power.

In the years after 2004 the EU did relatively little to ensure that Ukraine tackled its underlying problem of state capture, manifest in the enduring power of key oligarchs. Notwithstanding an ostensible transition to a democratic government, politicians and oligarchs colluded to curtail reform. This collusion gave powerful economic actors access to national wealth and allowed the squabbling leaders of the Orange coalition to consolidate their power. Oligarchs initially fought against the 2004 Orange revolution. Having lost that fight, they adapted successfully to retain control over the now nominally democratic state. After a fleeting moment of democratic opening, Ukraine drifted back into soft authoritarianism.[1]

Commission aid to Ukraine for 2007–2010 was double the amount disbursed in 2003–2006. Allocations from the European Neighbourhood Partnership Instrument for 2007–2013 were a significant €1 billion, with an additional €100 million going through various regional projects and the Neighbourhood Investment Facility. The EU allocated Ukraine €22 million from the Neighbourhood Policy Governance Facility as a reward for democratic reform. Member states offered a range of new military cooperation. Technical assistance increased, with the aim of strengthening accountability in public administration through twinning programmes. Ukraine's Association Agreement (AA) mandate was the first to have a dedicated civil society chapter.

From 2007, the EU made direct transfers to Ukraine's state budget, to be spent on reforms under jointly agreed conditions. Around 60 per cent of all EU bilateral aid in the years 2007–2013 was spent this way. The EU and Ukraine signed agreements on energy efficiency, trade facilitation, the environment, transport and border management for the overall sum of €389 million. However, in practice Ukraine received only one-third of this amount due to the deterioration in public procurement and budgetary transparency.[2]

1 S. Matuszak, *The Oligarchic Democracy: The Influence of Business Groups on Ukrainian Politics*, Warsaw: Centre for Eastern Studies, 2012.

2 E. Kaca, *A New Pact for Ukraine: Making EU Aid Work*, Warsaw: Polish Institute for International Affairs, 2014.

In 2009, the EU and Ukraine signed an association agenda to help prepare the country for the association agreement. This included forty pages of commitments to new committees, deeper support and twinning arrangements in a wide range of policy spheres. Detailed priorities included enhanced support for institution building; administrative, judicial and electoral reform; civil society; economic modernisation; the adoption of EU standards; and foreign and security policy alignment.[3] The EU's focus on rule of law initiatives strengthened. While this area of policy allowed for more input from Ukrainian actors over the definition of legal models, the increased EU attention failed to provide any tangible progress on deep reform.[4]

Ukrainians expressed bitter disappointment at being denied an EU membership prospect in the wake of the Orange revolution. Member states' aid flows to Ukraine were modest and in most cases declined. The UK closed its aid programme in 2008. Ukrainian civil society organisations strongly criticised the EU's backing of a (short-lived) deal struck between Prime Minister Yulia Tymoshenko and Viktor Yanukovich in mid-2009 that threatened to centralise political power in an opaque fashion. The EU took a notably low-profile position in the run up to the January 2010 presidential election, eschewing pressure for further democratic reform so as not to be seen favouring any candidate.

Backed by Moscow, Viktor Yanukovich took power in the 2010 elections. He quickly tightened executive control over the judiciary, restricted press freedom, imprisoned many members of the opposition, and appropriated the economic benefits of corruption and state capture in the hands of his own narrow circle of friends, relatives and supporters – the notorious 'Family'. He did this in particular through control over kickbacks on public procurement contracts. The parliamentary elections of 2012 were less free than the previous round of elections. Yanukovich promised the EU reforms through 2012 and 2013, but few measures were actually implemented.

[3] European Commission, *EU-Ukraine Association Agenda*, Brussels, 2009.

[4] O. Burlyuk, 'An ambitious failure: Conceptualising the EU approach to rule of law promotion (in Ukraine)', *Hague Journal on the Rule of Law* 6/1, 2014, 26–46. O. Burlyuk, 'A thorny path to the spotlight: The rule of law component in EU external policies and EU–Ukraine relations', *European Journal of Law Reform*, 1, 2014.

In response the EU elaborated a policy mix of cooperation, incentives and conditionality. At the end of 2011, the EU and Ukraine concluded association agreement negotiations and initialled the accord in March 2012. The EU then put the agreement on hold mainly in response to the imprisonment of opposition leader Yulia Tymoshenko. Gradually, the EU widened its conditionality, pressing the government to reform the public prosecutor's office and the electoral law. The EU suspended budget support, although it continued various strands of aid into 2013.

The Ukrainian elite formally remained committed to meeting reform requirements linked to the association agreement. The government did implement some reforms, including to NGO and media laws, ombudsman powers, anti-fraud provisions, gender rights and minorities legislation. Yet, Ukrainian commentators increasingly worried that the EU's decision to drive the AA forward despite Yanukovich's violations of basic democratic norms was now primarily driven by geopolitical considerations.[5] One expert lamented that the EU's focus on keeping Ukraine outside of Russia's sphere of influence and increasing its own exports would undercut support for reform in Ukraine.[6] Corruption, police brutality and the return of 'super-presidentialism' stirred popular discontent well before the autumn of 2013.

The Russian pushback now began. Some suggested that President Putin was planning an intervention well before the 2013 eruption as it became clear that Yanukovich would probably lose power in 2015; the Maidan protest merely gave Russia a pretext to begin a whole new level of destabilisation. Moscow blocked Ukrainian chocolate exports – a measure aimed at prominent pro-European oligarch Petro Poroshenko. Pressed by popular opinion uneasy at Russian manoeuvres, Yanukovich made a rare appearance in parliament to press home his choice for the EU partnership. Ukrainian Prime Minister Mykola Azarov proposed holding trilateral consultations

[5] S. Kudelia, 'EU-Ukraine Association Agreement: Yanukovych's Two-Level Games', PONARS Eurasia Network, 20 September 2013.

[6] E. Paanukoski, 'End of era of cognitive dissonance should do Ukraine good', EU Neighborhood Guest Blog, 29 August 2013. Available at: http://euneighbourhoodguestblog.wordpress.com/tag/association-agreement.

between the EU, Ukraine and Russia's proposed Eurasian customs union.[7]

This uneasy situation continued to the eve of the EaP Vilnius summit in November 2013. The regime promised reforms but held out against the more specific demands of EU conditionality, in particular the release of Yulia Tymoshenko. Despite Yanukovich's constant promises, his formal reform commitments and his professed unease at Russian pressure, he increasingly wavered over the association agreement. One week before the Vilnius summit, he announced that Ukraine was pulling out. In a dramatic series of meetings, Poland and Lithuania persuaded other member states – most crucially, Germany – to drop the conditions attached to the agreement, as Russia's success in enticing Yanukovich away from the EU became clear. However, this change came too late, and the president duly announced that Ukraine would cease preparations to sign the association agreement.

Revolt

This triggered protests in Kiev's central Madian square. Underlying pressure had been building-up for some time. The 2004 protests had been driven by the political opposition; this time, the Maidan protests were much more spontaneous and driven by civil society and unaffiliated citizens with few ties to organised political parties. When Yanukovich eventually fled at the end of February 2014, Ukrainian citizens were wary of the new government, which included several faces from the discredited Orange coalition. When Tymoshenko spoke to the crowds after her release, the chant was 'No to messiahs'. Amidst the protests, Ukraine's economy teetered on the edge of a precipice. The country's foreign currency reserves fell to their lowest level since 2006. The drop continued even after Russia paid the first $3bn tranche of a bailout offered to the regime in return for withdrawing from the EU accord.

The EU sought to find the means to persuade Yanukovich to meet the protestors' demand that the government sign the association agreement. On 10 February 2014, the conclusions from a meeting of

[7] 'Azarov proposes trilateral talks between EU, Ukraine and Customs Union on Association Agreement', *Black Sea News*, 27 September 2013. Available at: www.blackseanews.net/en/read/70935.

EU foreign ministers offered the tantalising statement that the AA was not the EU's 'final goal' – which some member states played up as referring to the possibility of EU membership. As commented in the previous chapter, Commissioner Füle went out on a limb to insist that the EU should bring into play the membership carrot. Most member states declined to support him. High representative Catherine Ashton talked of a new Ukraine plan when she visited Kiev, but she did not make clear exactly what this would consist of. The EU committed €600 million as part of an IMF package – although this was several times less than the $15 billion that Russia promised to Yanukovich.

These were measures designed to influence the government's policy choice. Tangible support more specifically targeted at the protestors was limited. The European Endowment for Democracy released €150,000 worth of projects quickly providing medical supplies and helping the independent Kyiv Post replace computers destroyed by security forces. However, most EU funds were locked into long-term aid cycles and already committed to government bodies. Calls for funding were still in the pipeline; the EU switched only a very limited amount of longer-term capacity-building projects to protect protestors. European donors had helped set up a Lifeline Fund to protect civic groups around the world: but this was not mobilised to protect Ukrainian civic groups. European institutions were flooded with desperate pleas for help from Ukrainians in the Maidan; while a number of European embassies provided covert medical and travel assistance, funding mechanisms struggled to respond quickly. Reflecting disappointment with EU support, Ukrainian reformers launched a website called 'Deepconcern.com', poking fun at the tendency of European leaders to express concern at regime violence against protestors without offering tangible support. Given the limited EU backing, several opposition figures announced that the protests should no longer be labelled 'EuroMaidan'.

The EU held Yanukovich to be the legitimate president. When Ukrainian opposition figures called for external mediation, EU figures said they could not 'mediate' but only 'facilitate' dialogue. The EU placed its faith in a dialogue-based solution to Ukraine's turmoil. Despite the new depths of Ukraine's tumult, the EU refused to 'give up' on President Yanukovich. It did not back opposition calls for the president to step down or for an institutional overhaul. Prior to deadly street battles on 18 February 2014, the opposition berated the EU for its reluctance to impose sanctions on Yanukovich.

The president continued to juggle. On the one hand, he intimated the possibility of reform, an EU-orientation, concessions and dialogue. On the other hand, he pursued opaque deals with Russia and reverted to authoritarian repression. Despite repeated setbacks, the EU was reluctant to give up on the prospect of the president following a path of moderation and modernisation. EU officials felt that they watched and monitored so closely that they pulled the regime back from more brutal methods and from introducing draconian emergency laws.

At this stage, the EU's hope was for some mutually acceptable exit from the crisis. Russian foreign minister Sergei Lavrov seemed to be proposing a new deal for Ukraine: Ukraine as a 'neutral' country belonging neither to Russia's nor to the EU's direct sphere of influence and free to cooperate with both.[8] US Assistant Secretary of State Victoria Nuland made headlines when in a leaked phone call with the US ambassador she swore colourfully to express her disdain for the EU, believing it was not doing nearly enough to engineer certain outcomes in domestic Ukrainian politics. Violence intensified and over 100 protestors and security officers were killed. Opposition members insisted on major constitutional amendments. While German chancellor Angela Merkel expressed her support for the opposition's goals of pressuring for constitutional reform and a new government, she disagreed with calls for sanctions against Ukrainian top officials.[9]

Then, as the situation deteriorated, the EU approach changed. There was much talk of Germany assuming a more proactive lead role. Several coordinated speeches from senior German political figures heralded an end to German passivity. Angela Merkel's government invited opposition leaders to Berlin. High-level diplomatic engagement was now stepped-up. The Polish, French and German foreign ministers went together to Kiev. The violence visited on Ukrainian protestors now finally prompted the EU to threaten and then impose sanctions.

When the regime asked the EU for €12 billion to offset Russia's economic measures, the EU refused to get drawn into a bidding war. As the crisis deepened, the EU offered to look at ways of doing more

[8] 'Russia Tells the West it's Time for Common Ground on Ukraine – or Else', *Christian Science Monitor*, 13 February 2014.
[9] 'Merkel Meets with Ukraine Opposition', *Deutsche Welle*, 17 February 2014.

to address the government's concerns. But it resisted a geopolitical approach based on simply offering a corrupt regime more money than Russia. Rather, the European influence was felt through the diplomatic efforts of the German, French and Polish foreign ministers. They played a significant part in finally getting the president to sign a power-sharing, unity deal. Yanukovich immediately disregarded this deal and fled the country.

Ukraine's constituency in favour of reform was broader in 2014 than in 2004, in part because the extent of corruption had deepened and more businesses were prejudiced by the regime's rent-seeking behaviour. In addition, unlike in Egypt in 2013, the army did not mobilise to quash the protests and uphold autocracy. The EU did not have a direct influence on the vibrancy and tenacity of the protests. It imposed sanctions when the president was already preparing to flee the country; these measures were not a causal factor in explaining the outcome of the confrontation. Indeed, civic activists argued angrily that if European governments had been willing to implement asset freezes in December, then pro-government MPs, fearing for their funds abroad, would have pulled Yanukovich back from deadly violence. They complained that Russia's behind-the-scenes manoeuvres against the protests were more significant than EU support to the Maidan civic groups – even if they lacked firm evidence to proof this assertion.

One concern that arguably played an insidious role in what followed was the presence of far-right nationalists in the new government. The EU expressed concern over the presence of right-wing activists in the protests, but insisted the revolution was a genuinely democratic movement. Nevertheless, in the name of building as broad a coalition as possible, the French, German and Polish ministers assented to the right wing being included in the coalition accord, with a presence well in excess of its limited share of the popular vote. Russian and other critics accused the EU and some European governments of turning a blind eye to the violence carried out by the vigilante groups that attached themselves opportunistically to the Maidan revolt.

New European Support

After Yanukovich fled, European diplomacy focused on ensuring the orderly formation of an interim government under new constitutional provisions. The EU encouraged a mixed administration, with

Maidan civic leaders, non-aligned politicians, right-wing Svoboda and Tymoshenko's party all at the table. In fact, the selection of the new government in March 2014 was *ad hoc*, and involved almost self-selected Maidan representatives. This fed nascent complaints in the east of the country. The EU did not insist at this stage that a more balanced representation from the east be included in the interim administration.

The EU argued that it contributed to the immediate post-revolution context by forwarding Ukraine new areas of support. At the beginning of March 2014, the EU agreed to offer Ukraine new money totalling €11 billion. This would be made up mainly of loans for macro-financial assistance, along with European Investment Bank (EIB) and European Bank for Reconstruction and Development (EBRD) credits – all linked to IMF conditions. The amount also included €1.4 billion in new EU grants over a seven-year period.

The new government prevailed upon member states to pledge a quick signing of the political aspects of the association agreement. Member states agreed even in the face of some legal doubts over what exactly these elements could include. The interim administration also convinced doubters, including the French government, to agree to a speedy release of some of the newly promised funds. However, a March summit statement did not repeat the 10 February council conclusions language on the AA not being the 'final goal' of European policy.

Some doubts remained over this summit's outcome. Insiders reported that the most substantive, economic parts of the association agreement would be delayed by an agreement to hold technical talks with Russia.[10] It was not entirely clear what the 'political' parts, to be signed immediately, would include, and especially whether European governments were ready to extend military cooperation to Ukraine's new government. Germany was still hesitant over the AA, for fear of the Russian reaction at a moment of such sensitive diplomacy.

Policy-makers concurred that Putin's broader aim was to keep Ukraine out of NATO and the European Union. But member states showed no signs of pushing for these options anyway – even though support for NATO membership amongst Ukrainians rose to around 40 per cent, on a par now with opposed opinion. Francois Hollande stuck to his line that France would not support Ukrainian membership

[10] *Euractiv*, 7 March 2014.

of either body. France continued openly to block any mention of Ukrainian EU membership.[11] Whenever the membership question was raised it was generally dismissed as an option so far beyond the realms of the possible that it was not even worth advocating.

On 21 March 2014, the EU and Ukraine signed the political chapters of the association agreement. Governments believed that supporting Ukraine was where the EU could still make a real difference, and that the most effective way of holding Russian revanchism at bay was to help make Ukraine a viable and democratic state. Angela Merkel emphasised that the presidential elections scheduled for May would not happen in an orderly manner unless Ukraine received substantial financial assistance as soon as possible. She almost called into question IMF conditionality, and hinted at the fact that as a price for short-term stability the EU might have to accept that some money would go missing through nepotism and corruption.

After some debate, the political aspects of the AA included a commitment to political dialogue to strengthen common values. They upgraded the EU-Ukraine Cooperation Council to an Association Council; enshrined the 'gradual convergence' of Ukraine's foreign, security and defence policies with those of the EU; and bound the EU and Ukraine to 'intensify their joint efforts to promote stability, security and democratic development in their common neighbourhood, and in particular to work together for the peaceful settlement of regional conflicts'. The UK insisted on removing Justice and Home Affairs from the political provisions.

There was some discussion within the European Council on whether the split between the political and economic provisions of the AA would be temporary or longer term. The German government spoke out against the rapid implementation of any economic parts of the agreement. Instead, the EU promised unilaterally to remove many tariffs, giving Ukraine tariff-free access for many of its exports to the European market until a free trade accord came into force. The EU claimed this was worth half a billion euros a year to the Ukrainian economy.

A degree of recrimination followed over the decision not to sign the full AA. Some diplomats referred to technical obstacles. Others stressed it was a political decision, reflecting the desire to talk more to Russia

[11] *EU Observer*, 7 March 2014.

about the free trade rules before signing with Ukraine. Still others said it was a means to keep some pressure on the Ukrainian government to move ahead with reforms. Others reported that the main concern was to wait until after the elections, as such a substantive agreement should be signed by a new government with full democratic legitimacy. Some European officials defended the wait-and-see approach by claiming that the Ukrainian government was itself unsure it wanted the full AA prior to elections and that holding off was a sage gesture to eastern regions that their concerns were being taken on board.

Other reactions were downbeat. François Hollande repeated at the summit that, 'Ukraine cannot claim accession to the EU'.[12] The French line was that the EaP had enough on its plate to implement the AAs and then assess their impact, before considering any higher level of commitment. In private, senior member state diplomats commonly warned that, in the words of one foreign minister, 'Ukrainians' expectations of the EU are too high'. In support of their reluctance even to open a debate on a membership perspective, diplomats most commonly referred to the constraint of European public opinion – even though they invariably struggled to offer firm evidence that the EU population was firmly against Ukrainian membership, as shown in the previous chapter.

Ukraine's interim administration was not particularly committed to deep political reform and was in hock to powerful oligarchs.[13] Some key post-Maidan civic groups complained of government resistance to reform.[14] The EU pressed for a reform agenda to be respected. In its annual ENP review, at the end of March 2014 the EU pressed the interim government to draw up plans for further constitutional reform, improvements to the electoral law, stronger anti-corruption measures, police reform and stricter judicial independence.[15] EU officials insisted stricter 'control mechanisms' were being set up to guard against new aid funds 'disappearing into a back hole', in the words of officials in Kiev. Diplomats feared that IMF conditions would have negative short-term effects and that EU support should be directed at

[12] *Euractiv*, 20 March 2014.

[13] M. Natorski, 'A new social contract for Ukraine', *New Eastern Europe*, 26 March 2014.

[14] A. Wilson and O. Andreyev, *Ukraine: A Failing State, or Survival of the Old State?*, London: European Council for Foreign Relations, May 2013.

[15] European Union, *Ukraine ENP Progress Report*, Brussels, 2013.

preventing this. Representatives of some European democracy funders complained that in practice the interim government prevaricated on reform and did not fully welcome cooperation on issues such as corruption and the rule of law.

The EU promised to support economic reforms but without imposing such severe social costs that the population in eastern Ukraine would see Russian support as more attractive.[16] The EU promised to 'frontload' assistance to and cooperation with Ukraine, implying a more flexible use of conditionality and technical requirements.[17] The EU approved two crucial components of its package of economic and financial support to Ukraine, providing €1 billion in macro-financial assistance. The loans were still conditional on the signature of an agreement between Ukraine and the IMF. DG Trade officials tried to soften the way that IMF conditionality was imposed.

Ukrainian civil society organisations were increasingly critical of EU support. They judged the decision to sign only the political part of the AA as a German-led sop to Russia. Maidan leaders berated the EU for being insufficiently tough on the new administration's democratic reform commitments, while criticising European governments for being unwilling to provide essential security support. Ukrainian diplomats also expressed mixed sentiments. They stressed that Ukraine now needed help that was more immediate and different from the battery of twinning and institution-building initiatives supported by the EU during the previous decade; such initiatives were welcome but only useful if the EU reacted politically to the obstacles put in their way. Ukrainian officials lamented that while the EU talked now of its more 'geopolitical perspective' it was not willing 'to pay the price of geopolitics', either in its relations with Russia or in making really far-reaching commitments to Ukraine.

Help or Hindrance?

Conceptualising EU foreign policy towards Ukraine in this period requires us to break down the way that European aims differed and

[16] D. Gros, 'Restarting Ukraine's economy', *Project Syndicate*, 3 April 2014.

[17] European Commission and High Representative for Foreign and Security Policy, *Neighbourhood at the Crossroads: Implementation of the European Neighbourhood Policy in 2013*, JOIN(2014)12 p. 3.

evolved through three periods: the long run-up to the protests; the weeks of the Maidan revolt itself; and the immediate aftermath of the uprising.

The EU, along with the US, certainly sought to contribute to the Orange revolution. External actors helped both in maintaining a degree of open political space prior to the revolution and in pressing for the 2004 election results to be respected – even if EU policies were not the determinant factor in the breakthrough.[18] From 2005, the EU offered the nominally democratic government assistance and inducements to greater partnership. But it failed to prevent a gradual subversion of the Orange revolution's core spirit. Its approach was to support what were seen to be the 'good democrats' in power, without broadening its partnerships in ways that could have held the increasingly nepotistic elite to account.

To some degree, the EU's policy mix was effective under the Yanukovich government from 2010. Civil society was empowered, while conditionality weakened the president's position. Yet this was not quite a success story for EU foreign policy. The EU did help constrain the extent of authoritarian drift, but did not compel democratisation. Similarly to events in Egypt in 2011, while EU support for civil society and pressure on the regime were important factors, change happened through the kind of violent, unpredictable and polarising rupture that the EU wanted to avoid. In hindsight, many doubted whether Yanukovich was ever likely to meet EU reform conditions. Arguably, the conditions were sound, but imposed in a way that backed him into a corner; they may have worked better if deployed in a more subtle and oblique fashion.

The Yanukovich regime needed to be responsive to public opinion as Ukraine did have a relatively open political system, and this explained why the government at least kept the AA negotiations alive. This was off set by the president's need to retain his core power-vertical, however. This had contrasting outcomes: while the gradual narrowing of Yanukovich's political base militated against the EU agreement, the same procrastination on the AA also re-awoke civic opposition.

[18] M. McFaul and R. Youngs, 'Ukraine: External Actors and the Orange Revolution'. In M. McFaul and K. Stoner (eds), *Transitions to Democracy: A Comparative Perspective*, Baltimore: Johns Hopkins Press, 2013.

The EU kept a focus on the need for democratic reform, even when Russian provocations became stronger. Some argued the EU was naïve to do so: if it had signed the AA quicker, without such onerous preconditions, it could have locked Ukraine into a European orientation before domestic differences grew to the point where the agreement became a source of divergence. However, the situation was probably too complex to have produced such a tidy outcome. Signing the AA earlier with no political conditions may have undercut civil society and empowered Yanukovich enough for the regime to retain power. Moreover, it was the long-term reform focus that protestors latched onto and which inspired them to such stubborn courage. Several Ukrainian civil society organisations insisted the EU erred not in delaying the AA but in not imposing further-reaching conditionality and in scrambling to do a deal with Yanukovich at the last minute in February 2014.

Probably the most convincing lesson to draw was that conditionality needed more positive engagement on the ground to build up democratic capacity actually to fulfil those conditions. It was not sufficient just to impose conditions in such a 'take it or leave it' fashion. The EU's line had become unduly hands-off: 'here is our offer, now it is up to you to get your house in order'. This bred a view in some quarters that most member states were almost hiding behind democratic conditions – that they almost did not want Yanukovich to meet the conditions, as the EU would then need to step up and fulfil its side of the partnership in the midst of growing tensions with Russia. Some member states and EU commissioners insisted that the AA should be used as a means of anchoring Ukraine within the EU orbit. Others argued the new fraught context raised the importance of its values component – as the EU could now only sensibly cooperate with a democratic Ukraine.

What about support for the revolution, once the protests started in earnest in November 2013? Diplomats admitted that Ukraine's Maidan revolt exposed the EU's lack of an early warning system to identify the preliminary stages of regime breakdown and democratic crises. More favourably, some writers argued that EU pressure was enough to pull Yanukovich back from even more violent tactics against protestors.[19]

Insiders insisted that coordination in the heat of the crisis was good and certainly better than in the 2004 Orange revolution. The episode

[19] A. Wilson, *Ukraine Crisis: What it Means for the West*, Cambridge MA: Yale University Press, 2014, p. 88.

showed that EU foreign policy coordination was a matter of member states and EU institutions playing different types of roles, not simply out-sourcing foreign policy to a single Brussels-based figure. Ashton and Füle both played important roles, which were complemented by the weight of three major member state ministers going the extra mile of being present in Kiev. Germany promised leadership and engaged actively in high-level diplomacy, although it did not commit substantive resources.

However, the EU could undoubtedly have done more to support the civic protests. It gained the protestors' wrath by not insisting that civil society be given a seat at the table in any negotiated unity deal. The priority attached to reaching a negotiated solution was understandable. A consensual outcome was earnestly to be desired. But in the aftermath of mortal violence, one wonders if this was still a sensible premise upon which to base EU strategy. This, by now, appeared blind to some increasingly harsh realities of the power dynamics integral to the Yanukovich regime. The EU held Yanukovich to be the legitimately elected president even though he had fundamentally corroded and hollowed out the political system that had bestowed on him that legitimacy. Some insiders felt that European governments preferred to keep Yanukovich in power as any alternative inserted by President Putin could be even more difficult to deal with.

The EU effectively lowered its conditionality on President Yanukovich just at the moment his forces began gunning down citizens in the Maidan. After all his brutality, Ukraine's beleaguered president could have won EU money on easier and more generous terms than were available at the Vilnius summit before the uprising began. Punitive measures, targeted at regime members, came extremely late in the day. The EU had begun to congratulate itself that its critical attention on Ukraine had pulled the regime back from adopting repressive emergency measures. After the tragic events of mid-February, protestors perceived that the EU was helping to keep Yanukovich in power and its normative reputation suffered grievously. It terms of lives lost, the cost of indulging Yanukovich was extremely high.

Gradually the protestors were driven less by an EU vision and more by their confrontation with regime brutality; even if the regime had swung again in support of an EU orientation, this would no longer have saved it. Just as in Turkey, the EU reference point for reform had given way to domestic-orientated discourse. Increasingly, the protestors asked despairingly how many times the EU could allow the same tragic, red line of unacceptability to be crossed and how many times it would fall into the trap of having confidence in Yanukovich's promises of deals and concessions. Having been fooled several times already, the EU could no longer claim surprise as a credible excuse each time the regime shifted mode from dialogue to repression.

It was not clear to many protestors why Yanukovich fled so suddenly, just when he had secured a deal to keep himself in power until the elections. Did EU leaders really make an effort to ensure he did not escape? Would this have diverted the conflict that blighted eastern Ukraine in the following months? Given what happened after Yanukovich fled, it might indeed be contended that the EU had been wise to try to keep him in power. From the point of view of human rights concerns, the uncomfortable conclusion might be that a less clean-cut regime exit might have prevented the subsequent turmoil in Crimea and eastern Ukraine.

While this must certainly be entertained as a possibility, it was by no means certain that Yanukovich would have respected the terms of the deal in a way that brought stability. The accord might simply have bolstered a reconfigured set of elites and done nothing to assuage the ever-growing protests. By the latter stages of the revolt, divisions were so deep that instability might have been inevitable whether Yanukovich stayed or fled. In this sense, the EU's deal making left it out of tune with civil society. If it had erred initially by placing so much emphasis on the unity deal, having got this signed it did not insist enough on it being respected. Both steps in the process weakened the impression that it was thinking through the longer-term ramifications of its short-term crisis management diplomacy.

Into the next, post-revolution phase, the EU could also have offered Ukraine more generous means of support. Russia's critique was that the EU took sides and forced a zero-sum choice upon a country in which large parts of the population would never want to break relations with Moscow. While it would be unfair to accuse the EU of helping to cause the conflict that followed, it did little to pre-empt or forestall it. It is difficult to determine whether a membership perspective would have made a difference in reassuring Russian-speaking Ukrainians about their future under the new regime. Russian propaganda painted a pro-EU choice as synonymous with far-right desires to erase Russian identity. The EU at this stage did little to counteract this Russian misinformation; without such efforts a membership offer would have been unlikely to command the unified support of Ukrainian society.

Conclusion

How then can we extract from this evolving set of concerns from 2004 through to the 2014 Maidan protests conclusions that are directly relevant to the book's three core analytical enquires?

Categorisation

In the opening stages of Ukraine's crisis, the EU was hesitant and reactive and struggled to move out of its standard foreign-policy philosophy into a more geopolitical mode of operation. The EU's response contained a good deal of impromptu adjustment. It is difficult firmly to categorise the EU response in accordance with Chapter 2's four conceptual categories, as member states and Brussels institutions shifted somewhat inconstantly in reaction to events on the ground. Yet, the crucial early months of 2014 did witness the beginning of a change. The faint contours of a liberal-redux geopolitics could be discerned in the way that the EU and key member states sought to influence Ukraine's disrupted politics. The EU's response contained a mix of offensive and defensive geopolitics. This was evident in the precise ways in which European diplomacy, conditionality, aid projects and civil society support were deployed. It involved European diplomats sending some very finely balanced messages, holding President Yanukovich to be both the problem and a necessary part of the solution. The EU aim was to support political change, but also shepherd it towards consensual stability. It began to understand that relations with EaP states like Ukraine were not set on a smooth glide-path of technical approximation and win–win cooperation; member states began to ponder some highly geopolitical trade-offs.

Foreign Policy Dynamics

In this early period of the crisis, a familiar set of institutional patterns prevailed in EU decision-making; but they were also supplemented by new dynamics as the Maidan revolution reached its crux. The EU was focused on its own policy instruments as much as the accumulation of unsustainable political dynamics within Ukraine – a fact that indicated the institutionally embedded nature of EU foreign policy dynamics. The EU focused on getting the regime to sign the AA, almost as an end in itself, instead of broadening its partnership with other actors in Ukraine on reform issues when it should have been clear that Ukrainian democracy was deeply troubled. Member states' upgraded engagement on political reform was part of a geopolitical calculus, but this calculus was roughly hewn. Then, as the revolts reached their peak, a wider range of actors played important roles and more carefully rationalised different strategic options. An incipient and overdue geopolitical lens on reforms dampened EU enthusiasm for uncontrolled change – albeit in a way that seemed to misread many of Ukraine's domestic dynamics.

Impact

To summarise the extensive discussion above of the effectiveness of EU responses, there was a mix of positive and negative impact. The EU failed to act more pre-emptively to deal with what was an increasingly common situation around the world: that of a leader gaining power through democratic means and then chipping away at checks and balances. Yet Ukrainian protestors were inspired by the prospect of values-orientated EU partnership; this was to the EU's credit because it kept the focus on democratic reform as a long-term vision lacking in Russia's offers. In this opening chapter of the eastern crisis, there was much that went Europe's way. Vladimir Putin failed to keep a pro-Russian in power in Kiev and to entice Ukraine definitively away from a European choice. If Putin was really strategic, he might have left President Yanukovich in power to sign the AA, then worked to undermine reforms until Ukraine once again needed rescuing by condition-free Russian money.

The Maidan revolt was dubbed the Euro-revolution, very deliberately. Protestors flew EU flags, while banning political party symbols. This heightened expectations in European solidarity. European governments did not fully meet these expectations in the dramatic moment of revolution; again, the general tone of geopolitics-lite infused ambivalent EU responses. Andrey Kurkov, one of Ukraine's most famous and respected writers, complained that European governments reacted slowly, 'as if news were arriving not by internet but by messengers on horseback'. His overall judgement on the violence was sobering: 'The main reason for this is that Europe, so vociferous in her support during the Maidan protests, has subsequently fallen silent and walked away.'[20] The consequences of such laggardly and cagey indecision were about to become even more dramatic.

[20] A. Kurkov, *Ukraine Diaries, Dispatches from Kiev*, London: Harvill Secker, 2014, pp. 160 and 244.

8 *Ukraine II: Containing Conflict*

Compounding the shock of Crimea's annexation, armed conflict intensified in eastern Ukraine throughout 2014, 2015 and into 2016. After local separatists took up arms, Russia also supplied men and weapons to foment the hostilities. With large numbers of troops at the border, Russia signalled a potential willingness to intervene directly in eastern Ukraine under the guise of 'peace-keeping' operations. The conflict prevented Ukraine from functioning with normality as a unitary state. A peace accord was negotiated in Minsk in September 2014. However, violence worsened again in early 2015, with separatist rebels taking control of additional territory. A second version of the Minsk deal was agreed in February 2015, in an attempt to halt the spiralling conflict. While it partially succeeded in doing this, Ukrainian soldiers and civilians continued to die on a daily basis and the situation remained unstable through to the end of 2016.

The European Union (EU) and its member states incrementally put in place a response that focused on diplomatic mediation and an array of security support for the new Ukrainian government. This chapter uncovers the debates that occurred in relation to the EU's attempt to develop an effective and united conflict resolution strategy in eastern Ukraine. It charts the evolution of European efforts at conflict mediation, EU pressure for rebel-held areas in eastern Ukraine to be granted autonomous status and member states' cautious role in security assistance. The nature of the European response to the on-off conflict revealed much about its conception of asymmetrical and mixed forms of geopolitics. While EU engagement arguably helped temper what could have turned into a far more serious conflict, it did not prevent the crisis leaving a disquieting legacy – both for Ukraine and for European power.

Crimean Whimper

Well before 2014, some observers had feared – if not precisely predicted – Russia's takeover of Crimea. They had also intuited that the main concern was not so much President Yanukovich's strength as the fact that he had lost the support of President Putin and might leave power precipitately, leaving a power vacuum. This was reputedly one of the main reasons why EU leaders sought to keep him in power. After the disgraced president fled Kiev, Russia's annexation of Crimea followed in short succession – suggesting that Moscow was already prepared for this opportunity.

The EU had done relatively little to engage with Crimea or to present itself here and in eastern areas as a protector of minority rights, a source of investment or generator of social opportunities. The upheaval in Kiev reinforced the perceived imbalance in EU policy in the eyes of many in these regions.[1] Civil society leaders lamented that the predominant discourse across Ukraine quickly became one of identity, based on questions of language, religion, history and foreign policy orientation. These civic reformers felt they had pushed in vain for European sponsorship of inter-regional dialogue at all levels, including civil society, universities, political parties, NGOs and government.

Nor was the EU engaged sufficiently to prevent the Ukrainian parliament's attempt to repeal the law that protected Russian as an official language. The 2012 language law was introduced without consultation or parliamentary debate. It was a symbol of the Yanukovich regime and its whole way of conducting politics, which is why the interim post-Maidan administration moved to replace it. However, the move clearly heightened anxieties in Crimea and eastern cities. The interim president intervened to prevent the repeal. Parliament set up a working group to propose a new draft that would accommodate the needs of all ethnic groups, but much damage had already been done.

The EU's reaction to the Russian incursion into Crimea was timorous. While official statements were rhetorically firm in their defence

[1] K. Zasztowt, 'The radicalisation of separatists in Crimea', *PISM Bulletin*, 21, 17 February 2014.

of Ukraine's territorial integrity, concrete action was limited. As explained in Chapter 5, relatively limited sanctions were imposed against Russia in relation to the take-over of Crimea. Most EU governments expressed a desire to 'wait and see' and pursue diplomatic talks with Russia. The UK, Italy and Germany blocked proposals for an EU fact-finding mission to Crimea.

European leaders insisted that Russia enter into dialogue with a so-called Contact Group. In return, the EU would press the new government in Kiev towards a decentralised political system. As President Putin rejected this and backed the referendum on annexation in Crimea, the EU line toughened. Still, Germany in particular was not minded to insist that Russia withdraw from Crimea as a prerequisite to new dialogue.

As discussions proceeded inconclusively, the challenge widened. Russia moved in swiftly and with remarkable ease took effective control of Crimea. President Putin would subsequently boast (not entirely accurately) that not a shot was fired in the operation. The situation began to look like a fait accompli that would be extremely difficult to reverse. After the Crimea referendum, European leaders unequivocally condemned the vote. Yet they also engaged in dialogue with Russian officials to find a means of compromise.

Moreover, the first signs had emerged of Russia extending its covert destabilisation into the eastern part of mainland Ukraine. European Union ministers' deliberations on how to react to Crimea's annexation became more defensive. The talk soon focused on EU measures being adopted if a new 'red line' of Russian incursion into mainland Ukraine were crossed. As alarm bells sounded across EU foreign ministries, Crimea seemed increasingly forgotten – or at least, sacrificed in an effort to contain even more extensive Russian expansionism. Bulgarian Prime Minister Boiko Borisov accused Angela Merkel and François Hollande of having knowingly and cynically signed away Crimea.[2] Although human rights concerns deepened in the territory, European governments kept a low profile. In April 2016 Russia closed down the Tartar majlis in Crimea, with no discernible European reaction. Elections in Crimea in September 2016 reinforced Moscow's grip on the territory.

[2] *EU Observer*, 2 April 2015.

Mediation Efforts

As conflict spread in eastern Ukraine, the EU sought to mediate and facilitate dialogue with Russia. Indeed, as the violence worsened, most member states judged there to be greater need to reach accommodation with Russia – through a deal related in particular to the internal structure of the Ukrainian state. The deepening conflict was a shock that left EU diplomats disoriented. They acknowledged that under the rubric of the EaP there had been no strategic debate about Ukraine's geopolitical trajectory and the regional impact this might have. The working assumption had been that of a smooth and inexorable, low-politics approximation into an EU governance area. The conflict forced EU member states to adjust their geopolitical lens.

Russia proposed that it might desist from further escalation in return for a guarantee of Ukrainian neutrality and a say in the country's governance; many in the EU were not entirely unsympathetic to exploring such a possibility. In private, some European diplomats doubted whether President Putin's actions were any more threatening to global rules than the US-led invasions of Iraq, Kosovo and Libya.

Talks in Geneva at the end of March 2014 were led by Russia and the United States. European ministers played a secondary role. The talks produced an agreement that appeared to offer a way forward: pro-Russian separatist fighters would stand down and an inclusive political process would be guaranteed. The US and Russia now seemed to be battling for influence in a directly geopolitical sense that the EU still eschewed. The US was notably more assertive than the EU in pushing back against certain Russian demands, in particular Moscow's insistence on guarantees of Ukrainian neutrality.

The Geneva accord widened divisions between EU member states. Even as it became apparent that the terms were failing to stick on the ground, a majority of member states wanted to prioritise this new diplomatic track. The EU put an extension of phase two sanctions against Russia on hold. Poland and other states expressed frustration and a conviction that Russia was entirely disingenuous in its commitment to the accord. In contrast, Germany and France strongly favoured a stronger focus on mediation.

As new Russian-backed disturbances rocked eastern Ukrainian cities, German foreign minister Frank-Walter Steinmeier suggested again that Russia should join as equal partner with the EU in a contact group to reach mutually acceptable outcomes to the crisis.[3] Angela Merkel argued that the main priority was to support a 'Ukrainian roundtable'. When the US pressed hard for Ukrainian security forces to intervene against separatists, the Germans opposed this, instead calling for a reconvening of the Geneva forum. Germany was instrumental in mobilising the Organization for Security and Co-operation in Europe (OSCE) to assist this mediation.

Increasingly, European aid agencies orientated their funds to support mediation bodies to work with different sides in the eastern Ukraine conflict – the UK, for example, began a raft of new projects in late 2014. British diplomats in Kiev reported that their priority was to get Russians and Ukrainians together to talk informally in a non-official setting outside the country. The UK offered funds for the shared management of day-to-day community issues among border communities, funding a peace-building school in Kiev to this end.

President Putin again sowed confusion among member states as he surprisingly did not back Donbas separatists' referendums on succession. Putin recoiled from the notion of a people-led movement of separatists as it would cut across the power of oligarchs closest to him. The referendums in Donetsk and Luhansk were followed by calls from the *de facto* authorities there for these cities to be absorbed into Russia. Russia's response was ambivalent. Putin got the Russian parliament to revoke his right to authorise intervention in Ukraine that it had granted in March. European Union governments were divided on whether this represented a genuine de-escalation or a smoke-and-mirrors tactical change. Some thought Russia was covertly fomenting separatists only for the Kremlin then to claim that it alone could mediate between the different factions.

Some member states looked on aghast as Germany seemed to be overseeing some kind of neutral arbitration. A genuinely difficult strategic choice now presented itself: did the EU accept Putin's implicit offer of joint management of Ukraine? Was this to be the new geopolitics of the east? Putin's aims appeared to be clearer: he wished to retain influence over events in Ukraine, but not to hive off the east with full territorial control – in part because a full separation would leave a more cohesively anti-Russian rump Ukraine. Some comments, particularly from German ministers, were sympathetic to the idea of

[3] *EU Observer*, 5 April 2014.

new EU–Russia cooperation over Ukraine. French foreign minister Laurent Fabius apparently still believed that: 'Ukraine must be a bridge between Russia and the EU, instead of [it] having to choose between them.'[4], French diplomats approached conflict resolution as a matter of great power diplomacy rather than multilateral or EU rules.

France, Germany and the EU aimed to launch peace talks between Kiev and rebel leaders under the stewardship of the OSCE, including Russia. EU diplomats in the Ukrainian capital held meetings with OSCE delegates, even as sanctions lists were being drawn up in successive Brussels summits. The focus of diplomatic efforts centred on what came to be known as the Normandy format, of France, Germany, Russia and Ukraine. If Angela Merkel was by now losing patience with Putin, her foreign minister argued that inclusive mediation was more, not less, apposite, as the situation on the ground worsened. Some other member states noted the German–French process gave a place at the table to Putin henchman, Viktor Medvedchuk, actually helping Putin to gain a stronger foothold in Donbas. They also wondered how, after the MH17 tragedy, Steinmeier could still believe that separatists were legitimate partners within any mediation process – indeed, separatist-linked organisations entered into a number of working groups set up by international actors. One Ukrainian civil society leader blasted: 'Germany is acting as a tool of Russian imperialism.'

One noted expert described the EU's even-handedness as extreme: it called for restraint from Russian invaders and Ukrainian troops in equal terms – despite the conflict being about the invasion of Ukraine's sovereign territory, not an internal matter.[5] The government complained that the EU pushed it to agree a ceasefire in July 2014 when the rebels were on the back foot and could have been defeated. The resulting halt in fighting worked to Russia's advantage. When hostilities resumed the separatists recovered ground – armed now with Russian personnel and weapons that Moscow did not even try to cover-up.

The mediation focus tilted influence within EU foreign policy towards a select number of member state governments. It was notable that Putin chose to carry out diplomacy with his German and French

[4] AJC Global Forum, 13 May 2014.

[5] A. Wilson, *Ukraine Crisis: What it Means for the West*, Cambridge MA: Yale University Press, 2014.

counterparts, sidelining other member states and EU institutions. These and several other national governments were now fully engaged and high-level diplomacy was the dominant edge of EU policy. Insiders concurred that the Commission's role was now more marginal. For Russia, high-level diplomacy with Germany and to a lesser extent with France was unequivocally of primary importance.

The mediation route had ramifications for the vexed question of Ukrainian neutrality. A much-discussed issue was whether mediation should build in some form of guaranteeing Ukrainian neutrality as a means of placating Russia. Member states thought differently on this question. Germany and France exhibited some sympathy; indeed, they had effectively blocked any prospect of Ukrainian membership of NATO since 2008. Poland and others were less defensive: this, they argued, was a matter for Ukrainians themselves to decide democratically. They also noted that NATO could provide a useful deterrent to Russian meddling; that Moldova's neutrality had not protected it from Russian bullying; and that Ukraine had maintained *de facto* neutrality anyway. Nevertheless, the 'neutrality option' gained an increasing number of supporters within member states and the EU institutions, as a core element of a solution negotiated with Russia – even if this had to be agreed over the head of Kiev's elected government.

Germany and other member states stressed the mediation option even as rebel attacks intensified. Several EU states pushed President Poroshenko not to launch further operations against the separatists. The French government suggested that Russian incursions into the east were relatively limited and urged the Ukrainian government to cease operations there and offer negotiations. Hungary, the Czech Republic, Romania and Slovakia all doubted that Russia had 'invaded' eastern Ukraine and suggested the onus should be on mediated talks – and on the Ukrainian government to make concessions. At the NATO summit in September 2014, Germany diluted criticism of Russia in the final communiqué; Stienmeier again stressed the importance of impartial mediation.

Minsk I Fails

Mediation efforts appeared to pay off when a ceasefire and peace accords were agreed in Minsk in September 2014. As detailed in Chapter 3, these agreed a ceasefire in return for moves towards autonomy in parts of eastern Ukraine. Not everyone in the EU welcomed the Minsk accords. External Action Service officials were increasingly angry with Germany and France; they, rather than the EU as a whole, participated in the new peace process. Berlin and Paris had allowed Putin to pick the EU apart, and also to exclude the US from mediation talks. This had helped weigh the scales in Russia's favour, leaving the Ukrainian government far more exposed. In private, many diplomats talked of this representing a major unravelling of common EU foreign policy. France and Germany apparently even declined to inform their EU partners of when they were planning mediation meetings and exactly what was broached in the talks. Ironically, the Ukrainian government kept the External Action Service informed and pushed for EU officials to be included in some meetings, against French and German wishes.

The OSCE became deeply involved in mediation efforts and was highly instrumental in securing the newly agreed ceasefire. Germany was the member state keenest on using the OSCE; the latter was suited to Germany's preference for an inclusive and consensus-based approach to the conflict. A Tripartite Contact Group, including the OSCE, Russia and Ukraine, took a lead role in facilitating dialogue. An OSCE Special Monitoring Mission was gradually expanded to 300 monitors and 130 local staff. OSCE officials paid testament to the key role played by Germany in convincing Russia to accept the mission. European governments relied on the OSCE's ability to monitor the Ukraine–Russia border and enforce the Minsk ceasefire terms, as the organisation began regular military verification missions.

The limits to the OSCE mission soon became apparent, however. It could not gain access to rebel-held areas and could not fully monitor the border. Many diplomats saw the mission's formal impartiality as beneficial to Russia in practice. EU member states did not equip the OSCE to perform its monitoring role; they authorised the EU budget to top-up OSCE funds only by a modest €20 million but resisted calls for larger amounts of funding. Russia prevented Germany and France deploying drones to the OSCE verification mission. The OSCE ran several working groups aimed at filling in the details of the Minsk accord, but struggled to make progress. It did not gain access to the eastern regions to operate bridge-building or mediation dialogues there. Yet despite all these problems, member states did not support the deployment of a muscular EU security mission, but stuck to the 'softer' mediation and monitoring tools of the OSCE.

In broader terms, the OSCE struggled to move out of a phase of conflict containment into one of conflict resolution – and EU member states were not assertive in pushing it to do so. The OSCE launched a small number of programmes aimed at promoting dialogue among communities to foster longer-term harmony, but these were extremely small-scale and gained little traction. There was much talk of the OSCE fashioning a new security architecture for the wider European continent. While most agreed this was necessary, the process was held back by the failure to find a resolution to the Ukraine crisis.[6]

It soon became clear that Russia and the rebels were not fully respecting the ceasefire. Violence resumed, at a low-level but with gradually increasing intensity. Rebels set up parallel governing institutions in contravention of the Minsk accord. By November 2014, NATO's Supreme Commander said the ceasefire now existed in 'name only'.[7] Yet, EU member state diplomats insisted the aim was still to contain the conflict, even if in an uneasy frozen form. Polish and other member state diplomats criticised the (German) assumption that a focus on ceasefire arrangements would provide the foundation for sustainable security.

The German view was that the status quo of late 2014 was probably the best that could be hoped for. Russia could neither be militarily defeated nor driven out of the Donbas region. Berlin's red line was that Germany could not support any formal partitioning of Ukraine; this would be too redolent of its own post-war partition and President Putin was unlikely to be tricked into a deal that saddled him with Donbas in return for a rump Ukraine proceeding more smoothly into the Western orbit. Germany and France often held up the containment of the Georgian conflict in 2008 as a model of success; in contrast, Ukrainians dismissed this example as appeasement-lite that had merely encouraged Putin to intervene in Ukraine.

[6] S. Lehne, *Reviving the OSCE: European Security and the Ukraine Crisis*, Brussels: Carnegie Europe, 2015.

[7] 'Russia sends more convoys into Ukraine as cease-fire Collapses', *Time*, 12 November 2014.

The EU tried to dissuade the Ukrainian government from defining rebel groups as terrorists and from withdrawing social security payments from citizens in Donbas. These moves fed into EU criticisms that Kiev was not treating citizens in those areas in a fully inclusive manner. Member states pressed the Kiev government not to precipitate even more of a humanitarian crisis in a way that would nourish support for separatist actions. Mindful of this risk, the European Investment Bank released a €600 million loan that was earmarked specifically for development projects in the Donbas region.

By the beginning of 2015 the conflict was descending to new levels of brutality. A new round of Minsk talks was postponed; Angela Merkel pulled out as there appeared to be little willingness on Russia's part to make any constructive offer. By now, most people in the two occupied areas of Donetsk and Luhansk were losing faith in all sides, insisting they were neither pro-Russia nor pro-Ukraine, nor were they favourable towards the EU. Adding to a sense of unmanaged chaos, tensions increased between Russian commanders and rebel leaders. Regular and irregular forces were increasingly active, on both sides. More broadly, some speculated that Russia was now pushing for a land bridge to Crimea in part because it needed to regain support amongst a restless populace there.

Minsk II and Managed Defeat

Concerned that the conflict was spiralling out of control, Angela Merkel and François Hollande travelled to Moscow for talks with Vladimir Putin. In the first week of February 2015 a new Minsk accord was agreed between Putin, Merkel, Hollande and Poroshenko. Under this deal, separatists were granted additional territory; a new contact line was favourable to them. Unlike in the first Minsk agreement, there was no provision for OSCE monitoring of the Russian-Ukrainian border. The new accord spoke of more far-reaching autonomy for rebel-held areas, while more explicitly and formally placing financial responsibility for the region on Kiev's shoulders.

Many member states saw this latest phase of German–French diplomacy as another nail in the coffin for a united EU foreign policy. The Baltic states and Poland were highly critical; the Commission was furious that Merkel had allowed Putin to smuggle into the accords a commitment to new talks on changing parts of the EU–Ukraine trade accord to respect Russian interests. Whatever the gains of the second Minsk deal, Angela Merkel was clearly now not representing the EU as a whole.

When the strategically crucial city of Debaltseve fell to rebel forces in the days following the ceasefire, the French and German governments refused to declare that the peace deal had been infringed. The EU and member state leaders loosely threatened additional sanctions if Russia did not respect the Minsk accord. Yet despite the continued fighting, EU leaders did not take any punitive steps against Russia. Fighting spread close to Mariupol as the ceasefire failed to prevent militant attacks.

By mid-2015 the ceasefire stood comprehensively broken – by both sides. Member states pressed the Kiev government hard to respect its side of the accord, so that Russia would have no pretext for complaints. The level of violence then decreased and an uneasy stalemate appeared to have been reached. EU leaders pressed the Poroshenko government to respect the ceasefire against the tide of Ukrainian domestic opinion. Protests in Kiev strongly criticised European governments for reining Ukraine back from defending its territorial rights, and for doing so at Putin's behest.

The EU and member states tried to prevent president Proroshenko repeating his commitment to ensuring Ukraine's 'victory' in the conflict. Ukrainians were furious that the EU was beginning to describe the conflict as 'frozen' when Ukrainian soldiers and civilians were being killed every day. The EU leaned on Poroshenko not to declare martial law, despite strong popular pressure for him to do so. Most Ukrainians also believed that the EU was now holding back from offering Ukraine new money, visa liberalisation and trade benefits to keep Russia on board with the Minsk II accord.

The Ukrainian government requested UN or EU peacekeeping troops. EU member states refused this request. Russia and Ukraine agreed to double the number of OSCE observers to monitor the ceasefire. However, the OSCE mission was still denied access to most of the border and had powers only to monitor events, not to take action where the ceasefire was infringed. The EU did not support Ukraine's request for a military border mission based on the model of the EU's mission in Georgia. Talks about a possible observer mission in Donbas dragged on inconclusively, as France and Germany progressively diluted their ideas in response to Russia's concern that such a mission was a tactic to delay the granting of autonomous status.

However, most EU governments believed that the uneasy impasse was not comfortable for Russia: most working age people left Donbas, it was more and more costly to keep basic services going, industrial production plummeted, Kiev stopped paying pensions and the presence of Russian troops was increasingly unpopular with the local population.[8] Mariupol did not fall; the judgment was that the separatists did not have the capacity to create the much-discussed land bridge to Crimea.

Reflecting this uneasy balance, EU deliberations pointed towards a kind of managed defeat in the Donbas region. Many diplomats argued that a semi-frozen conflict might be the best that could now be hoped for, from the point of view of EU security interests. Representatives of several member states pondered that this might produce a manageable outcome, if fashioned in such a way as to ensure that Russia could not paralyse decision-making in Kiev. Such strategic realpolitik would be struck over the heads of many Ukrainians and sat uneasily with the EU's earlier insistence that it would defend the principle of self-determination. Many Ukrainian civil society interlocutors reacted angrily as such discussions and ideas gathered momentum. Their sense of betrayal grew.

Moreover, stability was extremely precarious and the conflict ebbed and flowed. Conflict dynamics fractured. Russian forces increasingly engaged against local rebel leaders not following Moscow's command, in an effort to regain control and shift from military confrontation to an effort to consolidate Donbas' political and economic autonomy. In turn, the Kiev government increasingly struggled to control maverick volunteer battalions. Many Ukrainians were strongly critical of EU deliveries of humanitarian aid to Donbas, fearing that these implied *de facto* recognition of Ukraine's loss of sovereignty. The rouble became the official currency in the two entities and Russia suggested it might issue Russian passports for Donetsk and Luhansk residents. A process of 'soft annexation' was creeping forward.[9]

President Poroshenko's representative to the Minsk process was angry that Germany and France were too ready to paint Minsk II

[8] A. Motyl, 'Out of Kiev's hands', *Foreign Policy*, 4 May 2015.

[9] 'Soft annexation in Donbas', *Radio Free Liberty*, 4 September 2015.

as a success. Ukrainian diplomats remonstrated that member states refused to provide practical help for tasks like border control. The EU said it supported democracy in Ukraine but was pushing Minsk provisions that a clear majority of Ukrainian citizens opposed. These provisions were generating a nationalist backlash and diverting civil society attention in a way that complicated reform efforts. Ukrainian officials felt that many EU states were putting all the onus on Ukraine fulfilling its side of the Minsk accord – somewhat unfairly, they argued, when it was Ukraine that had been invaded. In August 2016, hostilities spiked, almost back to the level of a fully resumed conflict. In September, Putin pulled out of Normandy format talks after a Russian agent was killed at the Crimea-Ukraine border. France and Germany insisted they would redouble their efforts to get Russia back on board to resurrect the Normandy format – provoking more grumbling from other member states about Paris and Berlin eclipsing a common EU line.[10]

President Poroshenko adopted a hard line in his September 2016 state of the nation address, refusing any further compromise over Donbas.[11] In October, the first Normandy format meeting for over a year was held, albeit without any breakthrough or tangible policy shifts. Merkel and Hollande still insisted on Poroshenko unblocking local elections in Donbas prior to considering any kind of new policing mission for the occupied territories. At the end of 2016, outright conflict had not returned, but the situation was tense and unpredictable.

While European diplomats admitted that they thought the Minsk plan was unlikely to hold indefinitely as the two sides read such different meanings into the text, they acknowledged that there was no other game in town. EU officials admitted with resignation that they were hoping simply for a roll-over of the prevailing impasse, even if the Minsk agreement was not fully respected by separatist forces. By the end of 2016, some were intimating the need for a Minsk III, simply to keep the uneasy peace. A form of bounded stalemate took root, with apparently no better option attainable.

[10] *EU Observer*, EU trying to re-launch Ukraine peace process, 3 September 2016.

[11] See www.president.gov.ua/en/news/shorichne-poslannya-prezidenta-do-verhovnoyi-radi-pro-vnutri-38077, 6 September 2016.

Autonomous Governance

One specific EU priority within these general diplomatic efforts was to press the Ukrainian government to allow separatist held areas some form of autonomous special status – or 'self-governance' in the EU's preferred language. Many in the EU saw such an arrangement as necessary for resolving the conflict. Most member states saw a far-reaching devolution of powers to Donetsk and Luhansk as the key political process that could assuage Russian concerns and aggression. The EU and member states constantly pushed the Ukrainian government to accelerate and deepen this process of devolution – keeping this separate from the broader process of decentralisation in other parts of Ukraine – and did so expressly to undercut Russia's case for aggression.

The Ukrainian government promised a more devolved political system with full linguistic rights for Russian speakers and it signed up to the Minsk agreement language on the Donbas areas being granted a special autonomous status. However, decentralisation progressed slowly in practice and become highly politicised by the conflict. In some ways the Minsk peace deal made decentralisation harder to design and implement. The government stalled on a full and balanced process of decentralisation, arguing that this would weaken state unity in dealing with the conflict.

Russia's model for Ukraine was neutrality combined with federalism. The sticking point was that Russia insisted that each territory would have power over Ukraine's foreign policy directions. Russia's notion of decentralisation was not about locally participative governance but the 'Russian population' gaining a guaranteed block of power. The Ukrainian government and civil society flatly rejected any discussion of federalism, because they insisted that this would be a route towards Russia prising off the eastern regions and dismantling the Ukrainian state.

Ukrainian officials complained bitterly that France and Germany in particular – although backed by others – were pressing for a degree of devolved power to occupied entities that put at risk the Ukrainian state. France and Germany and other EU states insisted it was the only way to allow the Ukrainian state to continue in existence. European support for decentralisation lacked any single strategic logic. Countries like Poland had been funding decentralisation projects for many years.

EU diplomats supported the decentralisation of powers to municipalities rather than regions, as this form of devolution would be less susceptible to Russian meddling. Yet, new initiatives were slow to get off the ground. By late-2015, the EU still had no decentralisation initiative of its own. Diplomats acknowledged that there was little detailed discussion of different possible models of decentralisation.

Diplomats from some member states expressed concern that the focus on decentralisation was being taken too far. Tensions in the east made decentralisation more necessary but also more risky: it now seemed to be forced as a means of assuaging Russian interference in a way that could indeed undercut the unity of the Ukrainian state. Some member states feared that far-reaching decentralisation would enable Russia to block any decisions taken on relations with the EU in Kiev.

Russia accused Ukraine of stalling on special status arrangements – as Poroshenko halted the bill providing for these measures – and insisted that this was why attacks continued. Ukraine countered there could be no special status or local elections in Donbas until a firm cessation of violence was guaranteed; trying to run elections in the midst of conflict was simply not practicable. Kiev was reluctant to hand power to rebel areas until the situation was fully stable and settled within Ukrainian borders. Ukraine's parliament voted in a first reading on a decentralisation package in September 2015. This did not resolve the question of a special status for Donbas. Moscow complained the package of reforms was not only delayed but also did not go far enough to meet the Minsk agreement.

Most actors in the EU adopted a position in between the Russian and Ukrainian stances. The EU pressured the Kiev government to grant additional concessions to militants and to accelerate local autonomy. Germany supported the Russian position on sequencing: there needed to be tangible moves towards handing powers to separatists and elections in the Donbas, and then *after* this peace and monitoring efforts could be stepped up. Ukrainian authorities complained that Germany was pushing too hard on the 'later' Minsk provisions ahead of the immediate imperative of guaranteeing a ceasefire and securing Ukraine's borders.

In December 2015, the French and German foreign ministers released a letter calling for the Ukrainian government to agree a draft law on local elections in Donetsk and Luhansk as soon as possible and for elections to follow within 90 days, with immunity for separatist fighters standing as candidates and an amnesty after the elections. The two ministers suggested that special status should then come into force for the two occupied territories – as long as the OSCE election observation mission judged elections to be in accordance with international standards. Concerned at the imbalance in Franco–German positions, some member states pushed the OSCE hard to engage more assertively and clarify that for elections to take place, violence had to cease. Disappointment with the OSCE's soft approach grew among some member states, while others pulled the OSCE back from any more critical or intrusive involvement.

Gradually, a raft of European-funded initiatives commenced. In December 2015 the EU awarded a €100 million grant for a new project to support decentralisation. This was for capacity-building and technical support for local communities, to set up sub-regional advisory centres, awareness raising, policy analysis, legislative drafting and donor coordination. The EU's decentralisation initiative was aimed at a very local level, to help build the capacity of governance structures below the level of oblasts; it was not directly related to the conflict in Donbas At a very low-level some member states shared experiences on asymmetric forms of devolution – for example in Scotland or Catalonia – as a possible means of offering special status to Donbas that went further than the general decentralisation package going through parliament. However, none of their initiatives were directly concerned with the conflict. EU donors were not able or willing to undertake initiatives supporting different kinds of institutional variation in the occupied territories, of the kind they supported in other conflict contexts around the word as a way of imbuing legitimacy to local governance processes. In Ukraine, the focus of debates and of EU policy efforts was much more centred on the high-politics of the Russia factor than on an exploration of possibly helpful forms of local institutional development in Donbas.

The Kiev government clarified in January 2016 that it would allow elections in Donbas only if a series of conditions were met: access for Ukrainian media, separatist disarmament, withdrawal of military equipment, full access for the OSCE, reinstatement of Ukraine's control over the border and withdrawal of foreign troops. Kiev insisted that the elections should be covered by Ukrainian rules stipulating that parties must be nationwide parties and that the contest should be run by the Ukrainian election commission; separatists wanted more flexible rules to allow independents to stand, and for the territories to have their own election commission. On all such detailed issues, the EU and member states supported compromise solutions, rather than overtly taking Kiev's side.

Debate intensified after Ukrainian MPs delayed a second reading approval of the decentralisation package in January 2016; they sought this delay in order to retain leverage over Russia. The Danish government intimated it might not support a renewal of sanctions on Russia if Ukraine now failed to implement decentralisation measures linked to Minsk. The EU Ambassador to Ukraine Jan Tombinski made a statement that Ukraine needed a completely new constitution, not decentralisation that excluded parts of the east. The EU delegation impressed upon Kiev the need to find a more flexible way forward to implement those elements of decentralisation related to the Minsk accord – in a sense the very inverse of Ukrainian views that wanted deeper decentralisation for Ukraine in general without ceding ground to the occupied territories.

In contrast, Lithuania's foreign minister expressed his disquiet that many in the EU were pushing Ukraine for decentralisation reforms prematurely, when they should have been pushing Russia to comply with the security elements of the Minsk accord.[12] One senior member of the presidential administration complained that a number of EU states had forced the government into accepting a link between the ceasefire and autonomous status in a way that prolonged the conflict. In practice, despite all the European pressure, at the end of 2016 there had been no progress on either elections or autonomous status for the Donbas occupied territories. Governance and human rights standards were by now declining fast in the two territories. Russia was trying to gain some kind of hold over political order there, while most of the local population was tired of both the separatists and the Kiev government.

Military and Security Assistance?

As the conflict evolved, EU member states debated whether to provide military support to Ukrainian forces. In mid-2014, Poland, Sweden and

[12] L. Linkevčius, 'Security before politics in eastern Ukraine', *Wall Street Journal*, 27 January 2016.

the UK formulated a proposal for an EU Common Security and Defence Policy mission focusing on medium term 'capability development' of the security sector. The majority of member states did not favour this option. Poland was sceptical that any political process could now take root and argued that the EU needed to concentrate more on directly boosting Ukrainian capabilities for providing order and security.

An EU Advisory Mission for Civilian Security Sector Reform Ukraine (EUAM) was set up in Kiev. This had a mandate that expressly excluded any role connected directly to the conflict. The mission would assist Ukraine with police and rule of law reform, and help Ukrainian authorities with the development of new security strategies.[13] Several member states diluted the mission, to exclude any remit to strengthen Ukraine's military capacities. Officials in the mission's office in Kiev revealed that member states pulled the EUAM back from any work in areas adjacent to the conflict zone. The mission was purely civilian, as member states refused to accord it any military function.

The mission formally started work in December 2014. It counted on over one hundred European officials plus local employees. It was based in Kiev and initiated work mainly on police reforms. It was set to work in several regions but was to keep clear of Donbas. It soon met resistance to security sector reform among parts of the Ukrainian security establishment. Ukrainian authorities constantly asked for cooperation that the mission's officials had to point out was beyond their mandate. The mission struggled to move beyond an advisory function into project support[14] – although in 2016 it was given a mandate to carry out more direct training and to set up centres in Kharkiv and Lviv. The EUAM had a fraction of the funds and staff of the EULEX mission in Kosovo. The mission's officials in Kiev lamented that on conflict-related security issues the US wielded far more weight than this European mission.

The EU focus was civilian and low-key. A €22 million package of Commission humanitarian and development assistance for the occupied regions in Donbas covered shelter, food, water, healthcare and psychological and social assistance. The EU delegation in Kiev began

[13] 'Ukraine: EU establishes mission to advise on civilian security sector reform', EU Neighbourhood Info Centre, 23 July 2014. Available at: http://enpi-info.eu/maineast.php?id=38065&id_type=1&lang_id=450.

[14] K. Zarembo, *EUAM's First Year: Ambitions versus Reality*, Kiev: Institute for World Policy, 2015.

new initiatives to keep basic services running in the east. An EU team prepared a Civic Assessment Evaluation to assess post-conflict reconstruction needs in Donbas. EU diplomats in Kiev spoke of new efforts to see how EU funds could indirectly feed into local Ukrainian funding for volunteer fighters. In September 2016, EU officials revealed that they were accelerating plans for reconstruction work in Donbas, presuming this would be the EU's main contribution to peace once the Minsk accords were fully respected. Still, EU states' ability and willingness to engage directly in the east to help temper the conflict in any immediate sense was limited.

Member states were still not willing to provide weapons to Ukrainian security forces. Donations from oligarchs and citizens to a new professional militia contributed most to improving the efficacy of Ukrainian security force operations. Crowdsourcing initiatives funded a growing amount of military equipment for the underfunded army, as local Ukrainian groups set up their own finding initiatives in response to the conspicuous lack of outside backing. The United States increased non-lethal military assistance, although not weapons. Diplomats in Kiev were concerned that EU meetings still did not link reform plans to the security situation.

As Russian support to rebels became more extensive and more explicit, the Ukrainian government made more strident pleas for European and American military assistance. Still EU member states prevaricated. Germany and France said explicitly they would not provide arms. Chancellor Merkel's line was that the international community could never supply enough weapons for Ukraine to stand a chance of defeating Russia – and that therefore sending arms would simply legitimise more unrestrained Russian involvement without any operational gain for Ukraine. German officials said that even if Minsk II collapsed Germany would not consider any military help. Nor would Germany support UN or EU peacekeeping forces; the only realistic option was to try to boost the OSCE mission. In contrast, Poland and the Baltic states intimated that they might begin to supply some arms. They stepped up supplies of non-lethal support such as medial supplies. Polish diplomats complained that successive NATO summits offered an excess of pro-Ukrainian rhetoric but very little concrete substance of any tangible use to Kiev. They complained that some member states were still supplying more military-related equipment to Russia than to Ukraine. The creation of the Lithuanian–Polish-Ukrainian armed unit was an attempt to strengthen local forces. In August 2015, training drills were organised for Ukrainian soldiers by a combination of US, UK, Polish, Romanian, Bulgarian and Lithuanian troops. Lithuania sent 150 tonnes of ammunition to Ukraine in September 2016.[15] The UK held a middle line, increasingly open to the idea of providing some military equipment. In March 2015, the UK announced it would supply Ukraine's army with a package of non-lethal military equipment and military training. NATO agreed to provide $15 million of support through its trust fund, although this was of relatively limited magnitude and was to be used for a general modernisation of the military not direct lethal support.

Overall, diplomats admitted that Ukrainian forces did not benefit from enough Western non-lethal advice and training to undercut Russian-backed separatists in Donbas. Ukrainian civil society contributions did more to shore-up the military than support from EU member states – even if European forces' training helped professionalise the military. Some writers believe Ukrainian defence reform made the most significant contribution to containing the conflict, and that EU states played a positive role in this success story. Yet it was a decidedly secondary role as several member states – in particular France and Italy – expressly narrowed the scope of EU security sector reform initiatives for Russia-related geopolitical reasons.[16] An October 2016 report highlighted the failure of international assistance to go beyond *ad hoc* training for immediate operations to a broader process of structural reform in Ukraine's security sector.[17]

Conclusion

Categorisation

The challenges covered in this chapter represented the areas of most marked caution in European foreign policy responses to the eastern crisis. Many elements of the EU response to the conflict in eastern

[15] *Radio Free Europe*, 3 September 2016.

[16] G. Gesssel, *Keeping up Appearances: How Europe is Supporting Ukraine's Transformation*, London: European Council on Foreign Relations, 2016, pp. 28–9, p. 38.

[17] Rand Corporation, *Security Sector Reform*, October 2016.

Ukraine resonated with the category of defensive geopolitics. The EU judged that major concessions were necessary to Russia and expressly declined any hard-power security profile in the crisis. When armed conflict began in eastern Ukraine, European leaders immediately took the military option off the table. Military engagement was never considered as an option; the EU did not contemplate an offensive, hard-power geopolitics of this nature. Rather, the EU attempted to map out a more engaged reforms-based geopolitics, under which its focus on decentralisation and consensual governance could act as a principal pillar to conflict resolution efforts. It was in this sense that EU conflict resolution efforts also contained some elements of the liberal-redux category of geopolitics.

In these efforts, the EU sought to strike a fine balance: increased commitment without confrontation; a defence of democratic self-determination at both national and sub-national levels within Ukraine; but a response also moulded to many unpalatable geopolitical realities of Ukraine's ongoing subjugation to Russian power. Such cautious realism won few plaudits from inside Ukraine. The EU understanding of geopolitics did not offer Ukraine the protection it most desired: an effective security guarantee in the event of military attack. Ukrainians attribute to themselves a cold, self-interested insouciance in their popular saying, 'My house is the furthest away'. They now routinely used this saying as a deflating and withering description of EU attitudes towards Ukraine.

Mediation was the core principle of EU conflict resolution efforts. More than the US, the EU was keen to keep channels open to the rebels and foster inclusive dialogue. The EU's mediation was of a relatively soft and malleable kind, and was not backed by muscular instruments of hard power intervention or support. Indeed, the External Action Service and the main member states were ambiguous even over formally playing a mediating role – as opposed to a looser role of encouraging and facilitating dialogue. The EU left formal mediation to the OSCE – an organisation with limited diplomatic and economic weight.[18] Ukrainian critics complained that the EU was pursuing conflict containment not conflict transformation – its aim was negative, not positive peace.

The European approach to conflict mitigation focused heavily on 'bridging the east–west divide'. This was also controversial within

[18] N. Mirimanova, *Peace-building in Ukraine: What role for the EU?*, Brussels: European Peace-Building Liaison Office, 2014, p. 4 and pp. 7–8.

Ukraine. It seemed to play into the Russian narrative of cultural cleavage that was not prominent before the crisis was provoked. With a stress on such bridge-building projects, the EU implicitly approached the situation as a civil conflict rather than as an invasion. The EU sought to use 'ethnic reconciliation' templates from the Balkans in the entirely different Ukrainian context – and Ukrainians fiercely admonished it for doing so.[19]

The boundary of European defensive geopolitics was a rejection of formal partition. There was no explicit EU support for the view that it might be good to split Ukraine in two, so that the Union could focus its cooperation on a western half that was more solidly pro-EU, better governed, and less weighed down by heavy industry and oligarchic structures. Notwithstanding their principled and robust rhetoric, however, many member states in practice seemed to accept that Russia's annexation of Crimea and the prospect of Russian influence in eastern Ukraine needed to be accommodated within some degree of normalised geopolitical adjustment. The EU's real concern lay in making a success of its positive engagement with the rest of Ukraine that would provide the effective counterpoint to an over-stretched Russia.[20]

Foreign Policy Dynamics

The conflict in Donbas was the element of the broader eastern crisis that most clearly ushered in new EU foreign-policy dynamics. The simmering conflict propelled greater diplomatic engagement, mainly from Germany and France. Indeed, Germany and France took a clear lead role, supplanting common EU processes. Although they did so alongside a raft of new EU policy initiatives on the ground, the weight of standard EU institutional approaches and processes diminished – and was weaker in this area of policy than in others. There was deeper division between member states on the Donbas conflict than on other aspects of policy towards Ukraine.

[19] See survey carried out in O. Burlyuk, *The Role of Culture in Reconciliation in the Ukraine Crisis*, *More Europe* Policy Paper. Available at: wwww.moreurope.org, 2014.

[20] J. Sherr, 'Putin is not master of the new world order', *Prospect*, 14 March 2014.

Many member states were unhappy with German- and French-led diplomacy, but they declined to make such a high-level strategic commitment themselves. The conflict shifted the driving force of European foreign policy away from EU institutions towards member states, but also towards a small subgroup of member states. Ukrainian interlocutors complained that these new driving dynamics tilted the EU away from a reliance on principled norms and rules to a geopolitics of expedient trade-offs. To them, the trade-off implicitly forced by Germany and France, and supported by some other member states, was unacceptable: Crimea and Donbas as the price for moving modestly towards the West. Ukrainians did not perceive Germany to be an impartial mediator; its foreign policy was characterised by 'Donbasisation' to the detriment of unequivocal support to resolve the conflict on terms favourable to Ukraine.[21]

Impact

In Crimea, the EU failed to pre-empt Russia's incisive move, even though some observers had begun to raise concerns over the fragility of the territory's political position. After the events of the preceding six months, the EU could no longer have the excuse of not being aware of how far Russia was willing to immerse itself in Ukrainian politics. Donors admitted that they began to focus on east–west bridge-building in Ukraine far too late. If the deal reached to keep President Yanukovich in power was conceived to head-off Russian incursions, it failed to do so.[22]

As Ukraine and Russia then hunkered down into a low-level conflict of attrition, the EU laid out red lines that were successively pushed back.[23] Germany and France effectively offered Russia a role in the joint management of Ukraine-related challenges. Member states differed on whether this was merely an uncomfortable tactical setback or a major structural defeat for EU security.

[21] A. Getmanchuk and S. Solodkyy, *Ukraine-Germany: How to Turn Situational Partnership into Priority One*, Kiev: Institute for World Policy, 2016, p. 9.

[22] M. Laurinavcius, L. Kascijnas and L. Kajola, 'What will determine Ukraine's future scenariois?', *Eastern Pulse Newsletter* 3/58, Eastern European Studies Centre, Vilnius, 2014, p. 3.

[23] L. Freedman, 'Ukraine and the art of exhaustion', *Survival*, 57/5, 2015, 77–106.

If the conflict was ultimately about some kind of autonomous status for Donbas, it must count as a failure that outside actors failed to prevent such extensive loss of life, violence and tragedy over such an eminently reachable settlement. Of course, many in Kiev and in some European capitals doubted that this was really what the conflict was about. They charged the Kremlin with seeking to use its new eastern foothold to unsettle the whole of Ukraine and pull it back from any significantly deeper partnership with the West. Russia preserved more influence over Kiev by keeping Donbas inside Ukraine than if eastern regions had broken away. Sceptics feared the EU focus on special status for parts of Donbas naïvely played into the Kremlin's agenda. Some member states believed that decentralisation could play a stabilising role that it was simply not capable of playing. While Ukrainians pushed the EU to decouple decentralisation from the Minsk agreements, France and Germany moved in the opposite direction, relying increasingly on just such a link.

As 2016 drew to a close, it was unclear whether the situation in Donbas had settled into a new, uneasy but sustainable equilibrium, or whether further violence was inevitable. This uncertainty made it difficult to evaluate EU policy in any definitive sense. It did seem clear, however, both that Russia now enjoyed a more embedded presence within parts of Ukraine and, conversely, that the limits to Russia's own power had been revealed. Without the European diplomacy detailed in this chapter, Ukraine would have been exposed to far greater geostrategic risk; with a more clearly enunciated EU geopolitics, Ukraine's fragility and insidious conflict could have been less debilitating.

9 *Ukraine III: Supporting Reform*

European governments and diplomats constantly repeated the refrain that the EU could most effectively temper Russian influence and power by helping Ukraine to be a strong and democratic state. Rhetorically, European diplomats argued that supporting political reform across Ukraine was the key to pushing back against Russia. It was such reform that would disrupt the political channels that had long benefited Russian political and economic interests in Ukraine. The EU insisted that building a successful Ukraine was the best way of undercutting sympathy for separatists in the east. This rhetorical line encapsulated a reform-as-geopolitics strategy – one aspect of the liberal-redux geopolitics category outlined in Chapter 2.

This chapter assesses how far the EU fulfilled its promise to support political reform and push Ukraine towards becoming a cleaner, more efficient and accountable state. The EU and member states offered many new projects of positive support to assist Ukraine's reform efforts and also sought a carefully calibrated use of conditionality to overcome the still-significant resistance to democratisation from Ukrainian vested interests. The chapter finds that the EU favoured particular routes to and types of reform that it judged most appropriate for a set of rationalised geostrategic considerations. The account also records Ukrainian perspectives on EU support for the reform process. The chapter concludes by relating the precise forms of EU reform support to liberal-redux geopolitics, and by pointing to areas of increased European impact over Ukraine's internal political developments.

Reform Trends

Taking office after elections in May 2014, new president Petro Poroshenko committed to a far-reaching process of economic and political reform. While the old, pre-Maidan parliament had initially blocked or diluted many reform proposals, elections in October 2014 brought in a more reformist legislature. Over half of MPs and four-fifths of ministers were now new faces. The new reformist Samopovich party finished in third place – behind the parties of Poroshenko and Prime Minister Arseny Yatsenuk. A group of 'Euro-optimist' MPs, made up of many former activists, provided a new link between civil society and party politics. A new National Reform Council gathered a wide range of stakeholders to take forward democratisation.

By 2016, over fifty major reform laws had been passed. The government set up six new anti-corruption institutions. Reforms included a new law to open up public procurement, for many years a major source of corruption. A new patrol police was rolled out across a number of cities to quell disorder. Laws were signed that strengthened judicial independence and parliamentary control of the security forces. The president presented his appointment of former Georgian President Mikheil Saakashvili as governor of the Odessa region as a major commitment to anti-corruption policies. New laws increased transparency in media ownership, parliamentary votes and customs management. In late 2015, the government introduced a law providing public funds for political parties, to reduce the influence of oligarchs. A civil service reform agreed in early 2016 promised to depoliticise state institutions and cut public sector payrolls by a third.

The government brought down inflation from over 50 per cent to under 10 per cent, increased currency reserves and cut energy subsidies. Economic reforms included major reductions in government spending. Public sector employment was cut, pensions and wage increases were capped and the government reduced subsidies in several sectors. A round of anti-corruption, economic and governance reforms cleared the way for IMF funding in August 2015, along with a write-off of 5 per cent of Ukraine's debt. Private creditors also agreed to write off 20 per cent of their debt in August 2015.

Ukrainian civil society was engaged in a more critical and sustained fashion than it had been after the first Maidan revolution in 2004. Civic activism embraced a much wider range of actors than the kind of professionalised NGOs that had led the Orange revolution. This time, a broader swathe of middle-class individuals had become politically active. The sense of Ukrainian identity strengthened. In the wake of the Maidan protests, the country addressed the challenge of forming a modern democratic state and a nation at the same time – processes that were separated by hundreds of years in Western Europe.

Notwithstanding all these changes, the pace and reach of reform disappointed many. While a significant amount of new legislation was passed, fundamental reform of governance structures was more limited. A familiar problem emerged of formally democratic laws being passed, but not fully implemented. The general consensus was that resistance to reform remained strong from within ministerial bureaucracies. The reform dynamic was still about a particular faction colonising state positions in the name of reform, rather than a fundamentally different set of rules. Most posts in the government were still bought. Civil society had come to fill the gap left by a still-dysfunctional state.[1]

After Ukraine returned to the 2004 constitution – which limited presidential power – wider issues of constitutional reform did not advance. There was no effort to strengthen the separation of powers or to clarify the division of responsibilities between president and prime minister. Some feared that Ukraine was drifting towards de facto super-presidentialism. The executive still exerted greater control over parliament than vice versa. Opposition within parliament was even weaker than before 2013. There was no increase in internal party democracy. Observers talked of the president creating a new 'power vertical', as he tightened control over many parts of the state. Many anti-corruption cases were blocked in the prosecutor general's office, controlled by a shadowy ally of the president. As indicated in the previous chapter, the government failed to win parliamentary assent for decentralisation reforms in early 2016.

The early months of 2016 were dominated by a political crisis that diverted the reform process. The economy minister resigned, bemoaning the slow pace of reform. Three out of five parties left the coalition and the government collapsed. Poroshenko eventually succeeded in pushing Yatsenuk out of office in April 2016, appointing a loyal acolyte, Volodymyr Grosyman as replacement prime minister. A new coalition was made up of only two parties and sufficient independent MPs to garner a parliamentary majority. The bitter haggling left the pro-reform parliamentary coalition severely weakened; power was more centralised in the hands of the president. In May 2016, Poroshenko controversially appointed a political ally lacking any legal background

[1] M. Minakov, 'Corrupting civil society in post-Maidan Ukraine', *Carnegie Russia Eurasia Outlook*, 11 April 2015.

or qualification as new prosecutor general. The new prime minister managed to stabilise the political crisis but the pace of reform slackened in the second half of 2016. In July 2016, the death of a prominent journalist gave rise to concerns over government intimidation of the media. In October 2016, Saakashvili resigned, citing the government's unwillingness to bear down on corruption as his reason. Many Ukrainian NGOs were so disillusioned with the reform process that they intimated a third Maidan uprising.

Ukraine's deep-rooted oligarchic power dynamics were difficult to dislodge. To some extent the pluralistic competition between oligarchs had assisted the Maidan breakthrough; the oligarchs had turned against President Yanukovich as he hoarded ill-gotten economic rent for his own family clan.[2] However, from mid-2014 onwards, many oligarchs frustrated democratic reform. Several flirted with separatists as a means of enhancing their leverage over the administration in Kiev. Oligarchs' control over the media tightened. The Kiev government was reluctant to implement reforms detrimental to these vested interests.

Politics in parliament were still structured around groupings of loyalties to particular oligarchs. Ukraine's pluralism was one of competing oligarchs more than competing ideologies. Opposition parties remained the personal projects of different oligarchs and failed to develop alternative ideological or programmatic identities.[3] Oligarchs still controlled whole groups of MPs. Poroshenko eventually removed the oligarch governor of Dniepopotrovesk, Ihor Kolomoisky. He insisted this was a first step towards tackling the oligarchs; government critics said it was merely a case of the president, himself an oligarch, removing an increasingly powerful opponent.

The Donbas conflict both helped and hindered democratic reforms. On the one hand, it created a sense of solidarity in adversity, which meant that the five-party government coalition held together for longer than many expected. On the other hand, the war bred a fear that pushing ahead too hard with sensitive and costly reform would debilitate resistance and unity in the east. Critics charged Poroshenko with using

[2] M. Laurinavcius, L. Kascijnas and L. Kajola, 'What will determine Ukraine's future scenariois?', *Eastern Pulse Newsletter* 3/58, Eastern European Studies Centre, Vilnius, 2014, p. 3.

[3] I. Lyubashenko, 'Democracy in a time of war', *New Eastern Europe*, 26 October 2014.

the security situation in the east as a pretext for delaying reforms.[4] Civic engagement was directed towards the conflict, through a wave a volunteerism; local activists lamented that this diverted civil society attention from democratic reforms. A big challenge remained: to merge irregular paramilitary volunteers into the national security forces. A growing strain of military-edged nationalism was evident among Ukrainian civil society.

Overall, the government implemented select and *ad hoc* measures of change but failed to define a comprehensive reform agenda. Even if oligarchs were not quite so prominently in charge, the influence of nepotistic parliamentary networks if anything increased. Ukraine's long-standing dynamic of political-patronage rent distribution – the basis of all post-independence politics – persisted. The elite remained highly predatory. Ukrainian politics were long characterised as a pluralistic competition for rents; this pluralism militated against absolute authoritarianism but also against deep-rooted democratisation. Parts of Ukraine were still, even increasingly, in the grip of feudal clans, functioning on the basis of corrupt and clientelistic nepotism.

European Reform Initiatives

As outlined in Chapter 7, the EU offered Ukraine €11 billion of new funding. Of this, €8 billion were credits from the European Investment Bank (EIB) and European Bank for Reconstruction and Development (EBRD). Of the €3 billion in new development aid grants, the largest slice – €1.6 billion – was for macro-economic assistance. The EU offered another €350 million as direct budget support through a state-building contract. The Commission's contribution represented one of the biggest support packages ever offered anywhere in the world. The new programmes were designed and implemented in the record time of three months, using derogations from formal EU procedures. It was, one senior diplomat pointed out, a huge risk: while the interim government remained unproven, the EU felt that the geopolitical crisis was such that support needed to be delivered quickly.

The EU set up a Ukraine Support Group that met for the first time in July 2014. This was an unprecedented initiative to accompany reforms

[4] A. Moshes, *The War and Reforms in Ukraine, Can it Cope with Both?*, Finnish Institute for International Affairs, 2015.

across all major sectors in one country. As mentioned in the previous chapter, the EU Advisory Mission added another layer of technical advisory services in the spheres of police reform and law enforcement made up of both EU and Ukrainian police and legal advisors. The mission had a €13 million budget for 2015. Senior officials in the mission's Kiev headquarters spoke in mid-2015 of an increased involvement in the incipient constitutional reform process and ongoing efforts to reform the police. The mission had only one human rights expert (like other EU missions) and was focused mainly on the state's capacity for effective law enforcement; senior officials in the mission stressed that their mandate had been narrowed down, away from having a broad political or security character.

The EU drew up a roadmap with local civil society groups. The Association Agreement (AA) was to include a coordinating committee with Ukrainian civil society and the Economic and Social Committee. A €10 million programme for civil society was introduced to fund groups to monitor government reform commitments under the so-called state-building contract. This would 'support the establishment of a structured dialogue between the authorities and civil society'.[5] Officials in Kiev stated that a priority would be to support reconciliation work, as well as to monitor benchmarks attached to budget support. Several European donors – in particular the UK and the Commission – supported the National Reform Council in its efforts to get different parties agreed on a reform agenda.

In 2015, the EBRD launched an initiative for mentoring reforms, placing technical experts in ministries. The EU ran an €8 million project on judicial reform, taking the form of twinning experts in the ministry of justice. The EU and Ukraine jointly put in place an anti-corruption unit of over 30 detectives to investigate the potential misuse of EU funds. The Council of Europe's Venice Commission was the main player on rule of law issues. The EU Anti-Fraud office helped to set up anti-corruption structures. At the end of 2016, the EU announced another raft of anti-corruption and administrative reform support. Also in late 2016, a large EU civil society initiative began, designed to improve coordination between civic actors. The Union provided

[5] 'EU steps up support for civil society in Ukraine', EU Neighbourhood Info Centre, 16 September 2014. Available at: http://enpi-info.eu/maineast.php?id=38377&id_type=1&lang_id=450.

an important €110 million to support SMEs and entrepreneurship in Ukraine.[6] The EU defined Ukraine as being subject to a 'crisis declaration' that enabled the delegation in Kiev to identify projects proactively for some funding, outside the scope of calls for proposals.

The European Instrument for Democracy and Human Rights allocated around €1 million of additional funding. The European Endowment for Democracy supported Maidan activists in the setting up of political parties; it was also was one of the very few outside organisations that worked in Donbas; here it supported independent journalists to provide an alternative perspective on the conflict. The Commission stepped up support for the Black Sea NGO Forum; the crisis breathed new life into this initiative, which held its first large-scale meeting in Kiev in December 2014. One official highlighted that this reflected the aim to reinforce 'bottom-up, development-oriented' approaches to the geopolitical crisis, with a particular stress on regional cooperation around the Black Sea. The different strands of EU support are summarised in Table 2.

Increases in member state bilateral aid were more limited than the additional funds flowing through the Commission.[7] Only three member states were willing to extend bilateral loans to Ukraine.[8] Diplomats in Kiev reported that by the end of 2014, the US and Canada were the most prominent donors in most reform sectors. A collection of Open Society initiatives funded by George Soros aimed at monitoring and cohering the reform process seemed to gain far greater prominence than member states' efforts.

Nevertheless, several member states did increase their level of funding for reform projects in Ukraine. Germany announced a new €500 million package of support to Ukraine and increased support, especially for economic governance reforms. It gave a €25 million allocation to humanitarian aid as the crisis worsened. German priorities were: humanitarian aid; local elections and constitutional

[6] European Commission, 'Press release – International Conference on Support for Ukraine: EU announces €110 million benefiting SMEs and entrepreneurship in Ukraine', 28 April 2015. Available at: http://europa.eu/rapid/press-release_IP-15-4868_en.htm.

[7] Institute for World Policy, *How the World Helps Ukraine*, Kiev: Institute for World Policy, September 2014.

[8] F. Wesslau, 'EU needs to step up its game in Ukraine', *EU Observer*, 31 August 2015.

reform linked to the Minsk accord; and training border guards. Germany's reform initiatives were especially linked to the conflict, said its diplomats in Kiev. The German government supported Democracy Reporting International to run projects with youth and student groups to increase their engagement in the political reform process. By 2016, Germany was Ukraine's third largest door after the Commission and the US. A new government strategy proposal for Ukraine at the end of 2015 promised further upgrades, offsetting at least partially Kiev's perception of German 'neutrality' over Donbas.[9]

The Swedish development agency Sida built on a long-standing presence in Ukraine to find a niche role in providing more core support for around a dozen civil society organisations. Several recipients were well-established bodies that had been receiving funds for over a decade, such as the Kharkiv Human Rights Group and the Committee for Ukrainian Voters. At the same time, Sida sought to focus on new Maidan actors and, in particular, efforts to agglomerate efforts of the now-large number of NGOs active on similar reform issues. Another growing concern of Swedish support was grass-roots civic activism in the regions; support was forthcoming for a 'Marketplace' initiative designed to filter the positions of such local groups.

The UK's development agency DfID returned to Ukraine after a six-year absence, because of the crisis. It launched a £10 million programme focusing on economic governance, public finances, anti-corruption and election preparations, working in conjunction with the World Bank and German development agencies. From this total amount, a £4 million fund was for technical assistance to help implement government reform priorities. In addition, the UK's conflict pool made £11 million available for the OSCE mission, the EU Advisory Mission and peace-building efforts. Like other states, the UK had defence advisors embedded in the Ukrainian government. Denmark led a new anti-corruption project from September 2016. Poland was increasingly active in some reform sectors in 2015, although the continuity of this support was uncertain after the Law and Order party won power.

Donors and civil society organisations (both local and international) embarked on a raft of projects designed to build-bridges

[9] A. Getmanchuk and S. Solodkyy, *Ukraine-Germany: How to Turn Situational Partnership into Priority One*, Kiev: Institute for World Policy, 2016, p. 9.

between east and west. Many of these started but were interrupted by the violence in several eastern cities. Funds were made available for new EU centres in east Ukrainian universities, as a means of increasing understanding of the EU, thereby counteracting Russian media. EU officials in Kiev insisted that the worsening conflict dynamics in the east rendered support for local-level, grass-roots civic initiatives even more important as a counter-balance to security-focused geopolitical diplomacy.

European donors were not strongly focused on the lack of internal party democracy, the main impediment to a less-personalised party system; a number of US organisations prioritised this area of reform more systematically than any European donor. One issue was that several recipients of European support decided to stand for election; donors worried that this was premature, as they were likely to see their credibility as civic organisations undermined. Donors worried that their various initiatives aimed at bringing civil society organisations together were being undone as political rivalries sharpened.

By means of comparison, the US development agency, USAID allocated around $250 million to Ukraine. This was negligible compared to the EU's overall €11 billion figure, but according to diplomats in Kiev US aid grants played a prominent role in relation to key aspects of democratisation. USAID counted on 120 staff in Ukraine and a new high-level appointment to give more coherent political direction to US aid on the ground. Practitioners in Kiev spoke of the focus moving back towards US initiatives on the most sensitive questions of political reform.

Pressure and Conditionality

As political developments unfolded, so the EU's attempts to exert influence evolved. One of the most important debates between member states was over the degree of conditionality that should be used to encourage reforms. Perspectives on conditionality were increasingly informed by geopolitical considerations. The EU and member states sought to strike a balance between leniency designed to help a much-beleaguered new administration and pressure for overdue reform. Some member states expressly saw the question of conditionality through the lens of their relationship with Russia.

Table 2: ***Summary of EU Support to Ukraine***

Type of Support	Amount, Instrument, Time Frame
Macro-financial assistance	€610 m: First package (Decision 2010) €1 bn: Second package (Decision 2014) €1.8 bn: Third package (Decision 2015)
CFSP-related actions	€42 m: Instrument contributing to Stability and Peace (election observation, OSCE Special Monitoring Mission, support to conflict-affected population and IDPs), 2014–2020 €15 m: Common Foreign and Security Policy (CFSP) 2015–2020
Trade support	€500 m/year: tariff reductions, 2014–2016 (estimate by the European Commission)
Technical and budgetary support	€355 mi State Building Contract ('Special Measure') 2014–2015 €70 m: Special Measure in Support of Private Sector Development and Approximation 2015 €1 bn (indicative): ENI, 2014–2020
Humanitarian aid	€42 m: European Commission 2014–2015
Investment project financing (Dependent on bankable projects)	Up to €3 bn: European Investment Bank, 2014–2020 Up to €5 bn: European Bank for Reconstruction and Development 2014–2020 €200–250 m: blending finance from Neighbourhood Investment Facility, 2015–2020
Civil society support	€10 m: Civil Society Support Programme, 'Special Measure' 2014–2015 €10 m civil society support, ENI, 2015–2020 €4.5 m: EIDHR, 2013–2017

Source: European Commission 2015, reproduced in J. Chromiec and N. Koenig, *Supporting Ukraine's difficult path towards reform*, Jaques Delors Institute, 2015, p. 16

The head of the National Reform Council highlighted that reforms were tightly moulded around the EU's 35 Copenhagen criteria; Ukraine's aim was to 'qualify for membership', whether or not member states were willing to grant an accession perspective. The EU required procurement and anti-bribery laws to be passed before authorising the release of IMF and Word Bank funds. These were seen as steps towards creating a stronger and more independent middle class in Ukraine. European embassies and the EU delegation in Kiev insisted that they pressed hard to reduce oligarchs' influence through applying strict conditionality in particular to opening up public procurement and various transparency initiatives. The EU also increased the number of individuals targeted by EU sanctions in connection with embezzlement of Ukrainian public funds – although in 2016 the European Court of Justice ruled that there were insufficient grounds for including several of these figures. The EU saw conditionality aimed at oligarchic power as an area where the EUs technical, economic governance rules could play a strategic role in giving the Ukrainian state greater resilience. A view commonly expressed by European diplomats was that offering additional money was not the main issue: Ukraine should be a rich country. Rather, the challenge was to get the huge amounts of money siphoned off by oligarchs re-invested in new projects to develop a stronger set of state structures.

The EU Court of Auditors insisted on a strict monitoring of whether the Ukrainian government was meeting benchmarks attached to EU budget support funds. A portion of these funds was held back at the end of 2014, in light of Venice Commission criticisms of new lustration and constitutional reform proposals. Indeed, the Venice Commission forced the government to backtrack on efforts to tighten its own control over the technical management of the judiciary at several stages. The EU also pressed President Poroshenko to rein back plans to use a new ministry of information for blatant propaganda to counter Russian tactics. Diplomats suggested funds might be held back if these plans extended too far and the ministry misused. EU officials insisted they wanted to see, in particular, actual corruption cases brought – not just formal reforms written – before releasing more money. Several big EU projects on aspects of administrative reform were delayed over disagreements with government authorities.

The 2014 ENP Country Progress Report for Ukraine contained strong criticism of delays to reform.[10] In mid-2015, the Council of Europe pushed the president to drop proposals that would give him stronger powers to disband local councils. The EU also pressed hard on the government's reluctance to implement full judicial independence, citing this as a reason for new funding being delayed. EU pressure increased as progress on implementing AA requirements was slow. The government alluded to more pressing priorities, especially in the realm of security. It also complained that external deadlines were taking precedence over those set internally by the coalition government itself.

EU diplomats said that the granting of the visa-free regime was by far their strongest leverage in pushing forward reforms. As Ukraine introduced the final pieces of anti-corruption and anti-discrimination legislation stipulated as a precondition to visa liberalisation, the EU still sought to push the implementation of reforms further before granting the new visa provisions. This caused considerable friction with the Ukrainian government in 2016. The government complained that the EU delayed granting visa liberalisation too long, and that the delay was serving not so much as useful leverage over reform as it was turning citizens against the EU. The Commission played a role in eventually putting a limit on the conditionality attached to the visa regime – against the efforts of some member states, nervous about additional migration inflows, to add to the more than 400 reform stipulations already included.

The EU's conditionality reflected a genuine concern with funds disappearing into a black hole of corruption. However, this focus also had a geopolitical corollary. Some member states' critical stance towards the Poroshenko government was connected to their desire to maintain a balance in their relations with Russia. Germany in particular became more critical of the Poroshenko government's record on reform, and this played into Berlin's increasing impatience to re-normalise relations with Russia. It was curious that countries like Spain and Italy insisted that strict conditionality be applied before Ukraine was rewarded, when these states pushed for a condition-free approach with partners in the southern Mediterranean. By 2016 reformist Ukrainian

[10] European Commission, *ENP Country Progress Report 2014 – Ukraine*, March 2015.

politicians feared that some member states were being overly critical of the government as a cover for keeping a distance from Kiev and giving primacy to relations with Russia. They also made this charge against the Support Group, whose reception was not generally positive amongst either Ukrainian officials or civil society.

The financier and philanthropist, George Soros caused a media stir when he criticised the EU for being too strict on conditionality. He accused the EU of insisting on reform as if the war in the east did not exist.[11] Diplomats disagreed with this assessment and insisted some degree of pressure was necessary to help reformers unblock progress on Ukraine's thorniest problems. Several locally based diplomats worried that the government lacked adequate absorption capacity for large-scale loans and grants.

Yet the EU and member states also insisted that on some questions the geopolitical situation with Russia pushed them towards greater flexibility. They sought to press forward reforms but were mindful of the broader strategic context with regard to Russia. Pressure needed to be firm enough to help reformers overcome vested interests, but not so onerous that it undermined an extremely fragile pro-reform coalition and inadvertently played into Russia's hands. Diplomats based in Kiev tended to feel that the likelihood of serious conflict was greater than member state governments back in European capitals realised or were willing to acknowledge.

A number of member state diplomats expressed the view that the new government should not be pushed too hard on economic and political conditions because of the short-term imperative of retaining stability and securing the association agreement. One member of the National Reform Council bemoaned the fact that behind closed doors most EU states sought to dissuade the government from implementing far-reaching and speedy reforms, to the extent that these might be inimical to stability. Diplomats generally argued for a flexible implementation of trade liberalisation requirements, in anticipation of Russia being able to blame future economic difficulties on the EU agreement. As detailed in Chapter 5, trade preferences were front loaded, offering immediate trade benefits prior to reforms being undertaken. The EU opened up its markets through autonomous trade preferences without waiting for the new government to implement reforms. This appeared

[11] G. Soros, 'Wake-up Europe!', *New York Review of Books*, October 2014.

to work, as Ukrainian exports to the EU increased 25 per cent in the six months after they were introduced.

Diplomats from some member states worried that the EU was pinning its hopes and credibility too exclusively to the new president. Officials based in Kiev acknowledged that conditions were not placed on specific areas of change like electoral reform, even where these were necessary for far-reaching democratisation. EU member states largely left the lead role on such reform to the Council of Europe, even though they acknowledged that the latter functioned at a relatively technical level and lacked political weight to put pressure on reform spoilers. The EU supported select aspects of constitutional reform related to the conflict, but did little to engage critically with the need for overarching change to embed a firmer separation of powers.[12]

The political crisis of 2016 sharpened the EU's dilemma and began to change member states' strategic calculations. The economy minister's resignation in February 2016 rang alarm bells in several European capitals. As the governing coalition appeared increasingly fragile and the possibility of early elections widely rumoured, many European diplomats expressed exasperation with the government. Others feared that pushing too hard would now push the government over the edge and that new elections would unleash a cycle of great political uncertainty. The UK now favoured a tougher use of conditionality. Those member states more sceptical of favouring Kiev, muttered their disapproval of the crisis and pushed for a tilt back towards a 'Russia first' strategy. The European Commission and member states indicated they would channel a lower share of their funds as budget support in order to increase their control over how Ukraine used aid.

Amidst the uncertainty, and with key reform pledges stalled, EU macro-economic aid was now held back – this aid being linked to a decision to delay a further tranche of IMF support. The EU postponed its summit with Ukraine in May due to the political crisis and reform delays. Once the worst of the political crisis passed, many European governments were keen to resume support, even though few reforms were taken forward towards the end of 2016. In September 2016, the IMF board agreed to release the delayed third tranche of funds for Ukraine. However an IMF mission to Ukraine at the end of November

[12] G. Sasse, *Constitution Making in Ukraine: Refocusing the Debate*, Brussels: Carnegie Europe, April 2016.

2016 concluded more critically that the government needed to do more before additional support was released. By the end of 2016, the full resumption of EU economic aid remained pending. Once again, the EU's delicate balance between leniency and pressure was evident.

Civil Society Perspectives

Ukrainian civil society representatives warmly welcomed their new European funds, but were not entirely positive in their assessment of EU reform support. Civic leaders concurred that peoples' expectations of the EU were now lower than in 2005. There was greater realisation that Ukrainians had to lead reform processes themselves, and that EU help could be useful but would always prioritise Europe's own interests. The absolute bottom-line for Ukrainian reformers was that the EU should deal with Ukraine as an independent nation-state directly and not via Russia.

In general, most Ukrainian reformers thought external donors were not capturing enough of the new local level civic activism that prospered after Maidan. A common refrain from civil society leaders was that the nature of civic activity was changing faster than Western donors were aware of. One civil society leader said: 'The EU needs to go back to the drawing board as it still does not understand Ukraine's power dynamics.' This became the standard critique. EU diplomats felt this was unfair, as they monitored trends to understand the nuances in such dynamics.

Significantly, most civil society organisations spoke of their concern that the EU was being too soft in its conditionality – that it was thinking in terms of supporting President Poroshenko rather than what was needed for far-reaching reform. While the EU relied on Prosohenko and Yatsensuk to lead the reform process, Ukrainians believed these two figures – each with their own extensive and shady business interests – to be reluctant to push democratisation beyond a certain point. The EU was seen as too ready to accept the government's line that the conflict made it necessary to delay reforms. The EU needed to press the government to grant civil society a more formalised role in policy-making.

Ukrainian civil society representatives worried that the EU moved back to relying on large amounts of direct budget support, devoid of conditionality. Ukrainians complained that too much aid was still going through the central government rather than local authorities that might be more committed to reducing corruption. Ukrainian civil society representatives complained that the Support Group was slow to get working and remained relatively inactive well into 2015. They judged the EU to be providing useful assistance but to be insufficiently proactive. Civil society leaders typically complained that it was still easier to get US funds for political objectives than it was to obtain European support. Even into 2016, civil society representatives were saying that the EU still under-estimated how much the government needed to be pushed to implement its reform promises.

NGOs in Kiev complained there was still not enough transparency in EU aid. They accused European donors of not doing enough to reach new and grass-roots civic groups. EU instruments were still not flexible enough and still too heavy in *acquis* approximation requirements. While Poland was the most welcomed provider of democracy support, there were some grumblings among recipients that it saw Ukraine too much through the lens of its own 'pacted' transition. One civic leader lamented: 'Euro-pessimism is growing in Ukraine.' Some centre-ground political figures in Kiev felt that the EU was not willing to engage with potentially new opposition forces emerging from the discredited Party of Regions – held by many to be necessary to a balanced and robust democratic pluralism – as donors were still drawn to a narrow sector of familiar NGO activists.

A constant criticism from Ukrainian reformers was that the EU failed to press hard on the government's delays to get an anti-corruption bureau working effectively. A group of civil society bodies pushed for a specialised law enforcement agency focused on high-level corruption and asked for the EU to put more pressure on the government to get this through parliament. Another struggle was to get the government to reform political party financing, as there was still little information on who financed which parties and the connections between various oligarchs and the parliament. While EU micro-assistance and the state building contract programme did include very specific anti-corruption provisions that reflected civil society demands, civic leaders in Kiev argued that the Union needed to put much more effort into monitoring and follow-up than it did between 2005 and 2013. These common Ukrainian views contrasted with external experts' complaint that by the end of 2016 the EU was stilling holding back its promises of really generous support despite Ukraine having fulfilled conditionality requirements.[13]

Ukrainian civil society organisations pleaded for more assertive EU pressure to defend the human and citizenship rights of Ukrainians in Crimea, as post-annexation repression increased in particular against the Tartar population. The EU did little to redress the increasingly brutal abuses suffered by Crimean Tartars – although the EED was active in Crimea. Local groups also thought the EU did little to protect civil society organisations in Donbas as civic leaders were hounded out of the region. Pro-democracy, pro-EU groups were sceptical of debates over 'minority linguistic rights', seeing the EU has being somewhat taken in by Russia on this question: Russian was already in full use and permissible formally in state bodies, with President Putin pushing this issue not as a minority rights question but as a means of extending the influence of the Russian state.

Most in Ukraine thought the EU should not support civil society in a neutral way and that it should be more geopolitical in backing pro-Europeans. Indeed, they were puzzled at the EU's reluctance to be explicit in this when Russia was pouring millions into creating its own 'civil society' in the east. One Ukrainian civic leader lamented in Kiev that European donors still needed to focus more on preparing NGOs for conflict prevention work in addition to more traditional human rights and anti-corruption work. NGO representatives from outside Kiev complained that they still got very little support. The EU did little to support the emergence of a new political elite, beyond its existing NGO and party interlocutors.

By 2016, a consensus view expressed by civil society organisations in Kiev was that there was by now almost too much technical assistance provided by external actors. The deficiency was not so much a shortage of technical expertise in Ukraine, but the EU's reluctance to put pressure on the high-level political obstacles to deeper reform – a constant theme in conversations in Kiev was that such pressure was coming from the US ambassador but not equally from his European counterparts. Civil society interlocutors recognised that by now

[13] A. Aslund, *Does Ukraine Receive the Western Aid it Deserves?* Waterloo, ON: Center for International Governance Innovation *Policy Brief* 92, November 2016.

European support was gaining critical mass, but that this relied too heavily on training and not enough on political pressure to unblock deep reform. They complained that external actors like the Venice Commission were asking Ukraine to adopt standardised templates of reform that were not tailored enough to the country's political specificities. Reformers stressed the lack of coordination and strategic focus in external support, and how most money was going to external advisors not core support for Ukrainian civic organisations.

Conclusion

As the dust of the Maidan uprising settled, reformers in Ukraine got down to the drawn out business of trying to install deep institutional change. Many vested interests stood in their way. Conflict in the east cast a complicating shadow over the democratic reform process. Unsurprisingly, some observers stressed the extent to which democratic reforms advanced, while others lamented the limits to political and economic change. The shifting sands of Ukraine's reform process raised issues for EU foreign policy responses that were closely related to the book's three core analytical concerns.

Categorisation

Crucially for our concern with identifying EU approaches to geopolitics, the precise way in which European support for economic and political reform was delivered reflected increasingly careful and subtle geopolitical deliberation. Most member states and the External Action Service saw upgraded support for democratic and economic reform as core to the EU's geopolitical comparative advantage over Russia. The EU sought to maximise a window for leverage as the government needed EU funds and agreements to show tangible results from its pro-European choice. Yet the EU was also mindful of the risk of instability and the strategic context that complicated the reform process. The EU inched towards a more considered degree of pressure and conditionality. It was also mindful of the need for inclusive reform in eastern Ukraine, reflecting a concern with stable and consensual reform. Such deliberations were not completely absent before 2014, but as Chapter 4 made clear the EU had not previously strategised so deeply on the complex links between reforms and geopolitics. From both EU and

Ukrainian perspectives, trade offs were juggled: the granular detail of the reform process was now not simply a matter of domestic politics but of regional geopolitics.

Foreign Policy Dynamics

Compared to the sphere of conflict management described in the previous chapter, EU-level institutions and instruments were a more prominent driver in support for Ukrainian political and economic reforms. This was the sphere where standard EU processes and initiatives came closest to acting as the leading edge of overall European responses to the eastern crisis. EU-level actorness was more important for reform support than member state initiatives. At the same time, the way in which many of these familiar EU initiatives were rolled out and fine-tuned suggested an increasingly instrumental and purposive logic to EU policy-making. Curiously, this logic both propelled a firmer backing for deep reform and gave EU policy certain *limiting* features. Support for Ukrainian reform was based on strong elements of embedded internal EU processes and policy orientations but also entailed more tangible reaction to external strategic factors than had been evident before 2013.

Impact

The EU assisted Ukrainian reforms in valuable and often generous ways. Prominent critics insisted the scale of EU support was woefully inadequate and that the Greek crisis simply took further funds and attention away from Ukraine, even though the latter should have been the greater priority.[14] By 2016 this looked like a harsh judgment. While assistance for Ukrainian reform was not what dominated the headlines, it was where the EU's impact was greatest.

In many arenas of reform, the EU leveraged significant influence. President Poroshenko needed to demonstrate a commitment to democracy to keep a wavering Europe engaged; in response to European pressure he pushed through areas of reform the government was initially reluctant to implement. Reforms to areas like public

[14] G. Soros, 'Ukraine and Europe: What should be done?' *New York Review of Books*, October 2015.

procurement undoubtedly owed much to constant EU pressure. Yet, the EU could not help surmount some of the obstacles to Ukrainian reform. While it offered much useful support for reform it grappled uncertainly with the challenge posed by Ukraine's resilient oligarchs. The EU struggled to find a way of engaging with key oligarchs and enticing them to accept rule of law improvements. The EU's concern to see a reform process marshalled to geopolitical imperatives led it to rely heavily on a small number of reformist ministers and politicians; European support made a more modest contribution to widening out the pro-reform constituency in a way that would keep democratic change moving forward.

By the end of 2016, Ukraine had not fully democratised; its economic reforms had not been entirely successful and the weakening of the pro-reform coalition threatened to reverse many of the gains made since 2013. The political regime changed, but the structures of the Ukrainian state less so. The EU hoped the former would lead to the latter, but its approach to reform failed to usher in deep-rooted democratic change; much more time would be needed for the EU to have this kind of qualitative impact on Ukrainian political and economic systems. The Ukraine crisis suggested that state- and regime-change needed to proceed simultaneously to produce resilience and stability. The EU now worked harder to engineer such a holistic reform process. Often, however, it was reduced by circumstances and its own mind-set to more *ad hoc* reform initiatives that fell short of playing such a role.

More broadly, this chapter shows how debates over reform and the Donbas conflict sometimes stood at odds with each other. Many Ukrainians insisted that the clearest division in Ukraine was not between east and west but between reformers and anti-reform vested interests. In this sense, the challenge of supporting reform did not always sit easily with the EU's approach to containing the Donbas conflict. As both reform and conflict dynamics stumbled unsteadily though 2016, the eastern crisis presented with the EU with increasingly thorny geopolitical trade-offs.

10 *The Impact on Other Eastern Partners*

The eastern crisis was not only about Ukraine. Geopolitical aftershocks also rippled outwards from eastern Ukraine to the other five Eastern Partnership (EaP) states. This chapter shows how the EU shifted its strategy and aims towards Georgia, Moldova, Armenia, Belarus and Azerbaijan – taking the EaP states in the order of how positively engaged and cooperative each partner was with the European Union (EU). The chapter finds that EU responses to the wider EaP region corresponded to the liberal-redux category of geopolitics and that they entailed bounded changes to European foreign-policy dynamics. The EU sought to find new modes of engagement and rapprochement with EaP states, but also sought to dampen expectations of how far its offers of strategic alliance would extend. The EU's policy awkwardly sought both to embrace EaP partners and keep them at bay; to demonstrate solidarity with them and acknowledge Russia's role in the region. After 2013, there was greater variation in EU policy towards the five states than there had been before the crisis started. The forms and tactics of EU cooperation were increasingly moulded with geopolitical imperatives in mind. The eastern crisis pushed the EU's policies in EaP states in contrasting directions, depending in large measure on the domestic political conditions of each country. The crisis had a profound impact on EU strategy but was not sufficient to propel a radically altered or clearly defined form of EU geopolitics in the EaP region.

Georgia

The crisis with Ukraine arrived at a moment when the EU's relations with Georgia stood at a moment of re-definition. The Georgian Dream coalition won parliamentary elections in October 2012 and presidential polls a year later, ejecting the mercurial Mikhail Saakashvili from power. Georgian Dream was the creation of billionaire businessman

Bridzna Ivanishvili. The new coalition's victory raised hopes that democratic reforms would be revived after Saakashvili's government had become increasingly autocratic in its final years. However, Georgian politics remained highly personalised under the Georgian Dream government. Moreover, the legacy of Russia's 2008 invasion lingered on. In the summer of 2014 Russia used various tactics to engineer changes of leadership in the territories of Abkhazia and South Ossetia, to leave in place more pro-Moscow administrations.

The EU had provided the pro-Western Saakashvili with much support after he led the Rose Revolution in 2003. The Commission doubled its aid package to Georgia immediately after the revolution. The EU was relatively silent on Saakashvili's gradual undermining of democratic checks and balances. The Russia-Georgia war in 2008 belatedly encouraged European governments to focus more on the country's security vulnerabilities, as well as the weakness of Georgia's democratic institutions. The EU pushed the government to offer dialogue and policy coordination with the opposition. Tensions grew with Saakashvili as his model of deregulation clashed with EU rules and regulations.

The EU and member states played a role in ensuring parliamentary elections in late 2012 were free and fair and that Saakashvili accepted defeat. Nevertheless, the change of government presented the EU with a challenge. The Georgian Dream coalition included both pro-European parties and Russia-leaning nationalist parties hostile to the EU.[1] The new government bent to these parties' illiberal views. The church played a powerful role in the ascendant agenda of conservative social values. Ivanishvili displayed a strongly populist streak. His personal influence and financial resources served to hollow out political parties.

The new government lowered the temperature of Georgia's fraught relations with Russia. The two countries resumed trade after a six-year interruption. Yet, the government quickly stressed that events in Ukraine should lead Europe to speed up the process of integrating Georgia with the EU. The new government immediately discussed with EU leaders how to strengthen economic cooperation. Joining NATO was now even more of a priority for some Georgian ministers. Georgia signed an agreement on cooperation with EU security and

[1] S. Cornell, *Getting Georgia Right*, Brussels: Centre for European Studies, 2014, p. 46.

defence policies at the Vilnius summit. EU policy-makers worked on an active 'association agenda' to guide relations after the signing of the Association Agreement (AA), focused on measures that would bring quick, concrete benefits to Georgia.

Geopolitical concerns intensified. After signing the AA, Georgian leaders hoped the EU would be more obliged to confront Russia's determination to push the enclaves' boundaries deeper into Georgia. Russian troops resumed the construction of barbed wire fences along a buffer zone close to South Ossetia. Foreign Minister Maia Panjikidze said the events 'deepen our suspicion that Russia is preparing many provocations before the association agreement is signed'. The prospects for further Russian pressure on Georgia intensified. The government was cautious in its statements about the events in Ukraine so as not to antagonise Moscow.[2] Complete freedom for Georgia's civic sphere was still held back because of Russian infiltration.

Counter-balancing the desire to deepen relations with Georgia in response to Ukrainian events were the EU's concerns over political trends. The EU exerted pressure to rein the government back from a politicisation of the justice system, as a number of ministers from the former government were detained and thousands of opposition party members questioned; eventually Saakashvili himself was called for trial. An EU special advisor on constitutional and legal reform worked with the administration on judicial reform. EU diplomats stressed that rule of law conditionality was now becoming tighter, as the issue of selective justice came under closer scrutiny. In the European Parliament, the European Peoples' Party – closely allied to Saakashvili – sought to ramp up the pressure on Georgian Dream.

While the EU was concerned over democratic conditions in Georgia, it was now more anxious to move forward with signing the AA as quickly as possible. Some member state diplomats suggested that the EU was turning too much of a blind eye to the new government's somewhat undemocratic use of the legal system in order to rush through the agreement. The US was notably more critical towards Georgian Dream than was the EU. The EU addressed political concerns through new aid initiatives designed to promote transparency and state reform.

[2] J. Parkinson, 'Uneasy Georgia waits for Russia reaction to Ukraine', *Wall Street Journal*, 25 February 2014.

The European Commission and Georgia launched negotiations for the country's accession to the Energy Community.

Georgians talked of 'creeping occupation'. The Geneva International Discussions on Georgia's breakaway regions of Abkhazia and South Ossetia, co-chaired by representatives from the EU, UN, and OSCE, became more fraught and even less productive.[3] The Georgian government criticised EU member states for using Russia's occupation as a reason for holding back new cooperation, on the grounds that Georgia was now a 'divided territory'. While the US came out in favour of now offering Georgia a NATO Membership Action Plan, the majority of EU member states were against this. France and Germany were particularly prominent in dashing Georgia's NATO aspirations. The Georgian government pushed without success for NATO to deploy defensive assets in Georgia in response to Russia's actions in Ukraine. Georgians berated the EU for leaving Ukraine unprotected, increasing support within Georgia for an accommodating line towards Russia.

While cautious on these security issues, EU member states supported an acceleration of the AA. The agreement was signed at the historic EU summit in June 2014. Georgia and the EU signed an accord to provide Georgia with €19 million to help implement the agreement. About 80 per cent of the Deep and Comprehensive Free Trade Area (DCFTA) came into force in September 2014. The EU allocated €30 million to Georgia under its 'more for more' mechanism of positive conditionality and pledged to increase its financial assistance to Georgia for the period 2014–2017, well beyond the €450 million allocated in 2007–2013. Georgia was included in a range of EU cultural, social and technical programmes. It received a €50 million macro-financial loan from the European Union in mid-2015. However, Georgia's quest for an EU membership perspective was not successful.

The EU's focus on political developments inside Georgia continued to balance concerns over democratic standards against encroaching Russian influence. The EU stressed the need to strengthen the independence of the judiciary, as well as the accountability and democratic oversight of law enforcement agencies. In late 2015, Georgian civil society was given scrutiny over implementation of the DCFTA. After heated local elections in July 2014 and further political arrests, the EU

[3] *RFE/RL*, 19 June 2014.

Ambassador to Georgia Philip Dimitrov said that the signing of the AA did not mean that 'everything else ... is guaranteed'. This was widely taken to be a warning over the EU's willingness to withhold visa-free travel.[4] The Commission successfully pushed the government to adopt anti-discrimination legislation and a National Human Rights Strategy as part of the conditionality attached to the EU's Visa Liberalisation Action Plan. As a result, the Commission formally proposed that Georgia be granted a visa liberalisation agreement in March 2016. Demonstrating the EU's dilemmas, in the very same week the Georgian Dream government introduced legislation banning gay marriage, leaving many EU member states uneasy about upgrading cooperation.

Indeed, the Georgian Orthodox Church obstructed many 'liberal' reforms associated with the European Union. Priests triggered protests against Georgia importing EU anti-discrimination laws. Some parts of the Church had close ties to the Russian Orthodox Church and were a channel for Russian influence – although other parts were suspicious of Russian designs on Georgia. Opinion in Georgia was becoming more polarised. There was an increase in the number of pro-Russian rallies. Russian TV channels reached a wide audience within Georgia. Despite this, a May 2014 poll showed that Georgians' support for EU membership remained strong. Two thirds of Georgians agreed that Georgia should join the EU rather than the Eurasian Union.[5]

A political crisis rocked Georgia during the final months of 2014, as the Free Democrats party left the Georgian Dream coalition. The tensions were closely related to Georgia's difficulties in trying to pursue its goals of joining NATO and the EU without antagonising Moscow. The defence minister was dismissed after warning that the government was putting at risk Georgia's Euro-Atlantic course. The foreign minister and minister for European and Euro-Atlantic Integration resigned.

The US condemned the crisis as another step in the political manipulation of the judiciary. The EU was more equivocal. Federica Mogherini praised the government for 'further important progress' in the country's democratic development.[6] However, European leaders

4 M. Ellena, 'Georgia: Does rise of Euro-skeptics spell trouble for Tbilisi?', *EurasiaNet.org*, 15 July 2014, Available at: www.eurasianet.org/node/69031.

5 'NDI Survey: "More people see Russia as threat to Georgia"', *Georgia Today*, 9 May 2014. Available at: www.georgiatoday.ge/article_details.php?id=12227.

6 T. Schumacher, 'Letter from Tbilisi', *Open Democracy*, 2 December 2014.

became increasingly impatient as cooperation and reforms both seemed to stagnate. Georgia stalled on implementing many EU laws as it concluded that adaptation costs were high relative to the expected gains; this applied, for example, in the crucial energy sector. The EU reacted with strong criticism when the government attempted to take over control of Georgia's most independent and critical television station in what developed into another major domestic scandal at the end of 2015.

In November 2014, Russia and Abkhazia signed a Treaty on Alliance and Strategic Partnership. This foresaw the integration of Abkhazia into Russia. A similar treaty with South Ossetia followed. Against this background, the Georgian government complained that the EU's position of not recognising the enclaves but wanting to maintain engagement with them was increasingly untenable. Member states still disagreed on Abkhazia and South Ossetia, with Poland and Lithuania explicitly giving these the status of illegally occupied territories, but other member states like Germany reluctant to take this step.

The EU monitoring mission (EUMM), present since 2008, was hamstrung and several humanitarian organisations were denied access to South Ossetia and Abkhazia (although the United Nations Development Programme retained a presence in the latter). Russia refused to work with the EUMM in withdrawing its troops. As Russia stationed additional guards, France and Germany got the EUMM scaled back in size, with a budget cut from 26 million for 2014 to 18 million for 2015 and a 20 per cent reduction in staff. In March 2015, Moscow deployed soldiers to the border between Georgia and Abkhazia, because of Georgia's refusal to sign a non-use of force agreement against the breakaway region. The EU did not respond in any tangible fashion. Georgia complained it was not getting high-level weapons supplies from the West as Russia pushed the enclave borders further into its territory – although France signed a notable weapons sale with Georgia in 2015 and the NATO Training Centre was carried forward. Overall the EU position became more defensive as Russian proceeded with de facto 'absorption' of the two territories and new nationality laws in the enclaves forced out many ethnic Georgians.

Georgians' views of EU policies became more critical. Civil society leaders in Tbilisi feared that the EU's ambivalence in the crisis undermined support for 'European values'. Georgian NGOs insisted that, despite bringing forward the AA, the EU was 'losing Georgia'.

Most interlocutors in Tbilisi perceived the 2015 ENP review to be about 'accommodating Russia'. Georgians on both sides of the political divide routinely insisted that their country stood on the front-line between the West and Russia and thought the EU failed to understand this. They criticised the EU for moving back towards a strategy based on geography rather than on norms. European governments seemed to conclude that Georgia's territorial disputes made EU and NATO rapprochement even less advisable, not more necessary.[7]

One Georgian reformer observed that the EU was now very carefully balancing criticism and help, pushing reform on the one hand, while showing flexibility to shore up sovereignty on the other hand – a policy mix driven by a very much more geopolitical mind-set. While EU officials criticised the government's failure to follow through on its own promises to relinquish political control over the judiciary, they acknowledged their desire to reward Georgia as the most successful of the EaP states – and to avoid doing anything that could push the country towards Russia, especially as pro-Russian parties gained support in the run up to the autumn 2016 elections. In the event, Georgian Dream won these elections. While it continued in power without any apparent commitment to advance political reform, in October 2016 EU member states finally assented to move ahead with the long-delayed visa accord. Deeper political reform was a means of closing the space for Russian influence; but if pushed too assertively it could also rebound to the EU's disadvantage. In sum, the focus on reform was both the EU's geopolitical advantage and its potential Achilles Heel vis-à-vis Russia.

Moldova

Political turmoil in Moldova was a sobering geopolitical setback and divided EU member states. Before Moldova's 2009 civic uprising the EU was relatively soft on the government's questionable democratic commitment. Moldova was the highest per capita aid recipient in the whole neighbourhood after the Occupied Palestinian Territories. Most aid went direct to the government in the form of budget support, with very little to civil society organisations. Moldova was the first country

[7] T. German, 'Heading west? Georgia's Euro-Atlantic path', *International Affairs*, 2015, p. 608.

to be granted a pilot Mobility Partnership in 2008. The EU made tepid offers to mediate a solution for Russian-controlled Transnistria, but apart from a few travel bans against officials from the latter region, the EU did little to press any particular outcome.

The EU was critical of President Voronin's violent crackdown on protestors after the latter disputed the results of elections in April 2009. However, the EU's main focus was on mediation between the Communist government and opposition, through the figure of an EU special representative. The EU feared that if Voronin did not agree to an acceptable exit plan he would call in more direct support from Moscow. Opposition forces complained that the EU made it harder for them to secure a full democratic breakthrough by in effect giving Voronin the benefit of the doubt in the disputed elections. The Romanian government slated its European partners for agreeing new cooperation with Moldova under the Eastern Partnership just as the regime crackdown was taking place.

After elections were eventually re-run later in 2009 the EU backed an opposition-led coalition that took power, the Alliance for European Integration. The EU granted Moldova €300 million of aid for 2011–2013, in per capita terms one of the most generous aid allocations anywhere in the world. The unwieldy nature of the new coalition militated against stable government. In-fighting and oligarchic nepotism prevailed, even as the new administration made a raft of commitments to adopt EU laws and harmonise national legislation around European standards. After the government was defeated in a vote of confidence in early 2013, progress under a caretaker government slowed even further, before a reassembled Pro-European Coalition formed a new government in May 2013. Significantly, these governance pathologies kept the door open to Russian influence through shady business dealings with Moldovan oligarchs in various positions of power.

Moldova reacted to the Russia-Ukraine crisis with the clearest pro-European conviction of all EaP states. The coalition government exited a protracted internal crisis and redoubled its commitment to meeting EU reform requirements and targets for harmonising local laws with EU standards. In November 2013, a huge pro-EU demonstration took place in Chişinau. Russian attempts to destabilise the new government intensified in late 2013 and into 2014.

The EU increased pressure on Transnistria to accept EU rules to access cooperation initiatives and beefed up a border mission to stifle illegal activities upon which the enclave depended. The EU insisted that its EUBAM border mission became more active in reducing trafficking at the border and in galvanising rules convergence between Transnistria and Moldova. The EU presented this dynamic of rules convergence as its main contribution to conflict resolution – one based on norms and inclusion. The hope was that the conflict would be solved through a process of Europeanisation. The EU approach was to reach out to actors in Transnistria to address their concerns. Angela Merkel supported the notion of security dialogue with Russia partly with this case in mind. Yet, the broader geopolitical context provoked cool reactions from Russia and the EaP dynamic failed to shift embedded positions.[8]

In 2014 and 2015, Russian intimidation intensified. Russia threatened to expel Moldovan workers, and generally sought to provoke Moldova into taking rash action in Transnistria so that the EU would be obliged to withdraw cooperation. Russia imposed sanctions on Moldovan wine, and threatened restrictive measures in more sectors. It pushed to have Moldova ejected from the EU energy community. As an enticement, Russia offered €60 million for infrastructure projects. The EU's fear was that Russia would take control of Transnistria after Moldova signed its AA – although Moscow sought to dissuade Transnistrian demands formally to join Russia.[9]

The EU stepped up cooperation. A 'European package' discussed among EU officials in February 2014 included specific proposals for high-level diplomatic visits to Chisinau and public diplomacy efforts to highlight the AA's economic benefits. The EU offered Moldova a visa-free regime in March 2014. A sign of firmness was that the EU advanced with AA preparations even as Russian officials and ministers ratcheted up their threats to annex Transnistria should this agreement be signed.

As with Georgia, the signing of Moldova's AA was brought forward. The EU announced a new annual support package for Moldova. This aimed at supporting the modernisation of key public institutions in charge of implementing the AA and DCFTA. The EUs Single Support

[8] T. Tudoroiu, 'The European Union, Russia, and the future of the Transnistrian frozen conflict', *East European Politics and Societies* 26, 2012, p. 135.

[9] S. Secrieirn, *Can Moldova Stay on the Road to Europe?* London: European Council for Foreign Relations, 2014.

Framework set out strategic objectives and priorities for future EU-Moldova cooperation in 2014–2017.[10] The EU supported an initiative to re-export (Russian) gas from Romania to Moldova to reduce the country's dependence on direct Russian supplies. Some member states also increased support. In April, Romania released €100 million of financial aid to Moldova. Poland released €12 million in grants and €100 million in credits. Angela Merkel promised that Germany would provide Chisinau with all the necessary support against Russia.[11]

The new EU measures did not entirely satisfy either the government or public opinion. Against the backdrop of Russian actions, the absence of a membership perspective weighed more heavily. Moldovan Deputy Prime Minister, Natalia Gherman, argued that an EU membership perspective was now even more 'a matter of urgent necessity'.[12] Notwithstanding its formal neutrality, Moldova looked for enhanced practical cooperation with NATO. New political dialogue was agreed with NATO, along with technical cooperation. European governments were, however, wary of developing an overtly securitised focus and diluted the extent of this cooperation. They were keen to silence any Romanian talk of re-unification, so as to avoid provoking Russia.

While the EU made efforts to deepen cooperation and accelerate implementation of the AA, Moldova's domestic situation looked increasingly parlous. The AA was sped up in part to ensure that the agreement was ratified before elections in the autumn of 2014. The Communist party was predicted to do well in these elections and thereafter aim to slow the process of EU integration. Visa liberalisation was granted explicitly to help the pro-EU Alliance. This appeared to work, as the latter's sagging popularity held firm. Yet problems persisted: corruption, lack of judicial independence and weak, squabbling political parties. Many in the EU remained doubtful that the government had the will fully to implement the AA.

In a referendum in the autonomous region of Gagauzia, 95 per cent of voters supported integration with the Eurasian Union. The Moldovan parliament amended the country's election code to ban local

[10] EU Neighbourhood Info Centre, 'European Union supports key reforms in Moldova', 29 July 2014. Available at: http://enpi-info.eu/maineast.php?id=38095&id_type=1&lang_id=450.

[11] *Radio Free Europe*, 16 July 2014. Available at: www.rferl.org/content/merkel-moldova-russia-association-leanca-eu-visit/25453336.html.

[12] *Euractiv*, 18 March 2014.

referendums 'on issues of state importance'. The Moldovan authorities declared the referendum illegitimate and filed criminal lawsuits against its organisers. The EU ambassador visited Gagauzia and stressed that EU integration was not about choosing between Europe and Russia. He promised that the EU would seek to reconcile the Eurasian customs union with the commercial aspects of the AA.[13] The EU planned a three-year development program in Gagauzia worth €5 million.

Russia soon imposed temporary bans on Moldovan fruit imports as well as imports of canned fruit and vegetables, adding to the existing ban on wine imports. Russia insisted that the AA threatened to flood the Russian market with Moldovan imports and re-exported European goods. Russian trade retaliation was serious for Moldova: fruit, wine and tobacco production still accounted for half the country's exports and almost a third of employment.[14] The EU increased economic pressure on Transnistria again, pointing out that the enclave – which sent only 20 per cent of its exports to Russia – would be cut off from its main European export markets if it refused to adopt the AA. Diplomats acknowledged in private that the EU would accept the loss of Transnistria in return for a strongly EU-oriented rest of Moldova – and so probably would most of the Moldovan elite.

In March 2014, Russia and the US reaffirmed the common goal of achieving a special status for Transnistria inside a united and sovereign Moldovan state. The two sides agreed to renew regular consultations in a 5+2 format, with Russia and Ukraine acting as guarantors, the OSCE as a mediator, and the US and EU as observers. In contrast to the US's very security-orientated focus, EU approximation requirements were not about such high politics. These requirements also displaced any focus on making Moldova's security apparatus more robust and resilient – which according to local experts and policy-makers was what the country most needed.

In September, Federica Mogherini met with Moldovan officials in Chisinau and pledged increased support. The EU disbursed a second instalment of €13.2 million under its budget support programme for the reform of the justice sector, a response to the Moldovan government

[13] European Economic and Social Committee, 'The Gagauz People are not against Europe', Press release, Ref: 10/2014, 21 February 2014. Available at: www.eesc.europa.eu/?i=portal.en.press-releases.30905.

[14] *Bloomberg News*, 6 March 2014.

introducing a set of key reforms. The EU stepped up its efforts to help trade flows by doubling the previously agreed-upon import quotas for Moldovan fruit and vegetables. President Putin proposed a delay to Moldova's DCFTA similar to that agreed for Ukraine. Unlike in Ukraine, the EU did not agree to this.

Moldova held elections in November 2014. The state intervened in several subtle forms in the elections, to load the dice in a pro-EU direction. The EU did not respond critically to these tactics or to the exclusion of the pro-Russian Socialist party. Pro-European parties lost four seats in the elections. After internal personality clashes broke out, the new coalition was of two rather than three parties and more precarious as a result. The Communist party agreed to support the coalition, but wanted some AA-related commitments diluted. Voters punished the pro-EU Alliance for corruption. The pro-European elites' nepotism harmed the EU's wider popularity and legitimacy in the country.[15]

After the elections, a banking scandal broke involving members of the coalition government, who were accused of stealing over a billion euros of public money, nearly 12 per cent of GDP. Large-scale protests took place on several occasions in 2015. Moldovan civil society organisations increasingly criticised the EU for being 'too soft' on the pro-European elite because of its fear of Russian influence in the country. Moldovans' support for the EU halved from 63 to 32 per cent of the population between 2009 and 2015, while support for the Eurasian Union rose markedly to over 50 per cent.[16]

Pro-Russian protestors were those now able to position themselves as anti-corruption and pro-reform. The EU had been asking the government to reform the banking sector for many years; yet even in this tiny, impoverished country, highly reliant on external funds, the EU was either unable or unwilling to ensure that governance standards changed in any far-reaching sense. While EU conditionality succeeded in pushing the coalition to sign non-discrimination legislation in the face of stiff domestic opposition, it did not pushback against a dilution

[15] C. Ciurea, *Moldova after the Elections: Politics Overtakes Reforms*, London: European Council for Foreign Relations, 2015.

[16] V. Chirila, 'Moldova: More focus, flexibility and visibility for the European Neighbourhood Policy'. In A. Inayeh and J. Forbig (eds), *Reviewing the European Neighbourhood Policy: Eastern Perspectives*, Berlin: GMF Europe, 2015, pp. 32 and 34.

of the legislation and its incomplete implementation as it feared stirring anti-EU opinion.

As the banking crisis spiralled, the government and prime minister resigned. When a new government was finally cobbled together in January 2016, protestors stormed the parliament angry that they were to be deprived of new elections. Some of the protesters represented the pro-Russian Socialist Party and Our Party; some were from the Dignity and Truth Platform, espousing a pro-democracy and pro-European agenda and calling for a comprehensive clean-up of the banking scandal rather than another opaquely formed, EU-blessed coalition of the same elite implicated in that very scandal. When the new administration took power in February, it promised reforms of the banking sector, the public prosecutors office and energy policies. Yet the government now consisted of a disparate range of oligarch-backed political forces and was not certain to last long.

With belatedly toughened resolve – and indeed tougher resolve than the US in this instance – the EU suspended budget support to Moldova and temporarily held back some packages of EU technical assistance. While adopting a cooler and more hands-off position, however, the EU's aim was pragmatic: trying to make the new government work, despite the protests against it. While the EU demonstrated a new willingness to take tough action against corruption, it also wanted to avoid new elections, not least because it was aware of anti-European poll trends. Meetings related to implementation of the AA and DCFTA continued as normal. The EU proceeded with an advisory mission for security sector reform and a new dialogue with Moldova on cooperation with Common Security and Defence Policy missions – both these initiatives aimed at mitigating the country's security vulnerability. Diplomats hoped that the IMF would give a positive assessment of Moldova's macro-economic situation by mid-2016, which would trigger a resumption of EU budget support and judicial reform projects. The EU rolled out an €8 million support package for civil society, trying to engage with the protestors and with pro-Russian sectors of civil society. An EU mission in March reached out to the more pro-Russian and pro-Eurasian Union parts of Moldova's political spectrum. Moldova's constitutional court ruled in favour of direct presidential elections, in what many believed was a political ruling designed to deflect protestors' pressure for new legislative elections and an entirely new government; eschewing any critical involvement in this matter, the EU retained its low-politics areas of cooperation and harmonisation programmes.

As the interim, largely technocratic government advanced with its reforms, protests intensified once again. The formal EU position was still to help the interim administration stay in power until elections were due to take place. The EU worked with the new government to draw up a 'Roadmap' of 82 reforms to be completed by the end of July. After stalling during the political crisis, the implementation of AA commitments began to gain momentum again. For many Moldovans this reinforced the impression of the EU and local elite joining forces to push through reforms over the heads of the population – especially as technocratic ministers struggled to tackle the most sensitive issues of judicial and banking reforms. An inaugural EU-Moldova civil society platform met in May in an effort to ensure some link between the reforms and the somewhat unstable civic sphere. The EU and civil society organisations pushed for a new Commission for Integrity, while activists criticised the political elites for covering their tracks, winding up the banks before any criminal proceedings were able to proceed.

By this stage, neither new elections nor a prolongation of such a shaky and delegitimised administration were ideal options for EU interests. The EU's more defensive and less ambitious line was to move away from seeing its Moldova policy in terms of support for 'pro-European' parties against 'pro-Russian' forces. Diplomats acknowledged that the country's political dynamics had become more complex than this ritual dichotomy suggested – and more difficult to manage towards any far-reaching transformational ends. Pro-Russian candidate Igor Dodon won the October 2016 presidential election on a platform of recommending that Moldova ditch the European AA in favour of joining the Eurasian Union. Even if the presidency was a largely ceremonial post, this result was a shock that echoed the moment when Armenia decided to pull out of its EU agreement in 2013. As of late 2016, the EU had not resumed budget support to Moldova.

In a possibly more positive move, in early 2016 – and after long negotiations – Transnistrian authorities signed an accord with the Moldovan government to implement core elements of the DCFTA, to avoid losing autonomous EU trade preferences. This revived hopes among EU diplomats that low-profile customs and other economic convergence could help temper conflict across the region. Even if practical progress was slow on such convergence in 2016, Transnistria remained quiet; Russia remained the main power but its trade with the territory declined dramatically and Moscow did not use its *de facto* control as a base from which to stir open conflict – a clear contrast to events in Donbas.

Overall, in might be said that in Moldova the EU increased engagement and supported democracy as a geostrategic tool, but also overlooked the corruption of a nominally democratic government in the name of more directly possession-related goals – especially the aim of keeping pro-European allies in power. Moldova was a sobering indication of the limitations to EU influence; once the governing Alliance obtained the DCFTA and visa-free regime, reforms went backwards. For their part, Moldovan diplomats complained that the EU did not know how to convert the EaP into an instrument for protecting national sovereignty – as one politician put it, how to change it from being a 'fair weather to a foul weather' initiative – as the strategic context became more fractious.

Armenia

After Armenia opted for the Eurasian Union and pulled out of the association agreement, EU-Armenian relations stagnated. Neither side quite knew how to move forward. Government spokesmen in Yerevan insisted that the AA could have torn the country apart, like in Ukraine. Armenian officials referred to studies showing that the DCFTA would provide limited benefits compared to the Eurasian Union or an opening of the Turkish border. The choice in favour of the Eurasian Union was presented as being pragmatic: cheaper gas and export markets. It was significant that the Armenian business community was critical of the DCFTA for being too onerous in terms of regulatory alignment on the EU's terms and so did not push the government hard to choose this over the Eurasian Union. Opposition politicians berated the EU for not listening to these concerns. Armenian civil society leaders in Yerevan were furious as they insisted the EU had time to offer a more flexible package to Armenia, and to recognise the problems the government had in signing the DCFTA.

Despite the recriminations, European cooperation with Armenia did not cease. Projects continued under Armenia's €260 million aid allocation for 2007–2013. The Commission released a new aid package of €41 million to Armenia in December 2013. Only €6 million of this went to civil society, the rest was for government-run development programmes. Visa facilitation and mobility partnership talks advanced. A new action plan was drawn up covering five areas – justice, freedom, security, political cooperation, socioeconomic and infrastructure reforms. A new Single Support Framework for EU funding set strategic objectives and priorities for cooperation for 2014–2017. The framework identified the private sector, public administration and justice as the three priority sectors for implementing reform; support for the modernisation of public institutions and support to civil society would also be increased. The EU made a total of €170 million available to Armenia for 2014–2017, a year-on-year increase over the pervious period.

Signals from Armenia were mixed. The head of Armenia's National Security Council insisted Armenia-EU political cooperation was a priority.[17] The government indicated that Armenia had not definitively abandoned the association agreement. It insisted that Armenia wanted to deepen its cooperation with the EU. Prime Minister Tigran Sarkisian declared that signing only the political part of the AA would be 'the best path' for Armenia, following the model of the interim Ukrainian government. This would help Armenia become 'a little less exposed to Russian influence', suggested one high level official. As the Armenian economy was hit by Russia's economic difficulties, government officials in Yerevan said they now saw a need once again for some kind of economic agreement with Europe.

During a trip to Armenia in May, French President François Hollande urged the EU to find a unique model of cooperation with Armenia: 'Europe must accept an agreement for an association with Armenia ... [so that] Armenia can go [ahead] with a trade-commercial union with Russia.'[18] The French Ambassador claimed that Armenia's accession to the Eurasian Union need not impede better Armenia-EU relations.[19] While some European ministers cautioned that Armenia

[17] 'Armenia and EU Develop New Action Plan of 180 Provisions', *Aysor*, 19 February 2014. Available at: www.aysor.am/en/news/2014/02/19/armenia-eu/.

[18] *RFE/RL*, 26 May 2014.

[19] 'EU must know from Armenia what will be signed with EaEU – Germany ambassador', *News.am*, 11 July 2014. Available at: www.news.am/eng/news/218621.html.

had supported Russia over Crimea, the need for flexibility was generally acknowledged within EU deliberations.

In 2015, the EU indeed intensified efforts to revive cooperation. The EU invited Armenia to identify those elements of the AA in which it was interested and able to implement still – that would not clash with its Eurasian Union commitment. The EU accepted this tailor-made and demand-driven route towards drawing up a replacement agreement. Officials stated that they had no desire to compete with Russia and that the EU had to be pragmatic and offer Armenia a new mode of cooperation. They did not seem to be unduly worried about Armenia being in the Eurasian Union and not having a DCFTA, but still looking for a political partnership with the EU. After initial coolness in 2013 and early 2014, by 2015 the EU saw the country that had provoked the first big shock for the EaP in an apparently sanguine light.

A scoping exercise for the replacement agreement was carried out in early 2015. The technical difficulty was that it remained uncertain exactly what would be included within Eurasian Union commitments; Armenia was asking for a large number of derogations from the customs union in part to keep open the door for regulatory alignment with the EU.[20] Armenia wanted enhanced cooperation on institutional capacity building, regulatory alignment, civil society and democracy initiatives and most of the AA, except the DCFTA. Visa liberalisation continued to be the most attractive carrot. European aid still flowed, except programmes tied specifically to the DCFTA. Indeed, to compensate for the latter, officials sought to increase Armenia's allocation from other EU funding instruments. EU and member state diplomats in the Armenian capital believed that deepening democracy and rooting out corruption would help prize the country away from Russia. Civil society organisations were involved in drawing up proposals for a new agreement – indeed, more so than they had been with the original association agreement. Member states' bilateral programmes were not large, but did support modest initiatives on conflict mediation and judicial reform, in particular; Germany, Poland and the UK increased such funding.

The EU's flexibility was motivated by an increasingly fragile political–strategic panorama. Crimea's annexation encouraged

[20] H. Kostanyan, *The Rocky Road to an EU-Armenia Agreement: From U-turn to Detour*, Brussels: Centre for European Policy Studies, 2015.

Yerevan to press harder for full incorporation of Nagorno-Karabakh into Armenia. The Nagorno-Karabakh situation became more fragile, with significant increases in the number of contact line violations. Azerbaijan seemed to be pushing again to reopen the conflict. After ten years of military build up, its defence budget was six times larger than that of Armenia. While Armenia officially backed Crimea's annexation, its relations with Russia were not entirely harmonious. There was growing anger at increased Russian arms sales to Azerbaijan. In early 2015 there were anti-Russian demonstrations following the killing of an Armenian family by a Russian soldier. Tensions rose as Armenia pushed hard for Nagorno-Karabakh to be included within the Eurasian Union, yet Armenians stressed that the country needed Russian support primarily because of Turkey's perceived hostility. In the centennial year of the Armenian genocide of 1915, relations with Turkey steadily worsened.

In terms of strategic vision, EU and member state diplomats did not see themselves as competing for primacy with Russia. It was clear that Russia was the key balancing power between Armenia and Azerbaijan. The EU would not count as a security provider for Armenia. The Ukraine crisis had made this even more evident. The EU and member states were still reluctant to engage in military support; in contrast, the US did offer a modest amount of new military training. EU and member state diplomats set themselves modest objectives. They recognised that much of the country was strongly pro-Russian but were also concerned about the country becoming a vassal to Russia – the Crimea shock made most Armenians more determined to defend their national independence. The European aim was to enable Armenia to retain a degree of multi-vector pluralism in its foreign relations. The EU's geostrategic thinking was subtle: it would help Armenia to push back against Eurasian Union rules that would restrict the country's autonomy. Armenia was seen as a kind of experimental gateway between the Eurasian Union and the EaP.

In private conversations, senior Armenian diplomats stressed how uncomfortable the geopolitical context was for Armenia, as it made the pursuit of a multi-vector foreign policy more difficult. Member states' diplomats in Yerevan highlighted how they pressed Armenia to improve relations with Turkey, as the best way of undercutting the need for such a heavy Russian presence in the country's politics.

Armenian officials confirmed that what they most wanted from the EU was an indirect role, pressuring Ankara to implement the 2009 protocols on reopening the Turkish-Armenian border.

In addition to regional geopolitics, the EU had to factor in a domestic political crisis that rocked Armenia in 2015. The government pushed out the head of one of the main political parties, Prosperous Armenia, that had been supportive of the government. Semi-democratic Armenia drifted towards a greater degree of authoritarianism. President Serge Sargyszan won a referendum on constitutional changes in December 2015; these would move Armenia to a parliamentary system, allowing Sargyszan and the Republican Party to retain real power through the prime-ministership after leaving the presidency. The reforms also restricted human rights provisions. Opposition parties felt increasingly targeted; media pluralism suffered several blows; a proposed NGO law threatened to restrict civic space; and governmental control over the judiciary tightened. Protests accumulated during 2015, erupting in the so-called 'Electric Yerevan' uprising – large-scale mobilisations against rises in electricity prices.

The EU was critical of the constitutional reforms but did not interrupt talks on a new agreement. Armenian civil society organisations feared that the EU was so keen to sign a replacement agreement that it overlooked the worsening political conditions. Civil society groups criticised the EU for doing relatively little to keep democracy moving in the right direction; they saw member states as having an overly positive view of the president, describing him as a liberal democrat when all evidence suggested otherwise. One opposition leader even accused the EU of colluding in Armenia's increasingly palpable authoritarian drift. Civic leaders urged the EU to use the replacement agreement as a new opportunity to make democracy support its niche area of comparative advantage in Armenia, freed from the DCFTA's focus on heavy technocratic requirements.

In Yerevan interlocutors pointed out that most opposition parties were more nationalistic and pro-Russian than the government, and that this accounted for the EU's tepid stance on democratic reversals. Civil society organisations in the capital suggested that European funding levels were relatively generous but focused on generic training, while at a political level the EU as a whole did little to press the government to adhere to democratic norms. Those involved in the Electric Yerevan protests lamented the lack of EU backing. The EED supported the protests with legal assistance and media equipment, but other donors did not offer any such support. In Yerevan, NGO leaders accused the EU of prevaricating on the offer of a new agreement so as not to ruffle Russian sensitivities once again – effectively sacrificing a beleaguered Armenian democracy movement on the altar of Ukraine-related mediation concerns.

The EU and Armenia finally launched formal negotiations for a new agreement in December 2015, with each side accusing the other of not attaching priority to the accord. Adjusting the new agreement's trade elements to the Eurasian Union remained the thorniest obstacle, as this was technically new territory for DG Trade officials. It remained unclear whether Russia would scupper a new agreement as it had the AA in 2013. EU officials did not think this was likely and revealed that there was no EU dialogue with Russia to preempt any misunderstandings. Meanwhile, low-level EU cooperation continued, in an effort to keep relations on a 'normal' track. In early 2016, the EU launched a new support programme of €30 million to enhance employment opportunities, fiscal governance and civil society influence.[21] For all such efforts, a core tension remained unresolved: Armenian interlocutors all recognised that the country had to choose a geostrategic alignment with Russia, but stressed that society wanted European values – yet it was not clear if and how the EU could minimise the tension between these two orientations.

April 2016 witnessed the deadliest violence between Armenia and Azerbaijan since their 1994 ceasefire – an outbreak linked to the vulnerability and instability within both countries' governing regimes. Russia mediated a new ceasefire. With both countries engaged in a huge military build-up, the situation was more brittle and tense than for many years. The impact of the outbreak in violence on EU-Armenia relations was unclear. On the one hand, Armenia's dependence on Russian security protection increased.[22] On the other hand, Armenia's unhappiness with Russia's hold on events intensified and anti-Russian protests broke out in Yerevan after Moscow sold more weapons to Azerbaijan. While many European foreign ministries sensed a new opportunity to

[21] Available at www.mediamax.am/en/news/foreignpolicy/.

[22] T. Schumacher, *Armenia, Azerbaijan and the Nagorno-Karabakh conflict: Why the 'Black Garden' will not Blossom Any Time Soon*, Brussels: Egmont Institute, 2016.

tighten strategic engagement with Armenia, the conflict's flare-up once again revealed the EU's limited influence relative to that of Russia.

This question was soon overshadowed by dramatic political events inside Armenia. In July 2016, a new wave of protests erupted after the government detained an opposition leader. As gunmen from the opposition group took a number of policemen hostages, large crowds took to the street to demand the president's resignation. He did not resign but changed his government – appointing a Gazprom executive as prime minister, in part to reassure Russia. These events further slowed progress on the new EU agreement over the latter half of 2016. Part of the delay on this agreement was political, as the EU waited to see how the president would manage the transition to a parliamentary system in 2017–2018. There was also the more technical issue of Armenia now wanting flexibility to change any new agreement in the future in the case of new Eurasian Union rules. If the political will remained on both sides to strike a new accord, the political and technical conditions appeared to be causing ever-more daunting obstacles.

Belarus

The Ukraine crisis had profound but contrasting effects on Belarus. President Lukashenka sought a contorted strategic path through the new geopolitical context. He criticised Russia's annexation of Crimea as setting a 'bad precedent'. The Belarusian regime and population were increasingly anxious to safeguard the country's sovereign independence. Because of this, Belarus diluted Russian plans for the Eurasian Union. Russia failed to secure Belarusian support for sanctions against Ukrainian goods. The Lukashenka regime now saw a better relationship with the EU as a means of counteracting assertive Russian power.

However, the dire state of its economy meant that Belarus still needed Russian support. Belarus was hit hard by EU sanctions on Russia and it pushed Moscow for a deal on oil export duties and cheap energy supplies as preconditions for signing up to the Eurasian Union. Lukashenka argued that the lesson learned from Ukraine was that Belarus needed to maintain autonomy from both the EU and Russia. He was increasingly concerned to play the EU and Russia off against each other – and yet avoid a serious freeze in relations between the EU and Russia, as this would undermine the basis on which he maintained himself in power.

After a decade of sanctions, most EU member states wanted to see a new attempt at some form of engagement with Belarus. Belarus' new foreign minister professed to be receptive to this. Diplomats in Baltic capitals said they were more inclined to see Lukashenka now as a defender of Belarusian independence against Russia. After the Crimea annexation, efforts to revive EU-Belarus links took shape on both sides. Several EU member states argued that the crisis reinforced the need for engagement, to prize Belarus away from complete dependence on Russia, rather than having the relationship held up because of disagreements over a small number of political prisoners. President Lukashenka put out feelers to the EU with a view to returning to the 2008–2010 period of modest rapprochement. Polish premier Donald Tusk approached Lukashenka to explore the possibilities for new strategic cooperation.

However, ambitions were relatively modest. European diplomats in Minsk concurred that Russia's presence in the security field remained dominant, and that the EU simply could not compete with such influence. The EU could not hope to displace Russia in Belarus, only gradually influence a change in the 'rules of the game' that prevailed in the latter's internal and external politics. Diplomats in Minsk felt the Crimea-Ukraine crisis would not fundamentally change the policy equation vis-à-vis Belarus. The latter would not be a higher priority for most member states.

Member states were also scarred by the attempt at engagement made in 2008–2010. Diplomats in Minsk felt that the EU had been duped; that the president had pocketed new funds from Europe and the IMF, failed to reform, used the new Western engagement primarily to gain stronger influence over Moscow, and then clamped down hard in the 2010 elections – elections during which some European ministers visited Minsk promising benefits if the poll was genuinely competitive. Several diplomats suggested this experience now diluted their enthusiasm for a new post-Crimea rapprochement. European officials talked of 'small steps' rather than the kind of ambitious rapprochement offered in 2009. While the regime insisted it sought a multi-vector foreign policy, European officials took this with a degree of scepticism.

The EU kept sanctions in place targeted at regime members. Some member states urged conditions attached to political prisoners to be made more flexible. After a prominent political prisoner was released in June 2014, moves were made to reduce the number of individuals and entities included on the sanctions list. Belarusian advocacy groups were themselves divided on the question of sanctions. The issue reached its peak at the 2015 Riga summit: while the EU sought to entice Lukashenka into attending and agreeing to a range of new cooperation, the issue of political prisoners prevented this from happening. Insiders reported that a small group of member states, including Germany, the UK and Sweden held at bay some governments' calls for far greater EU flexibility on political prisoners at Riga.

Efforts were made to resuscitate a workable EU-Belarus Modernisation Partnership. In 2013, the Commission allocated half a million euros to extend the largely moribund Modernisation Partnership for another two years, and to include civil society organisations within this. It allocated €30 million in 2013 for small-scale educational, environmental and energy projects inside Belarus. Efforts were made to keep Belarus engaged in the EaP's multilateral tracks, as most member states insisted that negotiations on a bilateral accord were still not feasible. The regime agreed to engage in a technical dialogue as an 'interim phase' in May 2014, as long as this was not formally part of the process involving civil society dialogue. The EU's main approach was to inject technical, low-politics substance into the framework of the Modernisation Partnership.

The EU and Belarus began visa facilitation talks. These progressed, but slowly. This was the cooperation on which the regime was keenest, as a means of demonstrating its multi-vector foreign policy had produced tangible benefit for the population. However, preparations were slow and there remained little prospect of more ambitious talks on visa liberalisation rather than merely facilitation. Belarus had the region's second highest number of Schengen visa applications per capita. Lithuania and Poland offered visa provisions on a bilateral basis, but progress was held back on the Belarusian side. By mid-2015, the EU stressed that a far-reaching visa regime would be on offer if the regime released the last-remaining political prisoners.

The Belarusian government asked for cooperation on a range of technical issues. In March 2014 the EU Delegation in Minsk organised a meeting on new 'EU-Belarus Sectoral Cooperation'. EU officials hinted at an interim cooperation accord. The EU started initiatives on food standards, penitentiary management and energy efficiency, funding Belarusian organisations to adopt European-level standards. It also sought cooperation on rules that would attract more European investment and help the tentative privatisation of state owned enterprises. Each year Belarus was either the first or second highest recipient of twinning funding in the Eastern Partnership. Belarusian local authorities for the first time claimed funds from the EU's Non-State Actors and Local Authorities Budget line. Under the EaP's multilateral track, Belarus began to engage in justice and home affairs cooperation.

Belarus' signing of the Eurasian Union accord raised difficulties in this slowly accumulating range of technical cooperation. Officials were uncertain of the impact. The rules-based mode of engagement with Brussels remained alien for Belarusian officials used to, in a local phrase, the 'oil for kisses' trade-offs of diplomacy with Moscow. Belarusian diplomats insisted that the country was not interested in norms convergence but offered itself pragmatically as a bridge between EU and Eurasian integration. In this sense, the Eurasian Union was not all bad news: officials in the country pointed out that it increased the attractiveness for EU firms to invest in relatively cheap Belarus as a base from which to export into Russia.

Asked what the EU's interests were in Belarus after Crimea, a common response from diplomats referred to the need to step up security at the country's borders. The EU funded an initiative on integrated border management, one area where cooperation was unequivocally sought by the regime as it tackled illegal trafficking routes through the region. Lithuanian and Belarusian defence ministers agreed to step up bilateral cooperation. Lukashenka talked to NATO about possible security cooperation.

The Ukraine crisis had a clear impact on the civil society dimension of European policy. Belarusian civil society became more cautious, and was now at least as concerned about President Putin's actions as about Lukashenka's repression. This was a caution echoed by some European policy-makers who now feared that Lukashenka's overthrow could usher in a full Russian takeover. In addition, the regime was often astute in making some policy improvements in response to concerns on housing, health care and education; these changes acted as a decompression valve to cool civic frustration. The country lacked the kind of well-developed middle class that drove pressure for reform in countries like Ukraine. Three hundred civil society representatives were detained prior to the May 2014 world ice-hockey championships as a pre-emptive measure against possible disruption.

The EU stepped up network-building initiatives. Civil society support increased, to €20 million euros for 2013, but veered away from established opposition figures. The Swedish, Danish, Dutch and Norwegian governments increased civil society programmes, whether within the country, via bodies like the Visegrad Fund or through organisations based in Vilnius. The EU insisted it was broadening its range of partners in the country and undertaking initiatives aimed in particular at building cooperation between different civil society organisations, amongst whom rivalries were fierce and communication poor. The European Endowment for Democracy began projects on monitoring local elections and encouraging coalition building among different parts of the opposition. European delegations insisted they began to engage with a wider range of educational and research institutes and also with apparently more reform-minded technocrats in the economics ministry and central bank.

Ongoing events in Ukraine made the EU and Belarus even keener to develop a more constructive relationship with each other. Watching events in eastern Ukraine descend into full conflict, the Belarusian regime put out further feelers to the EU. President Lukashenka sought to position himself as the vital mediator in the Minsk meetings between Russia, Ukraine and Western powers. A new issue was that EU goods subject to Russian sanctions began finding their way into Belarus, where they were repackaged and then sold into Russia. Russia temporarily banned Belarusian food imports. Also causing some friction with Moscow, Belarus pushed back more firmly against the scope of Russian ambitions for the Eurasian Union.

Alongside regional shifts, internal politics entered another cycle. A seven-party opposition coalition briefly convened to coordinate positions in the run up to the 2015 elections. Several European organisations supported such platform-building efforts. Opposition parties sought to collect signatures for a 'people's referendum' covering a range of social and community issues. The regime began to allow space for NGOs promoting Belarusian sovereignty. New civic organisations were now working on community issues, with a different focus from the long-established political opposition. Donors shifted further their attention from groups based in Vilnius or Warsaw to more local, practical citizen-led groups.

A breakthrough occurred in August 2015, when the regime granted the remaining six political prisoners an amnesty. The EU suggested it would be willing to lift sanctions and offered the government new aid and loans. The EU's remaining condition was simply that the regime should not orchestrate violence during the election campaign; it did not insist that the vote be a democratic one. In the event, the election campaign was almost unnervingly calm, with no large-scale street protests against Lukashenka. The opposition was subdued and gained little support or traction during the campaign. Lukashenka allowed slightly more political space for small opposition gatherings than in 2010. The EU did not push hard or in any tangible way for a free vote.

Although the election returned Lukashenka to power with a record 83 per cent of the vote, because of the release of political prisoners and lack of violence in the election the EU agreed a four-month suspension of sanctions against 170 individuals and three companies – but kept measures against four individuals and an arms embargo in place. In February 2016 the EU lifted nearly all its restrictive measures. As quid pro quo, the regime agreed to a new human rights dialogue. The removal of sanctions occurred alongside Lukashenka refusing to host a Russian military base. Germany in particular pushed for various dialogue forums and an investment conference. Poland was also active in opening new routes for cooperation through its trade and investment forum with Belarus. In 2016 the EU commenced a series of projects that involved support for NGOs working on environmental and health issues. The Belarusian regime allowed civil society representatives to participate in talks about new EU cooperation. The EU planned to double its financial assistance to Belarus in 2016. The UK supported a conference on the death penalty, another sticking point that Minsk seemed to be willing to reconsider now. Parliamentary elections were held in September 2016. They were held without violence and two opposition candidates were 'allowed' to win seats, so the EU sent a high-level delegation to Minsk to push forward deeper cooperation with greater conviction.

Overall, strong Belarusian independence was the best geostrategic outcome the EU could hope for. The EU could not drop the issue of political prisoners, but looked for areas of cooperation related to technical governance reform that could be unblocked with parts of the regime. Officials in Minsk insisted that technical cooperation was gradually gaining ground and that the government was showing more commitment at this level. Low-key technical measures that were widely deemed insufficient in Ukraine were seen as a useful access point in Belarus. Still, the Belarusian regime complained that the EU did not give it enough credit for pushing back against Russia.[23]

Azerbaijan

Of all EaP states, the EU's relations with Azerbaijan were the least affected by the eastern crisis. Even here, however, there was some read-over. Azerbaijan maintained a strategic course relatively autonomous from both the EU and Russia. The government in Baku indicated early on that it wanted to form part of the EaP but would not seek the same kind of harmonisation with European rules and values as other EaP governments. Energy-rich Azerbaijan did not rush to sign an AA, although it did receive an EU aid allocation of €200 million for 2007–2013. Some of Azerbaijan's economic and energy governance rules were increasingly oriented to the EU as two-thirds of exports went to European markets and the new TAP pipeline would link directly to Italy; however, Baku rejected the range of other sectoral technical governance initiatives that the EU offered to EaP states.

Azerbaijan won the offer of a visa liberalisation agreement at the Vilnius summit. It chose not to sign the Strategic Modernisation Partnership offered by the EU as an alternative to the AA. President Aliyev's refusal to sign human rights language in the agreement was one reason for this decision. A European Parliament observation mission to Azerbaijan's 2013 elections was mired in controversy, when it was found that the MEPs providing a positive report on the election had received money and gifts from Baku. Unlike in Ukraine, protests did not erupt in Baku after the government refused to sign an agreement with the European Union.

As the Russia–Ukraine crisis deepened, EU diplomats felt both the need and greater possibility of a deeper relationship with Baku. Azerbaijan and the EU discussed the prospects for developing some kind of partnership during the course of 2014 and into 2015. The

[23] Y. Kryvoi with A. Wilson, *From Sanctions to Summits: Belarus After the Ukraine Crisis*, London: European Council for Foreign Relations, 2015, p. 4.

EU's desire to conclude some form of new agreement intensified; diplomats noted that the EU was now the clear demandeur in relations with Azerbaijan. Talks continued on upgrading energy cooperation; the EU offered new support for small and medium sized businesses in Azerbaijan. The EU even continued to channel direct budget support to the regime. While the number of political prisoners in Azerbaijan rose to over 100 by 2016, the EU did not impose a single travel ban or asset freeze on regime members. This contrasted with the sanctions imposed against Belarus in response to a small handful of political prisoners.

Azerbaijan opposed Russia's Crimea annexation. Given that Russia traditionally played a mediating role in the conflict with Armenia, the Aliyev regime measured its response, but refused to recognise Crimea's secession from Ukraine – fearing that this would set a precedent for Nagorno-Karabakh. Besides voting in favour of a UN resolution declaring Crimea's referendum on joining Russia invalid, Azerbaijan's embassy in Kiev issued a statement supporting Ukraine's territorial integrity. The US Ambassador to Azerbaijan noted: 'What is taking place in Ukraine makes Azerbaijan's relations with the US and EU even more important, and show[s] again why the Nagorno-Karabakh conflict must be resolved.'[24]

While Italy, Germany and France were Azerbaijan's biggest trade partners, Russia continued to have leverage due to its influence over Armenia and its power to escalate the Nagorno-Karabakh conflict. Azerbaijan bought new tanks from Russia in May 2014. In addition, Russian oil giant Rosneft signed a joint-venture agreement with the State Oil Company of Azerbaijan (Socar). Azeri officials spoke of feeling greater pressure from the Kremlin to join the Eurasian Union. Yet Baku was less vulnerable to Russian pressure than other EaP states, and Azerbaijan sought to maintain a relatively independent foreign policy. In response to the crisis, it announced plans to enhance Azerbaijani-Turkish military ties.

In April 2014, the EU proposed a protocol to the EU-Azerbaijan Partnership and Cooperation Agreement (PCA) that would allow Azerbaijan to participate in a wider range of EU cooperation

[24] S. Abbasov, 'Azerbaijan Divided Over Crimea's Implications for Karabakh Peace', *EurasiaNet.org*, 20 March 2014. Available at: www.eurasianet.org/node/68172.

programmes. The EU brought forward new initiatives for justice sector reform, education and renewable energy, and to support the government of Azerbaijan diversify its economy. Azerbaijan's oil and gas revenues rose from $1 billion in 2006 to $15 billion in 2014. The EU's support for the Azerbaijan-centred Southern Gas Corridor compounded the regime's empowerment. Tensions with Russia made this pipeline project more vital to EU energy security – even if Azerbaijan's potential share of the EU market was relatively limited. Justifying support for the Southern Gas Corridor, energy commissioner Maroš Šefčovič stressed that: 'This is the only project that guarantees us a major new gas supply from a new source.'[25] In addition, hard-security elements rose up the agenda, as NATO drew up plans to strengthen military co-operation with Azerbaijan.[26]

The EU weighed strategic priorities against human rights concerns. In May 2014, Azerbaijan took over the chairmanship of the Council of Europe. EU foreign policy chief Catherine Ashton and Commissioner Stefan Füle issued a joint statement voicing their concern over the increasingly repressive treatment of human rights activists in Azerbaijan and called on the government to honour its obligations and commitments as a member of the Council of Europe.[27] In September 2014, the EU announced a new Support to Civil Society Programme worth €3 million, to assist civil society organisations working on democracy and human rights.

However, the regime began a clampdown against civil society organisations in Azerbaijan. It sentenced the deputy head of the biggest opposition party and the leader of the largest human rights organisation to prison. Scores of human rights groups were hounded to close down and activists fled the country. The regime put several donors under investigation, including the European Endowment for Democracy, Oxfam and the Black Sea Trust. As the regime froze many EU funds, the Union reacted cautiously. One activist who had been forced to leave complained that the EU had failed to exert any

[25] 'Europe Relies on Azerbaijani Gas' *News.Az*. 16 February 2015. Available at: http://news.az/articles/economy/95716.

[26] *The Guardian*, 1 April 2014.

[27] EU Neighbourhood Info Centre, 'Azerbaijan: EU Concern at Treatment of Human Rights Defenders by Authorities', 5 May 2014, Available at: www.enpi-info.eu/eastportal/news/latest/37093/Azerbaijan:-EU-concern-at-treatment-of-human-rights-defenders-by-authorities.

pressure; it played up its new funding for civil society, but there were few independent civic organisations left to absorb the funds. EU leaders rejected the European Parliament's call for sanctions. President Aliyev used Azerbaijan's membership of the Council of Europe to neuter criticism, paralyse human rights investigations and build alliances with those European politicians who voted against attempts to sanction his regime.[28] Civil society in Azerbaijan accused the EU of being myopically focused on winning strategic support from Aliyev in light of the Ukraine crisis. Diplomats suggested that the only influence over internal developments would be to block oil and gas exports from Azerbaijan – a step that nobody in the EU was willing to contemplate.

The EU's position on the conflict with Armenia became a matter of greater concern. As noted above, Azerbaijan struck Armenian troops on the Nagorno-Karabakh line with increasing intensity and frequency. Both sides infringed ceasefire rules regularly during 2015 and 2016, until tensions erupted in the violence of April 2016. This was a clear spill-over from Russian meddling in eastern Ukraine. The Azerbaijani government increasingly complained of double standards: the EU assertively backed territorial integrity in Ukraine, Georgia and Moldova, but not for Azerbaijan – the latter having had part of its territory effectively prized away by Armenia at the behest of the Armenian majority in Nagorno-Karabakh. Azerbaijani diplomats insisted that the lack of clear EU support for Azerbaijan's territorial integrity took away their incentive for moving closer to the Union.

Azerbaijan finally presented its proposals for a new agreement at the Riga summit in 2015. Aliyev was invited to the summit but did not attend; while he said he could not travel due to a deadly fire that had broken out in Baku, some wondered whether he had been dissuaded by Moscow. After another rigged parliamentary election in November 2015, the EU said it was 'looking to continue cooperation' with the government. Relations reached a new low point, however, after a critical statement from the European Parliament led the Azerbaijani government to stop all contact and threaten to leave the EaP altogether. The EU put several official visits to Baku on hold.

Yet by 2016, cooperation was moving forward. The Baku government re-opened channels to EU institutions. In early 2016, talks began

[28] G. Knaus, 'Europe and Azerbaijan: The end of shame', *Journal of Democracy*, 26/3, 2015, 5–18.

to firm up the details of the prospective EU-Azerbaijan agreement. High representative Federica Mogherini visited Baku in March 2016 to add momentum to the negotiations. Azerbaijan now appeared slightly less belligerent and self-assured. The dramatic fall in oil prices shook the regime, which still depended on oil and gas for three-quarters of its budget revenue. In early 2016, the regime sought emergency support from the IMF. Moreover, Azerbaijan sided with Ankara in the brewing conflict between Turkey and Russia; this reinforced its need to deepen EU cooperation as a counter-balance to Moscow.

Germany and the UK led the pressure for a more geopolitically orientated pragmatism towards Azerbaijan. States like Sweden, Denmark and The Netherlands were reassured that the new partnership would include the EU's standard human rights and democracy clause, and so added their support for an agreement. There was by now a strong consensus among member states to move forward with a new type of flexible and bespoke agreement. The EU insisted that civil society protection remained a core element of its policy; the high representative pointedly met with civic leaders during her visit. The government released fourteen political prisoners in April 2016. Yet the regime brutally put down a new wave of protests triggered by a nearly 50 per cent currency devaluation, with little tangible European response.

After the April flare up in the conflict with Armenia, Azerbaijan hardened its position, making a resumption of violence more likely. Yet, the EU did not forward any new plan or deepen its engagement to prevent this from happening; rather, Russia was lead mediator. While Azerbaijan acted as aggressor to disrupt the status quo, it sought EU backing to balance Moscow's support for Armenia – although Baku also realised that Russia was the dominant player after the conflagration. The EU was now more willing to negotiate a new agreement on Baku's terms than it was when the Azerbaijani government had first proposed some form of alternative to the AA in 2013 – although it was still negotiating to keep some kind of reference to human rights clause, to have Azerbaijan accept full trade liberalisation and to resist the kind of unadulterated territorial integrity language sought by Azerbaijan on Ngorno-Karabakh. Even after President Aliyev extended his formal powers in a rubber-stamp referendum in September 2016, the EU's rapprochement continued. The EU and Azerbaijan found a way through their differences to agree on a negotiating mandate for a new, as yet unnamed, agreement at the end of November 2016. This represented a new step in the EU accepting provisions moulded more to its partner's interests than its own governance rules and norms.

In 2016, the geopolitics of energy relations also shifted markedly. Momentum gathered behind the Southern Gas Corridor. The initiative's governing consortium made a series of commitments to accelerate progress and pointedly did so during Mogherini's visit to Baku. Azerbaijan was not an easy energy partner, however. The government pushed for more direct control over the new project than it would have had under the Nabucco pipeline. The government was reluctant to base cooperation on EU energy market regulations, as these would reduce the regime's control over the energy sector and help competitors' supplies cross Azerbaijan into European markets. Azerbaijan had been planning to transpose some EU energy *aquis* into domestic legislation; from 2013 it shelved these plans.[29] Energy cooperation between the EU and Azerbaijan was set to assume a more directly geopolitical form.

Conclusion

While all eyes were on Russia and the conflict in Ukraine, the eastern crisis had broader regional ramifications. This chapter has outlined how the crisis changed the terms of engagement between the EU and the five EaP partners: Georgia, Moldova, Armenia, Belarus and Azerbaijan.

Categorisation

In these five cases, the EU made an effort to deepen and quicken strategic partnership and low-level cooperation. A complex geopolitical triangle took shape between EaP domestic trends, EU regional aims and Russian influences. The complexities of this triangle were reflected in the EU's delicate balance of assertive and defensive geopolitical dynamics. The category of liberal-redux geopolitics was useful for conceptualising EU responses to the post-2013 eastern crisis beyond policy towards Ukraine and Russia.

[29] F. Abbasov, *The Europeanisation of the southern gas corridor: Assessing the institutional dimension of the EU's energy security*, PhD Thesis, Sheffield University, 2016.

At the same time, this category's relevance varied between different EaP states. Liberal-redux geopolitics took contrasting forms in different parts of the region. The EU upgraded support for political reform as a geopolitical comparative advantage over Russia in Georgia and Moldova. EU policy centred on helping Georgia and Moldova hold their ground as independent states, with a degree of democracy and European orientation. In contrast, in Armenia, Belarus and Azerbaijan the EU sought more flexible, less norms-based forms of cooperation to counterbalance Russian pre-eminence.

The EU's focus on political and economic reforms tightened in some cases, diminished in other cases – and on very specific reform questions the EU adopted different or more flexible *tactics* of support. Paradoxically, the EU sought to extend its geopolitical presence through inclusive cooperation in non-reforming states that were ambivalent about partnership with the EU, while holding Euro-enthusiastic, reforming states at bay through limiting its offers of inclusion. The EU pursued policies of push and pull simultaneously, seeking some kind of equilibrium between geopolitical advance and retrenchment in the EaP area.

While it sought new avenues of practical cooperation, the EU did not extend offers of far-reaching inclusion into the EU-sphere to any of these five states. Some red lines of core EU human rights conditionality were maintained even where these held back the new avenues of engagement for which many member states pressed. In addition, the EU did not engage directly in conflict resolution in Armenia, Azerbaijan and Georgia in a way that helped protect the core tenets of national sovereignty – not least because it was aware that this would incur hostility from significant parts of these countries' populations. As the EU eschewed this kind of intrusive geopolitical engagement, it was more difficult for its traditional modes of external governance and diffusion to find fertile soil.

Indeed, the EU – along with other international actors – attempted an uneasily balanced approach to the contested territories that now littered the region, from Donbas, to Crimea, Transnistria, Nagorno-Karabakh, South Ossetia and Abkhazia. The EU did not accept 'separation' for these territories but nor did it press for the enclaves to be fully reintegrated back into their respective states. It neither completely shunned these entities nor fully engaged with them. If these territories existed in uneasy limbo, so did the EU's policy towards them. At most the EU pushed the national governments in question to allow more fluid contacts and trade with these territories.

Foreign Policy Dynamics

The chapter reveals that many policy initiatives based on the replication of EU norms and technical harmonisation continued relatively untouched by the apparent return of geopolitics. Liberal-institutionalist identities were, it seemed, to some extent embedded within the EaP's core essence. Yet, such continuity was overlain with more consequentialist strategic adjustment: EU policy moulded itself more tightly and instrumentally to both domestic specificities within each EaP state and to Russian policies.

In this sense, the chapter reveals variation in EU foreign-policy dynamics across the EaP region. In Georgia and Moldova, the processes and instruments of EU alignment and harmonisation continued to be the pre-eminent edge of overall European strategy. In Belarus, standard EU low-level politics seemed to offer the most propitious way forward in developing some degree of productive strategic engagement. Conversely, in Armenia and Azerbaijan, the EU began to move away from a focus on rules-extension towards more direct diplomatic tradeoffs. While some regulatory export still occurred in such cases, the EU's geopolitics of inclusion became less heavily dependent on rules and governance structures, seeking a more ends-oriented diplomatic partnership even where the political distance between the EU and such countries lengthened. European foreign policy became a more varied phenomenon across the EaP region, its mechanics, drivers and principle actors differing from one partner to another.

Impact

The chapter also reveals much variation in the effect of EU policies. In Moldova, Ukraine and Georgia much technical and legislative alignment proceeded, even in the context of political and strategic instability. Some EaP states benefited from the rivalry between the EU and Russia, as they played the two powers off against each other. The EaP partners had different types of external dependencies. Armenia needed Russia for security. Azerbaijan had such extensive income from energy resources that it was better able to retain a degree of autonomy from both the EU and Russia. All EaP countries struggled with internal divisions of some kind over the crisis. These were mediated through different types of political systems. In Belarus, alignment with Russia upheld authoritarianism; in Armenia it came after a period of genuine political reform. Internal politics in Georgia were not split overwhelmingly along EU-versus-Russia lines; in Moldova this was increasingly the case.

These domestic differences conditioned the impact of EU policies. In Belarus, reformers were too marginalised for any public policy constituency to lock onto EU conditionality; modest impact came from the regime's strategic desire to counter-balance Russian pre-eminence. In Moldova, the pro-European government was committed to reforms and saw EU linkages as the main way to bolster its own position vis-à-vis the Communist and pro-Russian opposition; yet it also saw itself as rather too protected by EU support to resist the temptation of deeply destabilising corruption. In Georgia, politics were personalised, party structures very thin, and the role of an illiberal church strong: all this was problematic for democratisation but not determinant in preventing approximation with the European Union. Compared to Ukraine, Georgia had made more progress in solidifying state institutions prior to incremental democratic reforms, meaning its relationship with the EU flowed more productively from a less fractured domestic base.

Overall, this chapter's account of the five EaP states beyond Ukraine shows the prominence of geopolitical balancing. The EaP was no longer so centrally an exercise in straightforward governance transfer outwards from the EU. The logic of balancing was increasingly evident at all levels. It conditioned internal politics and identities within EaP states themselves. It coloured the way in which the EU defined geopolitics; the foreign policy tools the EU chose and those it rejected; and the space that was available for EU leverage as EaP states sought to hedge their geopolitical bets between east and west and balance their Russia-related geopolitical calculations. As we will now see in the concluding chapter, these dynamics were set to represent one of the eastern crisis' most significant legacies.

11 *Conclusion: A Half-New European Union Eastern Policy*

At the end of 2016, the eastern crisis was far from spent. Conflict in parts of eastern Ukraine simmered and constantly threatened to explode into unrestrained violence. Mounting political uncertainty beset Ukraine itself. Instability intensified across the EaP region. Even if Russia had not achieved its most far-reaching aims, it was now a truculent and disruptive influence on an increasingly wide range of European foreign policy challenges. The crisis would yet have many unpredictable twists and turns. Yet, over three years on from the first rumbles of the crisis, an analytical retrospective is possible. In this spirit, these conclusions reflect on the book's three core concerns: the geopolitical categorisation of European responses to the crisis; the crisis' effect on EU foreign policy dynamics; and the impact of European policies.

Mapping the Geopolitics of Asymmetry

Chapter 2 laid out a template for conceptualising the European response to the eastern crisis. Guided by this framework, the book has charted the EU's level of commitment to the EaP; the shift in policy towards Russia; and the strategic role of support for democratic and governance reforms across the eastern region. The overall European response corresponded to a category of *liberal-redux geopolitics*. Table 3 encapsulates the main features of this response, in comparison with pre-crisis EU policy and relative to the options of offensive and defensive geopolitics that the Union could have pursued.

Commitment to the EaP

The EU's commitment to the east undoubtedly intensified. The EaP became more high profile and occupied much attention in EU foreign policy deliberations from the latter half of 2013. The leaders' summit

Table 3: *Categories of EU Responses*

EU Policy before 2013	Offensive Geopolitics Option	Defensive Geopolitics Option	The EU Response: Liberal-Redux Geopolitics
Low-level commitment.	Strong increase in commitment to EaP, including security protection, EU accession.	Pull back from eastern region, EaP neutrality.	Modest increase in support. Cooperative management of EaP space more cognisant of Russia. Neutrality-lite.
Formulaic cooperation with Russia.	Punitive isolation of Russia.	Acceptance of Russian interests.	Reduced engagement with and bounded containment of Russia. Combined with openness to dialogue on security order.
No hard-security element.	Strong build up and use of military capabilities. NATO prominence.	Softening of NATO.	Engage and hedge. Modest boost to defence, but hard security not prominent in policy mix. Avoidance of overt securitisation.
Technocratic, linkages approach to democracy. Logic of appropriateness.	Democracy support subordinate to relative power gain.	Low priority of democracy support, as too intrusive in post-Soviet sphere.	Democratic values as geopolitical tool, but instrumental variation across EaP states.
Led by EU institutions and processes.	Governments take over from EU institutions with standard diplomacy and security tools.	EU-level low-politics engagement.	Combination of national diplomacy and EU instruments.

in Vilnius in late November 2013 shone an intense spotlight on the region. The EaP became a matter of high politics, as it presented the EU with some of its thorniest strategic challenges. This dynamic deepened through 2015 and 2016, as Ukraine's crisis simmered and sent ripples across the region.

However, there was asymmetry between Russian and European understandings of the geopolitical imperative. For Vladimir Putin, the crisis was existential, the manner of its resolution crucial to Russia's status in global politics and its identity as a nation. For the EU, it was an annoyance – serious and unsettling, but not a matter of do-or-die Darwinian survival. Unlike the strategic impact of the post-2008 financial and Eurozone crises it was not judged to threaten the EU's very continuance. European rhetoric was similar to that heard after the terrorist attacks of 9/11 and the 2011 Arab uprisings; on both these previous occasions European leaders spoke of a watershed, while EU policies in practice exhibited as much continuity as radical change. The same was true of European responses to the eastern crisis of 2014. European governments spoke of a uniquely serious geostrategic threat, but did not act in way that was commensurate with their own rhetoric. There was still much debate in the EU about whether Middle Eastern or Eastern European problems were the priority, as if the EU would struggle to focus on both simultaneously. Many member states did not see the geopolitical imperative in the stark terms of having to hold at bay a wholesale illiberal threat to rules-based order.

The EU neither sought tighter control of, nor dramatically withdrew from the EaP space. Some experts insisted that the crisis presented the EU with a fundamental choice: either it had to offer deeper inclusion to EaP partners or reach an accommodation with Russia over 'sharing' the neighbourhood. European governments fudged this choice – at the multiple levels of EaP instruments, national policies and security commitments within NATO.[1] Some argued that this revealed that the EU was essentially a status quo power, and that this was evident in the east as much as in the long-turbulent south.[2] More conceptually, it might be said that while EU interest calculation was not geopolitical in the

[1] N. Tocci, *The Neighbourhood Policy is Dead. What Next for European Foreign Policy Along its Arc of Instability*, Rome: IAI, 2014.

[2] S. Biscop, *EU Foreign Policy between the Revolution and the Status Quo*, Brussels: Egmont Institute, 2014.

classical sense of seeking exclusive control over geographical territory, it did begin to incorporate a more variegated and sophisticated spatial awareness.

One argument commonly made was that the EU should deepen the extent to which EaP partners were incorporated into an institutionalised 'European space'. Diplomats commonly insisted that this would be the best way of pushing back against Russian tactics. The EU introduced many initiatives that deepened this logic of 'geopolitics as inclusion'. Yet this logic was not carried through in a comprehensive way. Most evidently, the crisis was not deemed serious enough to jolt member states into offering EaP states the prospect of membership to the Union.

The EU upgraded its policies but was keener to keep the EaP region as a 'middle-land' between it and a more abrasive Russia than it was to extend its own integration sphere. Many member states implicitly tilted to the view that EaP states constituted 'in-between lands'. While member states gave a positive twist to this, with much talk of Ukraine and other countries serving as a bridge between west and east, they gave at least some ballast to Russia's view that the region should be geo-strategically managed – juggled in an east–west balance, almost regardless of what its people might prefer. The EU insisted it did not see the Eurasian Union as a competitive strategic problem; Armenia's decision to join the Eurasian Union instead of signing an agreement with the EU was not seen as a major, zero-sum geopolitical loss.

Russia's presence within contested zones in Moldova, Georgia and Ukraine succeeded in dissuading many EU member states from fuller commitments to these countries; the Russian military presence meant that any offer of EU or NATO membership would inevitably drag European countries into conflict with Russia. Paradoxically, the more that Georgians, Moldovans and Ukrainians complained about Russian incursions the more, in a sense, they did Moscow's own bidding by frightening off EU governments from a deeper commitment to protect EaP states' territorial integrity and *de facto* sovereignty. In short, the EU offered managed inclusion but without the costs and (feared) overreach of enlargement. The EU's strategic coda was, in this sense, one of low-cost system maintenance.

European governments certainly did not raise their commitment sufficiently to become robust security protectors to EaP partners; they did not attempt geopolitics in the sense of defending EaP states from Russian intervention or low-level meddling. European governments did not extend unequivocal hard-security protection for EaP states' national sovereignty – the very thing that these states wanted. The EU as such struggled to deal with a paradox: it needed to protect the national sovereignty of eastern states while its own rationale and world-view were based on transcending sovereignty. The EU was still not attuned to the prerequisites of nation-building through its distinctive policy instruments; its policies attempted to standardise rules and governance quality in a way that presumed national identity and solidity already existed. Indeed, the EU as a whole implicitly held out a Faustian pact to Ukraine, Georgia and Moldova: extended and deeper partnership with Europe in return for accepting *de facto* loss of control over a portion of national territory.

While the EU showed intensified ambition in some areas, policy-makers were also more apt to acknowledge that it was no longer the only reference point or political actor in the region and to argue that ambitions of transformative impact had to be lowered. In many respects, member states' response implicitly accepted the criticism that the EU had dangerously over-reached in the EaP region prior to 2013: its promises and commitments had tipped balances within domestic politics but were then not followed through in a fully geopolitical fashion.[3] Some member states' primary geopolitical reflex was to call the US back into the region, in particular though NATO, rather than to seek any lead, autonomous European security pre-eminence.

European realism tilted more to the defensive than the offensive. Even more 'pro-Russian' governments, like that of Viktor Orban in Hungary, boosted defence and security capabilities as protection against Moscow. The crisis had a clearer impact on NATO defence provisions than on EU instruments. NATO commitments and deployments were primarily a matter of defending EU territory, a major step back from the aspiration to guarantee effective sovereignty in Europe's eastern neighbourhood. For many governments the priority was a profoundly defensive one of preventing Russia from undermining European unity; in particular dissuading Germany from drifting back into a balancing role equidistant between the east and the west.[4]

[3] N. MacFarlane and A. Menon, 'The EU and Ukraine', *Survival*, 56/3, 2014, 95–101.

[4] S. Rynning, 'The false promise of continental concert: Russia, the West and the necessary balance of power', *International Affairs*, 91/3, 2015.

One reason for the EU's pursuit of a measured response was a judgement that domestic factors drove President Putin's actions as much as any well-worked Russian plan fundamentally to overturn the geopolitical order. One of Putin's primary aims was to preserve the status quo *within* Russia. European diplomats often insisted that the crisis in Ukraine did not need to be interpreted as a clash between two completely incompatible geopolitical constructs. Although the EU did not play a particularly proactive role in Ukrainian reform, and discouraged the country's European aspirations, Russia was nevertheless afraid that a tide of Western-orientated economic and political restructuring could spread. One Machiavellian interpretation argued that European governments were happy for Russia to sink blood and treasure into EaP states, as the EU had more to gain from Russia being tied down in costly disputes than from running strategic risks to create a stable and democratic EaP zone.[5]

In sum, a degree of geopolitical logic gradually took shape across the different elements of European response to the crisis. Some writers concluded that the EU failed to develop any kind of strategic thinking during the crisis.[6] While this routine criticism seemed harsh from the vantage point of late 2016, it was certainly the case that the faint lines of EU strategic thinking did not denote a particularly high-definition variety of geopolitics. Assertive and defensive member states appeared almost to neutralise each other, meaning that the EU neither moved forward fully to embrace and defend EaP partners, nor fully retract. The EU logic towards Ukraine and some other EaP states might be termed *neutrality-lite*, given that Russia's interests and positions were now factored into European foreign policy initiatives in a way that was not the case prior to 2013.

Inclusion-Exclusion Towards Russia

The EU's response to Russia shifted from the logic of inclusion to one of partial exclusion. Russian counter-responses to the EaP or European Neighbourhood Policy were previously seen as a residual, nuisance variable; now they came to the forefront of how the EU defined its

[5] R. Gowan, 'Lacking security strategy, EU counts on nearby crises to absorb threats', *World Politics Review*, 28 July 2014.

[6] H. Haukkala 'A perfect storm; or what went wrong and what went right for the EU in Ukraine', *Europe-Asia Studies*, 68/4, 2016, 653–64.

eastern policy. Policy-makers often insisted that their key geopolitical switch was from partnering Russia to building resilient EaP states. If previously the geopolitical vision was that of influencing Russia through interdependence, from 2014 many aspects of EU policy aimed more at holding Russia's influence in Eastern Europe at bay. There was a tilt from 'power as inclusion' to 'power as exclusion'. European diplomats and businesses finally recognised that prioritising short-term gain with Russia risked undermining the EU's own long-term strategic interests.[7] While the EU had used restrictive measures elsewhere in the world, this was the most notable case of sanctions being used as a central pillar of European statecraft. Economic conflict was the most notable element of EU assertive geopolitics.

However, this change was not complete. Sanctions were designed to hurt but without completely destabilising Russia, and causing an even worse security implosion. Member states such as Germany performed diplomatic contortions to combine measures of exclusion with offers to Russia of ever-deepened cooperation over challenges arising from Eastern Europe and the Southern Caucasus. Several member states gave greater weight to the OSCE than the EU in managing the crisis precisely because it included Russia. What set the preference for a 'geo-economic' strategy apart from traditional offensive geopolitics was a degree of 'selective accommodation' and the pursuit of only a very modest form of strategic balancing.[8]

Some EU member states believed the only way forward was a foreign policy that was the very antithesis of geopolitical confrontation: joint negotiation with Russia over all core issues in the region. This emerged as a powerful dimension in some strands of the European response. This was the case even though some member states doubted that the strategy could be made to work, in light of Russia's apparent inclination to keep pushing for advantage and to disregard successive accords with the West. Despite the difficulties, most member states were not ready to accept that liberal cooperative-interdependence

[7] J. Nixey, *Russia and the EU are Signing their Divorce Papers*, London: Chatham House, 2014.

[8] M. Wigell and A. Vihma, 'Geopolitics versus geoeconomics: The case of Russia's geostrategy and its effects on the EU', *International Affairs* 92/3, 2016. This article applies the distinction not to EU policy towards Russia but Russia's shift from geo-economic tools to geopolitical conformation with Europe.

had definitively failed; some in the EU believed that Russia had been offered insufficient institutional inclusion rather than too much partnership.

The EU balanced this recognition of on-the-ground Russian power with an attempt to preserve core principles of self-determination. Some argued that EU interests would have been better served by the eastern regions of Ukraine opting for succession, defusing tensions with Russia while leaving a rump Ukraine free to integrate into Western and European structures. It was striking that EU member states did not see this as a remotely realistic option and did not contemplate such a radical, Manichean geopolitical shift. They did not engage is such creative manoeuvring in an attempt to outwit the agility of President Putin's tactics. Rather, they followed a script in which Ukraine would be a site of give-and-take coordination between Europe and Russia.

From within many quarters of EaP states all this seemed to leave the Eastern European region at risk of being unenviably conceived as a 'periphery' to both Russia and the EU. The EU effectively made it impossible for some EaP states fully to join either European or Eurasian integration projects, leaving them sandwiched between these two colliding behemoths. Yet, the EU again defended the need for balance: it did not allow its Russia policy entirely to dictate its EaP policy, but neither did its EaP policy entirely take precedence over its Russia policy.

From one critical perspective, the assessment was that the EU became just as aggressively expansionist and as committed to its own exclusive domination in the EaP states as Russia was. This line insisted that the EU was just as inattentive to the preferences of people in the EaP states as Russia and just as unaccommodating, uncompromising and zero-sum towards Russia as Russia was towards the EU.[9] One much-cited work claimed that the EU acted purely at the behest of US goals and therefore ended up mimicking Washington's zero-sum attitude towards Russia and ignoring Ukraine's dual east–west identity.[10]

[9] E. Korosteleva, 'The European Union, Russia and the Eastern region: The analytics of government for sustainable cohabitation', *Cooperation and Conflict*, 2016, 1–19.

[10] R. Sakwa, *Frontline Ukraine: Crisis in the Borderlands*, London: I.B.Tauris, 2015.

A common critical assessment was that the EU did not compromise enough to accommodate Russian positions and remained too concerned with democratic norms.[11]

These critical perspectives were surely right to insist that President Putin was not the singular cause of crisis and that the EU was driven by concerns over relative power rather than purely normative ideals. Yet their description of European policies was factually dubious. Much of EU policy was precisely about accommodation, shared management of geopolitical challenges and creating space for EaP citizens to choose their own identities. Critical accounts rarely proceeded from careful empirical study of the detailed variations in EU democracy support across the eastern region. While many commentators spoke of the US reverting to pure Cold War containment logic, this description simply does not fit the multifaceted strands of EU responses. Indeed, there were significant tensions between European and US responses to the crisis. To argue that, beneath a veneer of insincere Western liberal rhetoric, the EU, Russia and the US were all equally wedded to confrontationally exclusivist geopolitics would be to ignore all the nuances to European responses that this book has uncovered.

The EU's new distancing from and 'managed antipathy' towards Russia did not generate a uniform strategic logic. The EU orchestrated a selective and managed stand-off with Russia, calibrated to specific interests. Many in European capitals thought that the best that could be hoped for was a kind of contained mistrust with Russia. One expert described this as: economic containment, but well short of the complete geostrategic containment of the Cold War.[12] The EU's new preference was for *bounded containment*. This mixed elements that unwound interdependence with those that actually solidified the logic of inclusion in terms of talking with Russia on Ukraine's trade arrangements, internal political arrangements and conflict mediation issues. This was a more calculated and calibrated form of *engage and hedge* as prime geopolitical template.

[11] As seen in one good overview of prominent experts, C. Nitoiu (ed.) *Avoiding a New 'Cold War': The Future of EU-Russia Relations in the Context of the Ukraine Crisis*, London: LSE Ideas Report, 2016.

[12] H. Kundnani, *Containment and Economic Interdependence*, London: European Council for Foreign Relations, 2014.

Reform and Geopolitics

European governments concurred that increasing support for EaP states offered the most promising means of neutering Russian influence. The EU needed to move up several gears in its efforts to create the 'ring of well governed states' to which it had long aspired. As one writer put it: 'the EU became geopolitical in the sense of "trying to show Russia that it has the potential and the willingness to back up the promotion of its values and norms with strategic actions" and "being clear about the EU's interests and how they are pursued"'.[13] Diplomats agreed that the EU needed to deploy more strategic heft, precision and agility to create the conditions within which support for democratic and governance reform could prosper. The EU formally committed itself to a more strategic deployment of its core political norms – what might be termed a geopoliticisation of liberal values.

Yet, a crucial tactical question was what form such assistance should take. EU policy struck a new balance on its reform policies. The EU judged that democratic reform would help undercut Russian influence. However, its terms of engagement also became more flexible. Policy-makers generally realised that the sharper geopolitical challenge required lighter forms of conditionality and more direct assistance somewhat detached from heavy requirements for EaP states' legal approximation with European rules. The EU became more selective and instrumental in its use of conditionality, in pursuit of a more strategic engagement with EaP governments.

The EU sought speed and adaptability, but without subverting the long-term vision that represented its comparative advantage over Russia. The EU was both more insistent that is 'geopolitical advantage' lay in its focus on democratic reforms in EaP partners, and less rigid in the tactics through which it pursued that focus. One European diplomat summarised: the crisis was seen as a pushback against political modernity and thus a focus on defending such modern political values had to be integral to a more geopolitical EU strategy.

The EU sometimes veered towards a convenient disingenuousness: it insisted its aim was (simply) to ensure that EaP citizens could make

[13] C. Nitoiu, 'The Ukraine crisis is forcing the EU to abandon normative power and act more strategically in its eastern neighbourhood', *EUROPP LSE Blog*, 21 September 2015.

their own choices with full autonomy; yet the assumption was that for most those free choices would be pro-European. The EU's stock – and perhaps rather breezy – assumption was that a free and independent Ukraine would be a pro-European Ukraine. But more specifically, the EU prioritised those sectors of Ukraine's reform process that had direct geopolitical relevance, especially decentralisation and security sector reform. Some in the EU were still too ready to hold Europeanisation and democratisation to be synonymous; yet most policy-makers supported types of political reform that were managed, shepherded and controlled in a way that more instrumentally tallied with European interests.

As the crisis deepened, articles and commentaries routinely criticised the EU for blindly assuming that EaP states wanted 'more Europe'. Critics spoke of European influence over domestic democratic reform evaporating; many asserted that such reform was not highly in demand. In fact, the truth was more mixed, less spectacular and in some ways more encouraging from a European perspective. In many quarters of the EaP space, demand for support on political reform clearly increased. This gave European initiatives a niche that mattered in terms of social identities in EaP states.

However, the essential matter was again one of balance. Many experts advised the EU explicitly to renounce any intention to influence domestic political orders; this step would remove Putin's fear that the West was driven by a desire to destabilise his own hold on power and thus resolve the root cause of the crisis.[14] While the EU did not go this far, many in member states and in the Brussels institutions certainly became more circumspect about the blanket use of 'transformative power'. The EU and member states remained reluctant to engage in highly instrumental forms of ideas-based statecraft equivalent to Russia's use of information warfare. If the focus on political norms accorded the EU a clearer comparative advantage given the turn in Russian policy, the foregoing chapters show that the EU did not intensify its democracy support efforts to any overwhelming degree. The EU did not prioritise democracy policies as a conflict-resolution tool in the Southern Caucasus, but carved out a modest role for governance work that avoided the hard politics of frozen conflicts. It was

[14] M. Kaim, H. Maull and K. Westphal, *The Pan-European Order at the Crossroads: Three Principles for a New Beginning*, Berlin: SWP, 2015.

sometimes not entirely clear whether the EU's priority was to have democratic, stable or pro-European states in its neighbourhood: for at least some diplomats, Belarus represented the better outcome than Moldova.

There was a thin line between the EU downgrading support for reform, on the one hand, and encouraging reform helpfully in a more flexible manner, on the other hand. Harnessing values to the service of strategic interests was not easy. The EU still veered between promoting values with no consideration of interests in some instances and pursuing interests with no consideration of values in other areas of policy. Notwithstanding its rhetoric, the EU did not measure its response to the crisis only by milieu improvements that would make EaP states more resilient, but also in terms of relative strategic positioning vis-à-vis Russia.

Critics in Ukraine and other EaP states cautioned that support for domestic reforms could not be a substitute for more direct forms of geopolitical support. They commonly argued that the EU erred in relying too much on the belief that supporting domestic reforms was a 'soft' alternative to pushing back against Russia with hard power. EaP states did not need EU laws so much as they needed basic state capacity, security protection and more organised governance provisions. They needed resilience rather than Europeanisation per se. Governments and civil society in the EaP often complained that EU demands for reform sometimes weakened their resilience to external threats. In believing that support for select sectors of reform was the leading edge of European geopolitics, many in the EU underplayed the systemic, order-related dimensions of the crisis.

In sum, it can be said that the EU responded to crisis in the east with a more geopolitical tinge to its foreign policies. However, its understanding of geopolitics was distinctive. Critics often said that the EU needed to move away from soft towards hard power. But juxtaposing soft and hard power is not a useful lens of analysis in this case, as the distinction fails to capture the kind of options that European governments debated in response to the eastern crisis. The EU followed a path of *asymmetric geopolitics*. It adopted not overly adversarial geopolitics, but felt its way toward more purposive power in the region. For the EU, power was something to be safeguarded by being carefully rationed, not something to be amplified through maximised deployment.

EU Foreign Policy Analytics

These features categorise the nature of the European response to the eastern crisis. A follow on question is how that crisis changed the very essence, drivers, mechanics and processes of European foreign policy coordination itself.

Chapter 2 outlined the common view that EU foreign policy is driven by a *sui generis* dynamic, with its institutional structures explaining policy outcomes and an embedded, common identity setting the framework for EU foreign policy choices. Analysts argue that various forms and levels of embedded institutionalism have ensured a robust degree of unity between European governments and a distinctive set of common European global stances that transcend the calculation of narrow, material interests. Many argue that post-structural and discursive theories best explain EU foreign policy identity, with the norms referred to in European discourse conditioning the substantive evolution of external policies. A key question is whether such explanations were relevant in such a brutally geopolitical crisis in the east – or whether traditional, external geopolitical factors gained more significant explanatory weight.[15]

Taking the key analytical drivers in turn, a range of conclusions emerge from the book's chapters, as follows.

Institutionalist Continuity

Liberal institutionalist dynamics captured some aspects of the crisis response. The patterns of regular and socialised coordination in many areas of EU eastern policy quietly advanced. The crisis did not completely invert established EU foreign policy identities or narratives in the region. The EU's embedded power in the east was not negligible. The convergence on sanctions, from member states' very different starting points, showed that institutional dynamics were sometimes powerful. Russian officials admitted they were surprised at the degree of EU unity, especially on sanctions.

[15] For a summary and further references on these theoretical debates, see C. Hill and M. Smith (eds) *International Relations and the European Union*, Oxford: Oxford University Press, 2nd edn, 2012; R. Youngs, *Europe's Role in Global Politics: A Treat from Liberal Internationalism*, London: Routledge, 2009.

However, constructivist and institutionalist accounts help only to a certain extent and do not provide an entire explanation of the way in which European responses to the crisis were formulated. These dynamics were still relevant to some extent as member states delegated areas of low-level politics to EU frameworks; member states believed these low-politics had a modest, secondary and indirect relevance to the changed geopolitical context. However, they could not account for the switch from low-politics to crisis-mode in the overall European response to the eastern crisis, as member states sought to claw back diplomatic leverage and control from these structures. And acute crisis did not mould a common European understanding of the appropriate response across all aspects of strategy; rather it encouraged convergence between member states on some issues but drew them apart on other tactical questions. It also led to European governments adopting different positions on NATO's hard-security role in the east. On the EU role in the conflict inside Ukraine, in particular, the crisis made some member states less flexible towards Russia, but other governments more accommodating to Moscow.

External Drivers and Interest Re-calculations

In short, we need not just an inwardly orientated explanation but also an appreciation of how European governments reacted in carefully calibrated ways to alterations in the structure of the external order in the east. The shadow of a more eclectic geopolitical order in the east conditioned the parameters of European foreign policies. The standard charge was that the EU applied its *sui generis* foreign policy instruments on the basis of unthinking automaticity and as if the EaP region existed 'in a geopolitical vacuum'. By 2016, this was no longer entirely true.[16]

Governments' rationalist calculations both spurred and sapped European unity. The structural variables of the eastern crisis could have been predicted to tighten EU unity. To a degree this was indeed the case. The painfully revealed weaknesses of EU power against Russian actions encouraged member states to reinforce some areas of cooperation. However, the divergences engendered by the crisis also

[16] S. Biscop, *Geopolitics with European Characteristics: An Essay on Pragmatic Idealism, Equality, and Strategy*, Brussels: Egmont Institute, 2016, p. 3.

drove member states to break rank and secure quick-gain benefits for the national interest. This latter trend was compounded by the imprecision of the post-crisis European order. Uncertainty over the shape of that order militated in favour of multi-level external action. In aspects of their responses, member states dissociated themselves from their European partners and gave greater preference to bilateral interest-maximisation. National self-help was a powerful leitmotif of governments' response – even as simultaneously member states invested in strengthening the common European dimensions of the way that geopolitical interests were pursued in the EaP and with Russia.

EU Norms, Rules and Interests

The analytical dynamics and drivers of normative EU positions altered after 2013. Hitherto, the 'normative agenda' often owed much to a somewhat generic and abstract feeling that intrinsically European values were to be imparted almost by automatic mimetism to the outside world – a very constructivist notion of governments pursuing values they had come jointly to define as broadly appropriate for other states. After 2013, the EU deliberated its support for certain values in a much more strategic fashion. The common perception that the EU was a benign normative power and Russia a valueless geopolitical hard power looked far too binary a distinction. If the EaP's pre-crisis failure was that it had 'divorced soft power from the general foreign policy it is meant to serve and enhance',[17] after 2013 the EU went some way to addressing this shortcoming. The EU might not have adopted a classical or offensive form of geopolitics, but it did become more *instrumental* in the deployment of its different levels of policy tools.

The EU began to create a moderately different meta-narrative to underpin its foreign policy – a narrative that was more about interest preservation and slightly less about certain generic principles. The logic of geopolitical outcomes gained explanatory weight relative to the logic of appropriate values – a (further) slide from exclusively constructivist drivers towards a larger pinch of rationalism. Yet, this was a form of bounded rationalism: interests were more carefully defined but still in a less than systematic fashion and with a tendency to fall-back

[17] K. Nielsen and M. Vilson 'The Eastern Partnership: Soft Power Strategy or Policy Failure?', *European Foreign Affairs Review* 19/2, 2014, 243–62, p. 261.

on pre-existing EU institutionalised approaches in the face of strategic uncertainty. It was a rationalism that became slightly less tightly bounded as the crisis deepened.

More subtly, there was a *de facto* divergence of policy logics. In Ukraine, Moldova and Georgia the EU still sought to use the tools of approximation, alignment and external governance as the means to lock-in these states' geopolitical orientation. In Armenia, Azerbaijan and Belarus the EU and national governments in parallel developed more traditional forms of diplomatic engagement and dialogue, along with select functional cooperation. There was no single or uniform geopolitical response, but more of a flexible adjustment to EaP states' domestic conditions.

The eastern crisis was not the only factor pushing EU foreign policy in this direction – the euro crisis, the rise of China and turmoil in the Middle East all contributed as well – but it was certainly a major impact. Most assessments of EU foreign policy had hitherto focused on EU-centric questions: the extent of institutionalist convergence; the EU's self-definition as a normative power; how far its own narrative as a post-modern entity led it to assume certain external positions; and the dynamics of external governance. The post-crisis context called for more analysis of the strategic tactics adopted through different European initiatives on the ground in particular national contexts, and what was required for these to have desired outcomes.

The EU sought to strike more of a balance between ideational attraction, compliance and approximation, on the one hand, and transactional relationships, on the other. Elites sought to trade low-politics regulatory convergence for more tangible benefits. Of course, the Maidan protests suggested that identity was still a catalysing driver; but other events suggested that the EU could not rely on this explanatory dynamic so much in the future. The ostensibly quintessential EU preference for influence through multi-faceted cooperative 'linkages' was no longer quite such the pre-eminent descriptor of foreign policy in the east. The EU sought more of a balanced combination of linkages and leverage in the way it deployed its foreign policy instruments. Linkages were increasingly recognised to be insufficient to overcome tougher obstacles to reform. Lite-socialisation networks of dialogue at all levels could be detected, but many elites had clearly not yet modified their outlooks. The much-cited argument that EU influence is wielded effectively through linkages and rarely through tools of political leverage was not convincing in the context of the eastern crisis.

National Diplomacy

The EU's internal dynamics shifted. Member states assumed a higher profile role in overall European policy. The long-standing focus on the export of sectoral or technocratic EU rules was now complemented by far more engaged traditional diplomacy. A layer of geopolitical diplomacy was superimposed on pre-existing EU institutional initiatives. The latter exhibited much continuity. The new geopolitical diplomacy in part sought to supplement and harness EU-level instruments and practices, but in part to change their essential nature. In this sense, overall EU foreign policy came out of the crisis not quite as distinctive as it was previously assumed to be. The crisis gave increased prominence within EU foreign policy to a number of Central and Eastern European states, in particular Poland. It both raised the importance of these states and presented them with the challenge of meeting the expectations invested in their new international projection – a challenge that was only partially met.

In this sense, the prominent role adopted by Germany and France in the Minsk process was a sign of both strength and weakness. On the one hand, it demonstrated a willingness to pursue eastern policy through the prism of high-level national diplomacy, with two member states ostensibly representing the wider EU interest in a way that facilitated leadership-level negotiation with Russia and Ukraine. On the other hand, several strongly engaged member states felt that this *de facto* minilateralism was more or less imposed on them and reflected the fragmenting of EU unity. Several member states were deeply unhappy with the lines adopted by Angela Merkel and François Hollande; yet those member states had themselves ceded power to Germany and France to limit their own exposure and commitment to the crisis.

Of course, the crisis undoubtedly reinforced an incipient focus on German diplomatic leadership. The eastern crisis acted as a catalyst and test case for Germany's commitment to a more influential role in foreign policy. Unsurprisingly, the crisis revealed both the extended reach and limits to this new German ambition. The general view was that it propelled Germany to an uncontested leadership of European foreign policy. Some German analysts argued that Chancellor Angela

Merkel exercised successful leadership, keeping the EU together and finding the right mix of sticks and carrots to push President Putin back from his more maximalist agenda in Ukraine – and that this was indeed the most notable change in internal EU dynamics ushered in by the crisis.[18] From this perspective, Germany had demonstrated successful leadership over the Ukraine crisis, based on consensual networked diplomacy of which other member states were 'willing followers'.[19]

Yet, the evidence by 2016 looked a little more varied. At each step, German caution held back the potential for more effective EU responses. Member states certainly wanted things both ways: they wanted Germany to take primary responsibility but they were also bitterly critical of the German government and especially its foreign minister for acting in ways that dramatically worsened Ukraine's plight. The sharpest judgement was that Germany's response was so equivocal that it took the country another step out of the mainstream Western foreign policy camp.[20] Even if this criticism was somewhat harsh, it certainly captured some flavour of Germany's multiple levels of diplomatic balancing.

In sum, the post-2013 eastern challenges *tightened the interaction of internal and external explanatory factors*. The evolution of European policies was most potently explained by the way in which internal and external influences combined and interlaced with each other. It was in this sense that the *triangle of influences* was evident between internal EU policy-making structures, Russian geo-strategy and trends in the EaP states. The eastern crisis shifted the balance between these three levels towards the international-structural level – with these external factors mediated through the shaping influence of EU identities and EaP domestic structures.

Crucially, it was precisely this shift in analytical balance that dovetailed with the 'liberal-redux' combination of the European geopolitical response. The EU's embedded institutional structures, norms commitments and EaP path dependency militated against a pure raison d'état dominated by the large member states. The shifting and

[18] U. Speck, *The West's Response to the Ukraine Conflict: A Transatlantic Success Story*, Washington DC: Transatlantic Academy, 2016.

[19] G. Hellmann, 'Germany's world: Power and followership in a crisis-ridden Europe', *Global Affairs*, 2/1, 2016, p. 12.

[20] H. Kudnani, 'Leaving the West behind', *Foreign Affairs*, December 2014.

diverging domestic politics and expectations of the EaP states pushed the EU to combine normative support with geopolitical statecraft in permutations tailored to each partner state. Overlying all this, external shocks and challenges accounted for many of the 'redux' components of the EU's liberal-redux geopolitics. The crisis called for a profoundly composite picture of EU foreign-policy dynamics.

Results

Was the EU's mix of strategic logics a sign of muddle and inability to think in clearly geopolitical terms, or was it a carefully balanced response that traced the lines of an effective form of calibrated geopolitics? Was EU policy a factor in conditioning both Russian and other policy choices? Overall, the foregoing chapters demonstrate that the impact of the EU's asymmetric geopolitics was mixed – neither an unequivocal success nor a resounding failure.

On all objective indicators, the EU had more power than Russia, but came out of the crisis chastened in many senses. Crimea was lost and Russia had shown no willingness to concede on the other protracted conflicts through which it kept a toehold in the region. Russia was now in *de facto* control over territory in all EaP states except Belarus – over which it had effective tutelage anyway. President Putin seemed to have a losing hand: Russia was structurally weak and getting weaker; economically and militarily its power was modest compared to the combined weight of the West. Yet it gained successive short-term tactical victories. The EU struggled to get ahead of Russia in the fluctuating geopolitical brinkmanship of the eastern crises. EU policy sometimes seemed a rather hapless and insipid derivative of Russian strategy.

Critics constantly made the point that the EU was offering Russia little and asking in return for things that it could not deliver without a wholesale change to Putin's internal and external power strategy.[21] Many insiders believed that Putin's operating logic was beyond rational cost–benefit calculation, and that the EU's effort carefully to weigh up sticks and carrots was doomed to ineffectiveness. If Russia's aim was simply to make Ukraine so explosively unstable and fractured

[21] K. Liik, *The Real Problem with Mogherini's Russia Paper*, London: European Council for Foreign Relations, 20 January 2015.

that EU member states would pull back from offering it full inclusion in the EU's governance sphere, then it was at least partly successful.

In Ukraine, more than 9,000 lives were lost, engendering understandable anger there at the tepid impact of the Western response. The result of the overarching crisis was a 'new normal' of sustained instability in Ukraine, tension with Russia and less commitment from Moscow to joint problem-solving on global issues.[22] It was disconcerting that such extreme and damaging Russian meddling did not turn EU or EaP opinion against Russia nearly as strongly as might have been expected.[23] While the EU established its basic line of containment-lite combined with an open door to engagement with Russia, it seemed as if neither the negative nor positive side of that equation was pursued strongly enough to make a game-changing impact in Moscow or EaP capitals.

A number of paradoxes in EU positions detracted from the EU's impact. Member state governments said they did not see Russia as an overt, direct threat but as a second-order problem in the way Moscow kept EaP domestic politics tense and fractious. Yet the EU played into to the Kremlin's strategy by concluding that this very instability made a significant upgrade in EaP cooperation undesirable. Member states said they saw the biggest danger lying in Russia playing on differences within the West. Yet few member states made major concessions in order to defend EU consensus – they all spoke of the need for unity between EU governments, but in many areas of policy insisted on unity on their own terms. Before the crisis, Russia did not share the EU's notion of security order based on liberal values but did genuinely seek some kind of pan-European architecture. With the advent of the Eurasian Union, a dynamic of competing regional projects emerged. The EU said it sought to minimise the degree of clashing competitiveness, but its own rules held it back from effective palliatives – and it was also unable to convince Russia to show the flexibility necessary to make the two regional projects more harmoniously compatible.

However, there were grounds for arguing that the EU's measured responses were not entirely ineffective. Some experts insisted that any

[22] S. Charap, 'Ukraine: Seeking an elusive new normal', *Survival*, 56/3, 2014, 85–94.

[23] N. Popescu, 'After Crimea: Putin's Balance Sheet', *ISS Alert*, Paris: EU Institute for Security Studies, April 2014.

other geopolitical option would have been worse: on the one hand, blind and assertive expansion of liberal values was now likely to stir greater tension; but on the other hand, a traditional concert of powers could not realistically be made to work in cooperation with Russia.[24] No other state recognised Crimea. Other rising powers did not join with Russia to use the Crimea episode as a launching pad for rewriting the international order. The full-scale assault on European order that many feared and predicted did not take shape. Putin was reduced to more sporadic provocations and challenges. Ukraine turned westwards; the country suffered a tragic loss of life but its worst nightmare of Russian troops marching into Kiev did not materialise. The EU clearly gained the upper hand over the Eurasian Union – as Russia struggled to solidify the latter as a prospective Soviet Union-lite. At the same time, European diplomacy and bridge-building helped, to a very modest degree, to reduce Russia's brooding ostracism from the levels it might otherwise have reached.

The outcome was bad for Putin in many senses. Russia lost a huge amount of money in Crimea and the east. In some ways Kiev outmanoeuvred Moscow, making the latter assume much responsibility for Donbas as a protectorate and partly separating it from developments in the rest of Ukraine – exactly what President Putin did not want. Russia had to re-engage with OSCE cooperative rule-making. While Putin may tactically have played his hand to the maximum, Russia's structural weaknesses had, if anything worsened as a result of the crisis. The US returned to European security and NATO was reborn. The transatlantic relationship emerged at least partially revived. Russian nationalism intensified in a way that Putin struggled to manage for his own political survival. Russian-Ukrainian 'friendship' was sunk. Some EaP governments made a stronger commitment to 'European' and democratic values not so much due to EU policies but as a counter-reaction to Russian meddling.[25]

Putin, said many, did not care about Donbas per se, but about the West recognising that Russia had an unchallengeable sphere of influence in the region as a whole. Measured on this metric, the EU may

[24] S. Rynning, 'The false promise of continental concert: Russia, the West and the necessary balance of power', *International Affairs*, 91/3, 2015.

[25] L. Delcour and K. Wolczuk, 'Spoiler or facilitator of democratization? Russia's role in Georgia and Ukraine', *Democratization*, 22/s, 2015, 459–78.

have been pushed back against the ropes but it did not entirely cede ground. This was no small achievement. After all, in some senses, it was easier for Russia simply to disrupt politics in the EaP states than it was for the EU to fulfil its aim of changing those domestic politics in a long-term and structural fashion.[26] Russia's reputation was profoundly tarnished by the crisis, in the West but also beyond. The fact that the Russian government quite clearly told lies about its involvement in Ukraine meant that its trustworthiness on all matters was thrown into doubt. Splintered societies and identities were negative outcomes for EaP states themselves; but from a cynically realist perspective it was an outcome that at least prevented EaP states falling wholly into Russia's orbit. For some states the problem was not so much an all-conquering Russian sphere of influence, but that Russian engagement was – not unlike EU strategy – a half-way involvement bereft of the power or ideational appeal to guarantee stability.

Within individual EaP states, impact varied. In many places, the EU's much-cited transformative power patently struggled to gain traction in the geopolitical bear-pit of the EaP. The reasons why this transformative power reached an apparent limit were complex. Some factors had to do with domestic variables in eastern partners. Others had to do with broader structural changes in the international system and with the changing nature of the EU itself. Tactical mistakes by the EU compounded the turnaround in power vectors. Many in the region complained that the EU's ambivalence over 'values' made Russia treat it less seriously and was actually counterproductive for the EU's geopolitical impact. Some interlocutors feared that too much EU talk of geopolitics damaged the gravitas and impact of its liberal-cooperative approaches.

Notwithstanding these critical views, in some states EU cooperation gained traction and helped neuter Russian pressure. The EU was effective in maintaining a positive, ideational dimension to its policies that continued to draw many in the region away from Russia. Putin found that the new order was as much about states' resistance to his idea of civilisational identity as it was about declining Western power. With EU help, in some states governance reforms advanced further

[26] M. Laurinavcius, L. Kascijnas and L. Kajola, 'What will determine Ukraine's future scenariois?', *Eastern Pulse Newsletter* 3/58, Eastern European Studies Centre, Vilnius, 2014.

than prior to 2013. In other states, authoritarianism proved resilient. This variation in EU impact pointed to the primacy of domestic political structures: differences within EaP partners explained why in some the EU's approach was effective, but in others it did not register significant changes after 2013. The EU-governance dynamic persisted as one factor of influence but not necessarily the most dominant.

Indeed, after the crisis, discrepancies between EaP states were wider. EaP countries reacted differently both to EU offers and to Russian blandishments. Ukraine, Moldova and Georgia largely chose to veer towards the EU. Belarus tried to reduce its dependence on Russia, although not to the extent of bending much to EU conditionality. Armenia was left in a curious limbo, while Azerbaijan resisted both EU and Russian influence. Beneath their governmental positions, most of these states were more internally divided over western and eastern ideational choices. While the EaP purported to be a region-building initiative, the variation between different partners' paths became arguably its most striking feature. The EU gained little traction in Belarus or Azerbaijan and the EaP was not a high-profile policy concern in these countries. Armenia chose to drop its EU agreement with virtually no domestic debate or subsequent outcry. In Georgia, in contrast, a strong pro-EU consensus took shape and the country prioritised its association agreement, even as domestic political camps fought ferociously on most other issues.

Legacy

Beyond this mixed impact of EU policy responses was the question of the crisis' long-term legacy. Whose rules had come to predominate? Was the crisis the beginning of the end for the liberal world order or a false alarm?

In some ways the crisis forced the EU onto the back foot and forced it to recognise more prominently that Russia had interests and a presence in the region. The crisis bred an aura of 'manageable defeat' in EU circles. But it also made the EU more alert to Russian geo-strategy and less naïve – it was less liable to think that offering all-encompassing packages of positive sum cooperation would automatically get all sides of the geopolitical equation working together in harmony. There was no quick re-normalisation of relations with Russia as there had been after the 2008 invasion of Georgia. The silver lining was that this altered mind-set was probably overdue and arguably set the EU up for more effective influence in the future.

This book has covered a period of acute crisis and uncertainty, between 2013 and the end of 2016, which give birth to a more geopolitical EU eastern policy. One crucial question was whether the changes to EU policies would endure beyond 2016. Was this period the catalyst for a more geopolitical tone to general EU approaches to foreign policy that would last over time and spill into other areas of external relations too? Or as the situation in the east calmed down, would the EU shift quickly back to its standard approaches, devoid of the hybrid, liberal-redux geopolitics outlined in the book?

The crisis was certainly not 'just' about Ukraine; but neither did it signify that 'everything is now different', as many commentators and politicians announced with dread and anticipation. By the end of 2016 it was not clear whether the legacy would be persistent, unpredictable instability or a new stable equilibrium of rebalanced power across the European continent. The crisis certainly changed the parameters for the EU's efforts to keep global order intact over the longer-term. The precariousness of national sovereignty in the east remained. The future challenge would be to defend core territorial integrity, even as the EU espoused and sought to cultivate shared sovereignty.

A wider question was whether the EU devised a coherent response to the broader geopolitical contours of the crisis. Being 'geopolitical' should not simply have been about being 'tough on Putin'. However unjustifiably brutal, Russian actions did raise uncomfortable questions about the principles of European order. Putin's insistence that Crimea was no different to the West recognising Kosovo was obviously disingenuous. However, the episode revealed how the EU's whole approach toward self-determination remained replete with malleable principles and uncertainty.

Arguably, one unhelpful legacy of the eastern crisis was that it tended to force diplomatic, journalistic and analytical opinions into a 'pro-Russian versus anti-Russian' dichotomy. This skewered reflection away from more structural challenges to international order. If global order was indeed now under threat, the EU needed to look more broadly at how that order could regain legitimacy. Yet at least part of the European approach to the crisis seemed to suggest that some governments now saw the international political order as being maintained through a more pivotal reliance on great power dialogue and diplomacy than firm objective rules. Moreover, rising powers in other parts of the world were not convinced that this was an epoch-changing conflict, as opposed to a local European–Russian squabble: the EU–Russia relationship did not have quite the same systemic determinacy it might have had a decade previously.

In 1914, when British politicians weighed up the strategic costs and benefits of intervening to uphold established order in Europe, they were ultimately swayed by the likely impacts on the country's broader power and reputation: if Britain failed to protect the basic norms of order now, it would never be able to do so again.[27] The echoes of such deliberations were present 100 years later, as Europe was once again ripped open by conflict. In their response to the Ukraine crisis, European politicians certainly talked of the same long-term reputational and power considerations. Yet there was a powerful policy logic that was more managerial than strategically far-sighted. This contributed to the feeling that in this crisis the West and Russia had drawn: neither side was clearly victorious in ensuring that its understanding of order prevailed.

[27] M. Macmillan, *The War that Ended Peace*, London: Profile Books, 2013, p. 573.

Bibliography

Abbasov F., *The Europeanisation of the Southern Gas Corridor: Assessing the institutional dimension of the EU's energy security*, PhD Thesis, Sheffield University, 2016.

Abbasov S., 'Azerbaijan Divided Over Crimea's Implications for Karabakh Peace', *EurasiaNet.org*, 20 March 2014. Available at: www.eurasianet.org/node/68172.

Ademmer E., 'Interdependence and EU-demanded policy change in a shared neighbourhood', *Journal of European Public Policy*, 22/5, 2015, 671–89.

Agnew J., *Geopolitics: Re-visioning World Politics*, London: Routledge, 1998.

Al-Rodhan N., *Neo-statecraft and Meta-geopolitics*, Berlin: LIT Verlag, 2009.

Alieva L., 'Azerbaijan and the ENP: When soft power and security are tightly related', in Inayeh A., D. Schwarzer and J. Forbrig (eds) *Regional Repercussions of the Ukraine Crisis: Challenges for the Six Eastern Partnership Countries*, Berlin: GMF Europe, 2014, p. 12.

Allison R., 'Russian "deniable" intervention in Ukraine: How and why Russia broke the rules', *International Affairs*, 90/6, 2014, 1255–97.

'Security Policy, Geopolitics and International Order in EU-Russian Relations during the Ukraine Crisis', in C. Nitoiu (ed.) *Avoiding a New 'Cold War': The Future of EU-Russia Relations in the Context of the Ukraine Crisis*, London: LSE Ideas Report, 2016.

Arutunyan A., 'Putin's new foreign policy rulebook', Open Democracy, 3 November 2014.

The Putin Mystique: Inside Russia's Power Cult, Warks: Skyscraper, 2014.

Babayan N., *Democratic Transformation and Obstruction: The European Union, United States and Russia in the South Caucasus*, London: Routledge: 2014.

Behnke A., 'The politics of geopolitik in post Cold-War Germany', *Geopolitics*, 3, 2006, 396–419.

Bertelsmann Stiftung, *Free Trade from Lisbon to Vladivostok. A Tool for Peace and Prosperity: The Effects of a Free Trade Area between the EU and the Eurasian Region*, Gütersloh, 2016.

Birchfield V., 'A normative power Europe framework of transnational policy formation', *Journal of European Public Policy*, 20/6, 2013, 907–22.

Biscop S., *EU Foreign Policy between the Revolution and the Status Quo*, Brussels: Egmont Institute, 2014.

Game of Zones: The Quest for Influence in Europe's Neighbourhood, Brussels: Egmont Institute, Egmont Paper 67, 2014.

Geopolitics with European Characteristics: An Essay on Pragmatic Idealism, Equality, and Strategy, Brussels: Egmont Institute, 2016, p. 3.

Biscop S. and J. Andersson (eds) *The EU and the European Security Strategy: Forging a global Europe*, London: Routledge, 2008.

Bond I., *Europe and Russia: Continental Divide?*, London: Centre for European Reform, 2014.

The EU and Russia: Uncommon Spaces, London: Centre for European Reform, 2014.

Boonstra J. and L. Delcour, *A Broken Region: Evaluating EU Polices in the South Caucasus*, Madrid: Fride, 2015.

Börzel T. and V. van Hüllen, 'One voice, one message, but conflicting goals: Cohesiveness and consistency in the European Neighbourhood Policy', *Journal of European Public Policy*, 21/7, 2015, 1033–49.

Bouchet N., *How to Counter Russia's Anti-Democratic Strategy*, 2015, Washington DC: German Marshall Fund.

Burke-White W., 'Crimea and the international legal order', *Survival*, 56/4, 2014, 65–80.

Burlyuk O., 'A thorny path to the spotlight: The rule of law component in EU external policies and EU-Ukraine relations', *European Journal of Law Reform*, 1, 2014.

'An ambitious failure: Conceptualising the EU approach to rule of law promotion (in Ukraine)', *Hague Journal on the Rule of Law* 6/1, 2014, 26–46.

The role of culture in reconciliation in the Ukraine crisis, More Europe policy paper. Available at: wwww.moreurope.org, 2014.

Buzan B. and G. Lawson, *The Global Transformation: History, Modernity and the Making of International Relations*, Cambridge: Cambridge University Press, 2015.

Caiser T., 'Why the EU-Russia Strategic Partnership could not prevent a confrontation over Ukraine: EU just as zero-sum now as Russia', in C. Nitoiu (ed.) *Avoiding a New 'Cold War': The Future of EU-Russia Relations in the Context of the Ukraine Crisis*, London: LSE Ideas Report, 2016.

Charap S., 'Ukraine: Seeking an elusive new normal', *Survival*, 56/3, 2014, 85–94.

Chirila V., 'Moldova: More focus, flexibility and visibility for the European Neighbourhood Policy', in A. Inayeh and J. Forbig (eds), *Reviewing the European Neighbourhood Policy: Eastern Perspectives*, Berlin: GMF Europe, 2015.

Christiansen T. and B. Tonra (eds) *Rethinking European Union Foreign Policy*, Manchester: Manchester University Press, 2004.

Christou G., 'The European Union's human security discourse: Where are we now?' *European Security*, 23/3, 2014, 364–81.

Ciurea C., *Moldova after the Elections: Politics Overtakes Reforms*, London: European Council for Foreign Relations, 2015.

Cladi L. and A. Locatelli, 'Worth a shot: On the explanatory power of bandwagoning in transatlantic relations', *Contemporary Security Policy*, 34/2, 2013, 374–81.

Conceição-Heldt E. and S. Meunier, 'Speaking with a single voice: Internal cohesiveness and external effectiveness of the EU in global governance', *Journal of European Public Policy*, 21/7, 2014, 961–79.

Cornell S., 'European Union: Eastern Partnership vs Eurasian Union', in S. Starr and S. Cornell (eds), *Putin's Grand Strategy: The Eurasian Union and Its Discontents*, Washington DC: Central Asia-Caucasus Institute, Johns Hopkins University and Stockholm: Silk Road Studies Program 2014.

Getting Georgia Right, Brussels: Centre for European Studies, 2014.

Costa O., 'A force for and because of multilateralism: When is the EU a multilateralist actor in world society?', *Journal of European Public Policy*, 20/8, 2013, 1213–28.

Ćwiek-Karpowicz J. and S. Secrieru (eds) *Russia and Sanctions*, Warsaw: PISM, 2015.

Czech Association for International Affairs, *Conference Report: The International Conference 'Eastern Partnership Five Years On: Time For a New Strategy?'*, Prague, 2014.

Damro C., 'Market power Europe', *Journal of European Public Policy* 19/5, 2012, 682–99.

'Market power Europe: Exploring a dynamic conceptual framework', *Journal of European Public Policy*, 22/9, 2015, 1336–54.

De Jong D., 'Why Europe should fight Nord Stream II', *EU Observer*, 23 February 2016.

De Vries A., C. Portela and B. Guijarro-Usobiaga, *Improving the Effectiveness of Sanctions: A Checklist for the EU*, Brussels: Centre for European Policy Studies, 2014.

Del Sarto R., 'Normative empire Europe: The European Union, its borderlands, and the "Arab Spring"', *Journal of Common Market Studies*, 54/2, 2016, 215–32.

Delcour L., *The EU and Russia in their 'Contested Neighbourhood': Multiple External Influences, Policy Transfer and Domestic Change*, London: Routledge, 2017.

Delcour L. and H. Kostanyan, *Towards a Fragmented Neighbourhood: Policies of the EU and Russia and their Consequences for the Area that Lies in Between Brussels*, CEPS Policy Brief 17, 2014.

Delcour L. and E. Tulmets (eds) *Pioneer Europe? Testing EU Foreign Policy in the Neighbourhood*, Baden-Baden: Nomos, 2008.

Delcour L. and K. Wolczuk, 'Spoiler or facilitator of democratization?: Russia's role in Georgia and Ukraine', *Democratization*, 22/s, 2015, 459–78.

Delcour L., H. Kostanyan, B. Vandecasteele and P. Van Elsuwege, 'The Implications of Eurasian Integration for the EU's Relations with the Countries in the post-Soviet Space', *Studia Diplomatica*, LXVIII-1, 2015, 5–33.

Dias V., 'The EU's post-liberal approach to peace: Framing EUBAM's contribution to the Moldova–Transnistria conflict transformation', *European Security*, 22/3, 2013, 338–54.

Dreyer I., 'EU not yet ready to talk to Eurasian Economic Union as WTO cases mount', *Bordelex*, 7 December 2014.

'EU Ukraine DCFTA versus Russia-sponsored Eurasian economic union: Flexibility on implementation in sight', *Borderlex*, 28 August 2014.

Dufour N., 'France's D-Day diplomacy: Time for Paris to end its hedging on Russia', *PISM Bulletin no. 84*, Warsaw: Polish Institute for International Affairs, 2014.

Emerson M., *Russia's Economic Interests and the EU's DCFTA with Ukraine*, Brussels: Centre for European Policy Studies, 2014.

Erixson F., *How Trade and Security became Europe's Unhappy Couple*, Brussels: Carnegie Europe, March 2015.

EU Committee of Regions, *CORLEAP: Looking Forward to Democratic Reform in the Eastern Partnership Countries*, Brussels, 2014.

Eurasia Partnership Foundation, *Alternative Assessment Report, Implementation of the ENP Action Plan and EaP bilateral and Multilateral Roadmaps of 2013*, Tbilsi, 2014.

European Commission, *ENP Country Progress Report* 2014 – *Ukraine*, March 2015.

EU-Ukraine Association Agenda, Brussels, 2009.

European Commission and High Representative, *Review of the European Neighbourhood Policy*, JOIN (2015) 50 final, November 2015.

European Commission and High Representative for Foreign Affairs and Security Policy, *Joint Consultation Paper: Towards a New Neighbourhood Policy*, JOIN (2015) 6 March 2015.

European Commission and High Representative for Foreign and Security Policy, *Neighbourhood at the Crossroads: Implementation of the European Neighbourhood Policy in* 2013, JOIN(2014) 12.

European Council for Foreign Relations, *Annual Meeting Memorandum*, 12–13 June 2014.

Foreign Policy Scorecard 2014, London: ECFR, 2014.

European Union, *European Security Strategy: A Strong Europe in a Safer World*, 2003.

Ukraine ENP Progress Report, Brussels, 2013.

A Framework Strategy for a Resilient Energy Union with a Forward-looking Climate Change Policy, COM (2015), 80 final.

Eyal J., *Russia's Ukraine Strategy Ends Europe's Dream*, London: Royal United Services Institute, 2014.

Far S. and R. Youngs, *Energy Union and EU Global Strategy*, Stockholm: Swedish Institute for European Policy Studies, 2015.

Fischer S., *Escalation in Ukraine*, Berlin: SWP, SWP Comments, 2014.

Formuszewicz R., *Germany's Policy Towards Russia: Old Wine in New Wineskins*, Warsaw: Polish Institute for International Affairs, 2014, p. 4.

Forsberg T., 'Normative power Europe, once again: A conceptual analysis of an ideal type', *Journal of Common Market Studies*, 49/6, 2011, 1183–204.

'From Ostpolitk to frostpolitik? Merkel, Putin and German foreign policy towards Russia', *International Affairs* 92/1, 2016, 21–42.

Forsberg T. and H. Haukkala, 'Could it have been different? The evolution of the EU-Russian conflict and its alternatives', in C. Nitoiu (ed.) *Avoiding a new 'Cold War': The Future of EU-Russia Relations in the Context of the Ukraine Crisis*, London: LSE Ideas Report, 2016, p. 12.

Freedman L., 'Ukraine and the art of exhaustion', *Survival*, 57/5, 2015, 77–106.

Füle S., 'New Europe and enlargement in a new political context', reprinted by European Commission, SPEECH/14/323, 11 April 2014.

Garton Ash T., 'Angela Merkel has faced down the Russian bear in the battle for Europe', *The Guardian*, 22 December 2014.

Gast A-S., *A Shift In The EU Strategy for Central Asia*, Moscow: Carnegie Moscow Centre, 2014.

German Marshall Fund, *Transatlantic Trends 2014*, Washington DC: German Marshall Fund, 2014.

German T., 'Heading west? Georgia's Euro-Atlantic path', *International Affairs*, 91/3, 2015, 601–14.

Getmanchuk A., *Ukraine-NATO: A Hidden Integration or Undeclared Neutrality?*, Kiev: Institute for World Policy, June 2015.

Getmanchuk A. and S. Solodkyy, *Ukraine-Germany: How to Turn Situational Partnership into Priority One*, Kiev: Institute for World Policy, 2016.

Gessel G., *Keeping up Appearances: How Europe is Supporting Ukraine's Transformation*, London: European Council on Foreign Relations, 2016.

Giles K., P. Hanson, R. Lyne, J. Nixey, J. Sherr and A. Woord, *The Russian Challenge*, London: Chatham House, 2015.

Gowan R., 'Lacking security strategy, EU counts on nearby crises to absorb threats', *World Politics Review*, 28 July 2014.

Gros D., 'Restarting Ukraine's economy', *Project Syndicate*, 3 April 2014.

Haass R., 'The unraveling: How to respond to a disordered world', *Foreign Affairs*, November/December 2014.

Hagemann C., 'External Governance on the Terms of the Partner? The EU, Russia and the Republic of Moldova in the European Neighbourhood Policy', *Journal of European Integration*, 35/7, 2013, 767–83.

Haukkala H., 'From cooperative to contested Europe? The conflict in Ukraine as a culmination of a long-term crisis in EU–Russia Relations', *Journal of Contemporary European Studies*, 23/1, 2015, 25–40.

Haverluk T., K. Beauchemin and A. Mueller, 'The three critical flaws of critical geopolitics: Towards a neo-classical geopolitics', *Geopolitics*, 19/1, 2004, 19–39.

Hebel K. and T. Lenz, 'The identity/policy nexus in European foreign policy', *Journal of European Public Policy*, 23/4, 2016, 473–491.

Heisbourg F., 'Preserving post-Cold War Europe', *Survival*, 57/1, 2015, 31–48.

Hellmann G., 'Germany's world: Power and followership in a crisis-ridden Europe', *Global Affairs*, 2/1, 2016, 3–20.

Her Majesty's Government, *National Security Strategy and Strategic Defence and Security Review 2015: A Secure and Prosperous United Kingdom*, London: Stationery Office, 2015.

Hill C. and M. Smith (eds) *International Relations and the European Union*, Oxford: Oxford University Press, 2nd edn, 2012.

House of Lords European Committee, *The EU and Russia: Before and Beyond the Crisis in Ukraine*, London: EU External Affairs Select Committee, 2015.

Huntingdon S., *The Clash of Civilizations and the Remaking of World Order*, New York: Simon and Schuster, 1991.

Ikenberry J., 'The illusion of geopolitics', *Foreign Affairs*, May–June 2014.

Inayeh A., D. Schwarzer and J. Forbrig (eds) *Regional Repercussions of the Ukraine Crisis: Challenges for the Six Eastern Partnership Countries*, Berlin: GMF Europe, 2014.

Institute for World Policy, *How the World Helps Ukraine*, Kiev: Institute for World Policy, September 2014.

Ishkanian A., 'Engineered Civil Society: The Impact of 20 Years of Democracy Promotion on Civil Society Development in Former Soviet Countries', in T. Beichelt, I. Hahn-Fuhr, F. Schimmelfennig and S. Worschech (eds), *Civil Society and Democracy Promotion*, Basingstoke: Palgrave Macmillan, 2014.

Jakobik W., 'A return to business as usual', *New Eastern Europe*, 29 October 2015.

Kaca E., *A New Pact for Ukraine: Making EU Aid Work*, Warsaw: Polish Institute for International Affairs, 2014.

Kaim M., H. Maull and K. Westphal, *The Pan-European Order at the Crossroads: Three Principles for a New Beginning*, Berlin: SWP, 2015.

Kearns G., 'Beyond the legacy of Makinder', *Geopolitics*, 18/4, 2013, 917–32.

Kempin R. and M. Overhaus, 'EU foreign policy in times of the financial and debt crisis', *European Foreign Affairs Review*, 19/2, 2014, 179–94.

Keukalaire S., 'The European Union as a Diplomatic Actor: Internal, Traditional and Structural Diplomacy', in W. Rees and M. Smith (eds) *The International Relations of the European Union*, London: Sage, 2008.

Keukeleire S. and H. Bruyninckx, 'The European Union, the BRICs and the Emerging New World Order', in C. Hill and M. Smith (eds) *International Relations and the European Union*, Oxford: Oxford University Press, 2nd edn, 2012.

Keukelaire S. and T. Delreux, *The Foreign Policy of the European Union*, Basingstoke: Palgrave Macmillan, 2nd edn, 2014.

Kissinger H., *World Order*, London: Penguin, 2014.

Knaus G., 'Europe and Azerbaijan: The end of shame', *Journal of Democracy*, 26/3, 2015, 5–18.

Korfman M., How to start a proxy war with Russia', *National Interest*, 5 February 2015.

Korosteleva E., *The European Union and Its Eastern Neighbours: Towards a More Ambitious Partnership?*, London: Routledge, 2012.

'Evaluating the role of partnership in the European Neighbourhood Policy: The Eastern neighbourhood', *Eastern Journal of European Studies*, 4/2, 2013, 11–36.

'The European Union, Russia and the Eastern region: The analytics of government for sustainable cohabitation', *Cooperation and Conflict*, 51/3, 2016.

Kostanyan H., *The Rocky Road to an EU-Armenia Agreement: From U-turn to Detour*, Brussels: Centre for European Policy Studies, 2015.

'Examining the discretion of the EEAS: What power to act in the EU-Moldova Association Agreement?', *European Foreign Affairs Review*, 19/3, 2014, 373–92.

Kostanyan H. and B. Vandecasteele, 'The socialization potential of the Eastern Partnership Civil Society Forum', *Eastern Journal of European Studies*, 4/2, 2013, 95–110.

Krastev I., *Democracy Disrupted*, Philadelphia: University of Pennsylvania Press, 2014.

'Putin's world', *Project Syndicate*, 2 April 2014.

Krastev I. and M. Leonard, *The New European Order*, London: European Council on Foreign Relations, 2014.

Kryvoi Y. with A. Wilson, *From Sanctions to Summits: Belarus after the Ukraine Crisis*, London: European Council for Foreign Relations, 2015.

Kudelia S., 'EU-Ukraine Association Agreement: Yanukovych's Two-Level Games', PONARS Eurasia Network, 20 September 2013.

Kulesa L. (ed.) *Is a New Cold War Inevitable? Central European Views on Rebuilding Trust in the Euro-Atlantic Region*, Warsaw: PISM, 2014.

Kundnani H., *Containment and Economic Interdependence*, London: European Council for Foreign Relations, 2014.

'Leaving the West behind', *Foreign Affairs*, December 2014.

Kupchan C., 'Centrifugal Europe', *Survival*, 54/1, 2012, 111–18.

Kurkov A., *Ukraine Diaries, Dispatches from Kiev*, London: Harvill Secker, 2014.

Langbein J., 'European Union governance towards the Eastern Neighbourhood: transcending or redrawing Europe's East–West divide?', *Journal of Common Market Studies*, 52/1, 2014, 157–74.

Laurinavcius M., L. Kascijnas and L. Kajola, 'What will determine Ukraine's future scenariois?', *Eastern Pulse Newsletter* 3/58, Eastern European Studies Centre, Vilnius, 2014.

Lavenex S., 'The power of functionalist extension: How EU rules travel', *Journal of European Public Policy* 21/6, 2014, 885–903.

Lavenex S. and F. Schimmelfennig, 'EU democracy promotion in the neighbourhood: From leverage to governance?', *Democratization* 18/4, 2011, 885–909.

'EU rules beyond EU borders: Theorizing external governance in European politics', *Journal of European Public Policy*, 16/6, 2011, 791–812.

Lavrov S., 'Russia's foreign policy: Historical background', *Russia in Global Affairs*, 2016, English version available at: www.mid.ru/en/foreign_policy/news/-/asset_publisher/cKNonkJE02Bw/content/id/2124391.

Lehne S., *Reviving the OSCE: European Security and the Ukraine Crisis*, Brussels: Carnegie Europe, 2015.

Time to Reset the European Neighbourhood Policy, Brussels: Carnegie Europe, 2015.

Leonard M., 'Why Crimea matters', *Reuters*, 10 April 2014.

Liik K., *The Real Problem with Mogherini's Russia Paper*, London: European Council for Foreign Relations, 20 January 2015.

Linkevčius L., 'Security Before Politics in Eastern Ukraine', *Wall Street Journal*, 27 January 2016.

Litra L. and I. Chkhikvadze, *EU Membership Perspective for Georgia, Moldova and Ukraine: Impossible, Forgotten or Hidden?*, Kiev: Institute for World Policy, 2016.

Lo B., *Russia and the New World Disorder*, London: Chatham House, 2015.

Lucarelli S. and I. Manners (eds) *Values and Principles in European Union Foreign Policy*, London: Routledge, 2006.

Lyubashenko I., 'Democracy in a time of war', *New Eastern Europe*, 26 October 2014.

Maçães B., 'We are all Eurasian now', *Financial Times*, 25 November 2015.

MacFarlane N. and A. Menon, 'The EU and Ukraine', *Survival*, 56/3, 2014, 95–101.

Mackinder H. J., 'The geographical pivot of history', *Geographical Society*, 23/4, 1904, 421–37.

Macmillan M., *The War That Ended Peace*, London: Profile Books, 2013.

Major C. and J. Puglierin, 'Europe's new (in)security order', *IPG Journal*, 25 November 2014. Available at: www.ipg-journal.de.

Makarychev A. and A. Devyatkov, *The EU in Eastern Europe: Has Normative Power become Geopolitical?*, Eurasia Policy Memo 310, George Washington University, February 2014.

Manners I., 'The normative ethics of the European Union', *International Affairs*, 84/1, 2008, 45–60.

Marrone A., O. De France and D. Fattibene (eds) *Defence Budgets and Cooperation in Europe: Developments, Trends and Drivers*, IAI, IRIS, SWP, RUSI, 2016.

Matuszak S., *The Oligarchic Democracy: The Influence of Business Groups on Ukrainian Politics*, Warsaw: Centre for Eastern Studies, 2012.

McCormick J., *The European Superpower*, Basingstoke: Macmillan, 2007.

McFaul M., 'Confronting Putin's Russia', *New York Times*, 23 March 2014.

McFaul M. and R. Youngs, 'Ukraine: External Actors and the Orange Revolution', in M. McFaul and K. Stoner (eds), *Transitions to Democracy: A Comparative Perspective*, Baltimore: Johns Hopkins Press, 2013.

Mearsheimer J., 'Why the Ukraine crisis is the West's fault', *Foreign Affairs*, September/October 2014.

Meister S., *Putin's Plan*, London: European Council for Foreign Relations, 2014.

Melo F., 'Perspectives on the European neighbourhood policy failure', *Journal of European Integration*, 36/2, 2014, 189–93.

Menkiszak M., *The Putin Doctrine: The Formation of a Conceptual Framework for Russian Dominance in the Post-Soviet Area*, Warsaw: Centre for Eastern Studies (OSW), 2014.

Menon A., 'Divided and declining? Europe in a changing world', *Journal of Common Market Studies*, 52, Annual Review, 2014, 5–24.

Minakov M., 'Corrupting civil society in post-Maidan Ukraine', *Carnegie Russia Eurasia Outlook*, 11 April 2015.

Mirimanova N., *Peace-building in Ukraine: What Role for the EU?*, Brussels: European Peace-Building Liaison Office, 2014.

Monaghan A., 'Putin's Russia: Shaping a 'grand strategy'?', *International Affairs*, 89/5, 2013, 1221–36.

Moshes A., *The War and Reforms in Ukraine, Can It Cope with Both?* Helsinki: Finnish Institute for International Affairs, 2015.

Motyl A., 'Out of Kiev's hands', *Foreign Policy*, 4 May 2015.

NATO, *Sanctions after Crimea: Have They Worked?*, Brussels: NATO, 2015.

Natorski M., 'A new social contract for Ukraine', *New Eastern Europe*, 26 March 2014.

Nielsen K. and M. Vilson 'The Eastern partnership: Soft power strategy or policy failure?', *European Foreign Affairs Review*, 19/2, 2014, 243–62.

Nitoiu C., 'The Ukraine crisis is forcing the EU to abandon normative power and act more strategically in its eastern neighbourhood', *EUROPP LSE Blog*, 21 September 2015.

(ed.) *Avoiding a New 'Cold War': The Future of EU-Russia Relations in the Context of the Ukraine Crisis*, London: LSE Ideas Report, 2016.

Nixey J., *Russia and the EU Are Signing Their Divorce Papers*, London: Chatham House, 2014.

Nodia G., 'The revenge of geopolitics', *Journal of Democracy*, 25/4, 2014, 139–50.

O'Tuathail G., *Critical Geopolitics*, Minneapolis: University of Minnesota Press, 1996.

O'Tuathail G., S. Dalby and P. Routledge (eds) *The Geopolitics Reader*, London: Routledge, 2003.

Organization for Security and Cooperation in Europe (OSCE), *Back to diplomacy*, Final Report and Recommendations of the Panel of Eminent Persons on European Security as a Common Project, 2015.

Paanukoski E., 'End of era of cognitive dissonance should do Ukraine good', EU Neighborhood Guest Blog, August 29, 2013. Available at: http://euneighbourhoodguestblog.wordpress.com/tag/association-agreement.

Parkinson J., 'Uneasy Georgia waits for Russia reaction to Ukraine', *Wall Street Journal*, 25 February 2014.

Petrova T., *From Solidarity to Geopolitics: Support for Democracy among Postcommunist States*, Cambridge: Cambridge University Press, 2014.

Pew Research Centre, *Global Attitudes Survey*, Spring 2015, p. 52.

Pieniazek P. 'Last chance for European values', *New Eastern Europe*, 22 March 2014.

Pogodda S., O. Richmond, N. Tocci, R. MacGinty and B. Vogel, 'Assessing the impact of EU governmentality in post-conflict countries: Pacification or reconciliation?', *European Security*, 23/3, 2014, 227–49.

Polish Institute of International Affairs, *Learning from Past Experience: Ways to Improve EU Aid on Reforms in the Eastern Partnership*, Warsaw: PISM, 2014.

Popescu N., 'After Crimea: Putin's Balance Sheet', *ISS Alert*, Paris: EU Institute for Security Studies, April 2014.

'First Lessons from the Ukrainian Crisis', *ISS Issue Alert*, Paris: EU Institute for Security Studies, October 2014.

Portnov A., 'How 'eastern Ukraine' was lost', *Open Democracy*, 14 January 2016.

Raik K., 'The EU and mass protests in the neighbourhood: Models of normative (in)action', *European Foreign Affairs Review*, 17/4, 2012, 553–76.

'Liberalism and geopolitics in EU–Russia relations: Rereading the Baltic factor', *European Security*, 25/2, 2016, 237–55.

Rand Corporation, *Security Sector Reform*, October 2016.

Rettman A., 'The year history returned to Europe', *EU Observer*, 22 December 2014.

'Four fallacies of EU foreign policy', *EU Observer*, 13 March 2015.

Rinke A., 'How Putin lost Berlin', *IPG Journal*, 29 September 2014. Available at: www.ipg-journal.de.

Rodt A., R. Whitman and S. Wolff, 'The EU as an international security provider: The need for a mid-range theory', *Global Society*, 29/2, 2015, 149–55.

Rogers J., *A New Geography of European Power?* Brussels: Egmont Institute, Egmont Paper 42, 2011.

Russell Mead W., 'The return of geopolitics', *Foreign Affairs*, May/June 2014.

Rynning S., 'The false promise of continental concert: Russia, the West and the necessary balance of power', *International Affairs*, 91/3, 2015, 539–52.

Ryzhkov V., 'The new Putin doctrine', *Moscow Times*, 3 April 2014.

Sakwa R., *Frontline Ukraine: Crisis in the Borderlands*, London: I. B. Tauris, 2015.

Samadashvili S., *Building a Lifeline for Freedom: Eastern Partnership 2.0*, Brussels: Wilfired Martens Centre for European Studies, 2014.

Sasse G., 'Linkages and the promotion of democracy: The EU's eastern neighbourhood', *Democratization*, 20/4, 2013, 553–91.

Constitution Making in Ukraine: Refocusing the Debate, Brussels: Carnegie Europe, April 2016.

Schimmelfennig F., 'How substantial is substance? Concluding reflections on the study of substance in EU democracy promotion', *European Foreign Affairs Review*, 16/4, 2011, 727–34.

'Liberal intergovernmentalism and the euro area crisis', *Journal of European Public Policy*, 22/2, 2015, 177–95.

Schumacher T., 'Letter from Tbilisi', *Open Democracy*, 2 December 2014.

Armenia, Azerbaijan and the Nagorno-Karabakh Conflict: Why the 'Black Garden' Will Not Blossom Any Time Soon, Brussels: Egmont Institute, 2016.

Secrieirn S., *Can Moldova Stay on the Road to Europe?*, London: European Council for Foreign Relations, 2014.

Shapovalova N. and R. Youngs, *Civil Society Support in the Eastern Neighbourhood*, Madrid: Fride, 2013.

Sherr J., 'Putin is not master of the new world order', *Prospect*, 14 March 2014.

Shevtsova L., 'Don't be fooled, the Kremlin isn't back pedalling', *The American Interest*, 8 May 2014.

Simon L., 'The spider in Europe's web? French grand strategy from Iraq to Libya', *Geopolitics*, 18/2, 2013, 403–34.

'Post-European world', *European Geostrategy*, 7 June 2015.

Smith K., *European Union Foreign Policy in a Changing World*, 2nd edn, Cambridge: Polity, 2008.

Smith M., 'Beyond the comfort zone: Internal crisis and challenges in the EU's response to rising powers', *International Affairs*, 89/3, 2013, 653–71.

Smith M.E., 'Toward a theory of EU foreign policy making: Multi-level governance, domestic politics, and national adaptation to Europe's common foreign and security policy', *Journal of European Public Policy* 11, 2004, 740–45.

Snyder T., 'The battle in Ukraine means everything', *New Republic*, 11 May 2014.

Soros G., 'Wake-up Europe!', *New York Review of Books*, October 2014.

'Ukraine and Europe: What should be done?', *New York Review of Books*, October 2015.

Speck U., *The West's Response to the Ukraine Conflict: A Transatlantic Success Story*, Washington DC: Transatlantic Academy, 2016.

Sperling J. and M. Webber, 'Security governance in Europe: A return to system', *European Security*, 23/2, 2014, 126–44.

Stockholm International Peace Research Institute, *SIPRI Yearbook 2015: Armaments, Disarmaments and International Security*, Oxford: Oxford University Press, 2015.

Stokes D. and R. Whitman, 'Transatlantic triage? European and UK 'grand strategy' after the US rebalance to Asia', *International Affairs*, 89/5, 2013, 1087–1107.

Strachan H., 'Europe, Geopolitics and Strategy', Egmont lecture, 9 January 2015.

Stubb A., 'European Policy towards Russia', speech delivered in Berlin, 29 September 2014. Available at: http://vnk.fi/ajankohtaista/puheet/puhe/en.jsp?oid=426086.

Techau J., 'Ukraine: Birthplace of strategic Europe', Carnegie Strategic Europe blog, 18 March 2014.

Tèlo M., *Europe: A Civilian Power? European Union, Global Governance, World Order*, Basingstoke: Palgrave Macmillan, 2007.

Thomas D. (ed.) *Making EU Foreign Policy*, Basingstoke: Macmillan, 2011.

Tocci N., *The Neighbourhood Policy Is Dead. What Next for European Foreign Policy along its Arc of Instability*, Rome: IAI, 2014.

Tolstoy A. and E. McCaffray, 'Mind games: Alexander Dugin and Russia's war of ideas', *World Affairs*, March/April 2015.

Trenin D., 'Russia's great power problem', *National Interest*, 28 October 2014.

The Ukraine Crisis and the Resumption of Great Power Rivalry, Washington DC: Carnegie Endowment for International Peace, 2014.

Tudoroiu T., 'The European Union, Russia, and the future of the Transnistrian frozen conflict', *East European Politics and Societies*, 26/1, 2012.

Waever O., 'Politics, security, theory', *Security Dialogue*, 42/4, 2011, 465–80.

Walt S., 'NATO owes Putin a big thank you', *Foreign Policy*, 4 September 2014.

Wedgwood Benn D., 'On re-examining Western attitudes towards Russia', *International Affairs*, 90/6, 2014, 1319–28.

Wesslau F., 'EU needs to step up its game in Ukraine', *EU Observer*, 31 August 2015.

Whitman R. and S. Wolff (eds) *The European Neighbourhood Policy in Perspective*, Basingstoke: Palgrave Macmillan, 2010.

Wigell M. and A. Vihma, 'Geopolitics versus geoeconomics: The case of Russia's geostrategy and its effects on the EU', *International Affairs*, 92/3, 2016.

Wilson A., *Ukraine Crisis: What It Means for the West*, New Haven, CT: Yale University Press, 2014.

Wilson A. and O. Andreyev, *Ukraine: A Failing State, or Survival of the Old State?*, London: European Council for Foreign Relations, May 2013.

Wissel J., 'The structure of the 'EU'ropean ensemble of state apparatuses and its geopolitical ambitions', *Geopolitics*, 19/3, 2014, 490–513.

Wolczuk K., *Ukraine and the EU: Turning the Association Agreement into a Success Story*, Brussels: European Policy Centre, 2014.

Young A., 'The European Union as a global regulator? Context and comparison', *Journal of European Public Policy*, 22/9, 2015, 1233–52 – and others in this special edition.

Youngs R., *Europe's Role in Global Politics: A Retreat from Liberal Internationalism*, London: Routledge, 2009.

Europe in the New Middle East: Opportunity or Exclusion?, Oxford: Oxford University Press, 2014.

The Uncertain Legacy of Crisis: European Foreign Policy Faces the Future, Washington DC: Carnegie Endowment for International Peace, 2014.

Zarembo K., *EUAM's First Year: Ambitions versus Reality*, Kiev: Institute for World Policy, 2015.

Zasztowt K., 'The radicalisation of separatists in Crimea', *PISM Bulletin*, 21, 17 February 2014.

Zielonka J., *Europe as Empire*, Oxford: Oxford University Press, 2006.

'The EU as an international actor: Unique or ordinary?', *European Foreign Affairs Review*, 16, 2011, 281–301.

Index